# "WHAT DO YOU MEAN, MURDER?"

*CLUE* AND THE MAKING OF A CULT CLASSIC

# "WHAT DO YOU MEAN, MURDER?"

## *CLUE* AND THE MAKING OF A CULT CLASSIC

JOHN HATCH

Cover by Jason Francis
Back cover photo courtesy of Paramount Pictures
Edited by David Bushman
Designed by Scott Ryan

Published in the USA by Fayetteville Mafia Press
Columbus, Ohio

Contact Information
Email: fayettevillemafiapress@gmail.com
Website: TuckerDSPress.com
Instagram: @fayettevillemafiapress
Twitter:@fmpbooks

ISBN: 9781949024609
eBook ISBN: 9781949024616

For my dad, who took me to see *Clue* when I was nine,
and who instilled in me unceasing curiosity.

# CONTENTS

# PREFACE

In March 2020, everything came to a screeching halt. Restaurants closed, Broadway shuttered, and movie theaters went dark. Eventually, in fits and starts over the next several months, the world adjusted to the new normal brought on by COVID-19. As we acclimated to peaks and valleys of case counts and began to learn the Greek alphabet through new variants, some venues began to tentatively reopen. But with blockbuster film franchises like Wonder Woman and James Bond postponed, movie theaters were left without much to show. And so they turned to the classics—at least the modern classics. They were cheaper to screen at a time when theaters were running at 25 percent capacity and patrons were required to wear masks and sit at least six feet apart.

Reading the list of the top-grossing films only compounded the surrealism of the pandemic. It was like looking through a time portal: *Jurassic Park*, *The Empire Strikes Back*, *E.T.*, and *Raiders of the Lost Ark* topped the box office. George Lucas and Steven Spielberg, wunderkinds of the seventies and eighties, reigned again. Several chains, aware that even the most avid moviegoer might be uncomfortable sitting in a dark room with strangers, began renting out theaters. For fifty dollars on up—around the cost of four people going to a new release just six months earlier—anyone could have a whole theater to themselves. My family rented one at a local Cinemark and basked in *Back to the Future*. It was glorious good fun, and we joked that this was the only way to see movies: no latecomers blocking your view, no whisperers, no texters—just you and the movie. For a couple of hours, we felt normal again.

A few months after that, my wife booked a theater for my birthday so that we could watch Christopher Nolan's *Tenet*. This hooked me even further on the novelty of renting a theater, so I began to keep an eye out for other movies I'd like to see. For several weeks, nothing jumped out at me. Where were the old-school classics? Where was *Casablanca*, *The Maltese Falcon*, or *Citizen Kane*? Where was *Vertigo*? Where was *Chinatown*? Instead the options were a mixture of popular nineties movies and less exciting fare that shall remain nameless. But one day, as I scrolled absentmindedly through the latest list of available films, a movie jumped out that made me gasp with excitement. It wasn't a blockbuster. It wasn't an Oscar darling. It wasn't even adapted from a beloved novel; it was based on, of all things, a board game. It was a strange comedy from 1985 that landed to middling-at-best reviews, only to grow into the very epitome of a cult classic. And so it was that my family strolled into a theater to watch *Clue*.

By then, I'd seen it dozens of times. People often exaggerate how many times they've seen a movie. Die-hard fans insist they've seen *Star Wars* or *The Lord of the Rings* or *Ghostbusters* or *Pulp Fiction* or *The Avengers* "hundreds of times!" A hundred times is, to say the least, a lot. If you stop to really think through and count how many times you've seen a movie, you're likely to realize that even your favorites fall well short of the century mark. But if there was one movie I'd seen close to one hundred times, it was *Clue*. Admittedly, we'd have to define "seen" a little loosely. Often I'd throw on *Clue* for background noise, glancing up in the middle of some project to chuckle at a line I'd heard dozens of times before. Or, as happens when you fall in love with a movie, I'd laugh at the mere anticipation of a moment I knew was coming up.

I never tired of it. The dialogue was always funny, the action always welcome. At one rough time in my life, too worn out and too depressed to even climb into bed, I watched *Clue*, or at least parts of *Clue*, nearly every night for two months as I fell fitfully asleep on my couch. I'd thumb through my DVDs trying to think of what to throw on, but I kept coming back to *Clue*. It was familiar and comforting, and there was little I needed more than comfort. So I'd lie down, throw a blanket on, let my feet dangle off the edge of the couch, and hit play. The movie would pick up where I'd left off the night before, and I'd inevitably smile, usually my first smile of the day.

Pop culture affects us deeply, but we're often expected to pretend otherwise. Most of us, at one time or another, probably had a parent or a teacher or another well-meaning authority figure tell us, "It's only a movie!" But whether we admit it or not, the music we listen to and the movies we watch can transform us. We all have intense memories wrapped up in a song we heard with friends, a TV show we saw with family, a concert we went to on a date, a movie we fell in love with when we were young. I fell in love with *Clue*, and I'm still in love with it today, even as friends opine that I, as a supposedly sophisticated cinephile, should know better than to like this goofy little movie.

Millions of other people fell in love with it too. *Clue* is hardly the first film to go from flop to beloved icon. *The Princess Bride*, while not the bust *Clue* was, wasn't a box office smash. *The Big Lebowski*, *This Is Spinal Tap*, and *Dazed and Confused* also landed with indifference. Word of mouth and home video turned them into movies so well-known that the word "cult" seems inaccurate after a while. Is a movie a cult phenomenon if half of the population can quote it or at least recognize the dialogue? It may not quite be time to erase "cult" from *Clue*'s designation as a classic, but plenty of people who have never seen it know what someone is talking about when, in a fit of frustration, they sputter, "Flames—flames, on the side of my face!"

As I sat watching *Clue* in the movie theater for the first time in thirty-five years, I noticed things I hadn't spotted before. The set design jumped out at me. The costumes were suddenly more visible. The soundtrack was loud, and I heard lines I realized I had missed before. My mind started to race. Was that a portrait of US President William McKinley in the study—the one that swings open to reveal the secret passage to the freezer in the kitchen? (Read on for the answer.) Like many fans of the film, I had perused the Internet Movie Database's list of trivia for *Clue*, some entries sounding more plausible than others. (No, Lee Ving was not cast because his name sounds like "leaving," an actual trivia contention as of this writing.) I could also count myself among those die-hard fans who had read Adam Vary's wonderful oral history of the film, first published at *Buzzfeed* in 2013. But I had questions that articles or internet fan sites had never answered. Thus began my hunt for, ahem, clues (there will be more puns), so that I could write the story of this flop turned pop culture icon.

New details came fast, some from the daily trades like the *Hollywood Reporter* and *Variety*. Others came from archives I never dreamed would have *Clue* material, such as the Tom Stoppard papers at the University of Texas at Austin. Other details came in a trickle. But a picture began to emerge of how this movie came about. I know who did it, and furthermore, I'm going to tell you how it was all done. Follow me.

**John Hatch**
with the laptop
in the parlor

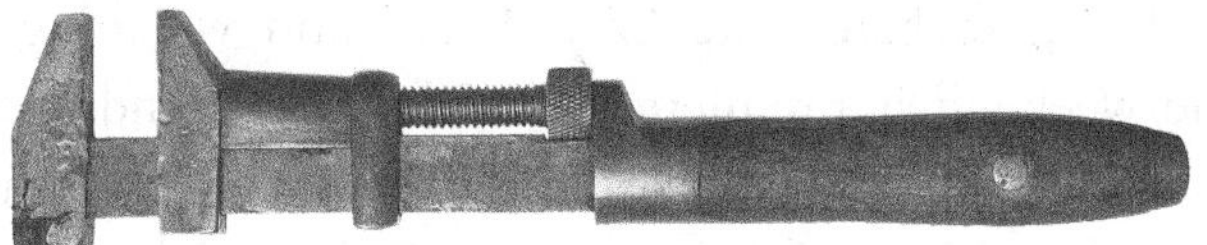

# INTRODUCTION

"I have a deadly serious commitment to farce."
-Jonathan Lynn[1]

And fans have a deadly serious commitment to *Clue*. I've spent countless hours pondering why that is—after all, I am one of those fans. What else could inspire someone to write a book about a movie that came out decades ago and grossed just over $13 million, not quite enough to earn back its production and marketing budget let alone break even once receipts were split with exhibitors. Other films that year are arguably more memorable, especially to Gen-Xers growing up in the eighties: *Back to the Future* and *The Goonies*, to name a couple. But it was *Clue* that famously flopped both critically and commercially only to become a cult classic thanks to a second life on cable television and home video. Even today, fans keep coming back to it.

There are all sorts of reasons why people fall in love with images on celluloid, twenty-four of them a second flickering through a projector and beaming onto a screen. In *Clue*'s case, it's nostalgia. Most fans discovered it as preteens and teenagers, and they remember it with fondness today. The movie appeals especially to kids, much to the amusement of writer and director Jonathan Lynn, who points out the abundance of sexual overtones in the film. But he also quickly explains that kids don't get those jokes. It's only when they grow up that the more adult themes of McCarthyism, blackmail, homophobia, sex workers, and government corruption pique their interest. The slapstick and farce

1 Farber, "Off the Board, onto the Screen."

hook them at a young age; the rapid-fire jokes, clever one-liners, and bigger issues keep them engaged as they get older.

I certainly didn't catch all those grown-up topics when I was nine years old, living in Salt Lake City, Utah, and watching *Clue* in a theater the weekend it premiered. The double entendres and sexual asides sailed over my naive little head. I was well into my twenties or thirties before Mrs. White's retort to Colonel Mustard's question "How many husbands have you had, anyway?" fully sank in: "Mine or other women's?"

*Clue* manages to operate on two levels: one for kids, another for when those kids become adults. Early in the film, as the characters gather around the ornate dinner table adorned with luxurious china, still suspicious of one another and unsure why they are there, Mrs. Peacock asks Mrs. White, "So what does your husband do?" Before she can finish the question, White blurts out "Nothing!" Realizing her defensiveness, she clarifies that he "just lies around on his back all day." It's then that Miss Scarlet admits, "Sounds like hard work to me." But it's only later, as all the characters' guilty secrets are revealed in the study, that we learn Miss Scarlet oversees others working on their backs, as a madam of a Washington, DC, brothel. Another joke that took me a good two decades to get.

None of these lines that fans can recite by heart were foreordained. In the twenty-first century, movies are adapted from comic books, theme park rides, video games, even phone apps and emojis. There are reboots of reboots of reboots. Over a twenty-year period, Spider-Man has appeared in at least thirteen films. But when producer Debra Hill obtained the rights to Clue in 1980, the idea of a movie based on a board game seemed . . . weird. A few news notices had an air of "What will those clowns in Hollywood think of next?" The static nature of the game raised eyebrows. The board never changes. The characters are colors with no backstory. Playwright Tom Stoppard, stymied in his own attempt to write the script, called them "stock characters" for a "stock situation."[2]

---

2 Stoppard to Landis, March 22, 1983, in Stoppard and Landis Correspondence.

Except Hill knew exactly what she was doing. *Clue* was going to be a London play before it was a movie. A play, performed night in and night out, made perfect sense. Agatha Christie's *The Mousetrap*, the longest continually running play in history, had only one set—the main room of a British boarding house. And that play had the same ending every night. Hill planned to follow the board game and change whodunit each night. Turning the board game into a stage play and then developing it as a movie was genius.

Hill's plans for the play fell through, so she focused on getting the movie made. The story of the development of *Clue* from this point on has been told several times, most memorably in a 2013 *Buzzfeed* article by Adam Vary. Hill hired John Landis to direct and brought on PolyGram's Jon Peters and Peter Guber to help produce. But the film wallowed in development hell as writer after writer backed out when all of the conditions placed upon the script by both Hill and Parker Brothers, the owner of the board game, seemed impossible to navigate. Not only was the movie supposed to have multiple endings, but Parker Brothers also wanted no profanity, and all the suspects, weapons, and rooms in the game had to appear in the final film. Playwright Warren Manzi finished two different screenplays, neither of which bears much resemblance to Lynn's movie. Stoppard labored for six weeks before telling Landis it wasn't going to happen.

Finally, Guber met with someone he thought might be able to crack the code. A popular British writer and stage director named Jonathan Lynn was the creator of the hit BBC series *Yes Minister*. The show lampooned British politics and won high praise for its smart writing and clever wordplay. Lynn believed that most writers underestimated the intelligence of the average audience, and after the success of *Yes Minister*, it was hard to disagree with him. Guber and Lynn sat down to breakfast, and before Lynn could tuck in, Guber was insisting *Clue* was perfect for him. Lynn met with the other producers, including Landis, who offered a very energetic pitch.

Lynn did what several other writers couldn't: he came up with a workable screenplay that included multiple endings and a sensical plot. What's more, he did it in a matter of months. He worked off of Landis's basic plot outline, and Landis is credited with part of the story, but the screenplay is Lynn's. By the time he was finished, the producers had another surprise for Lynn: Landis was busy directing *Spies Like Us*, so they wanted Lynn to direct *Clue* as well. Lynn had directed theater for years, though he had never helmed a Hollywood feature, and the idea was more than a little intimidating. But he agreed, and *Clue* was finally on its way to becoming a real movie, after five years. Lynn and his cast, including a couple of last-minute replacements, assembled with the crew on Stages 17 and 18 at Paramount Pictures for principal photography, which began on May 20, 1985.

It's here, after the writing and development, where much of the story of *Clue* vanishes in retrospectives. Most histories include a handful of anecdotes from the cast and some details about the oft-rumored deleted fourth ending, but they say little about the actual casting and production of the movie. There's good reason for that: most cast and crew members don't really remember much. They all seem delighted that *Clue* was passionately embraced by so many fans after its theatrical disappointment, but all of them moved on to do different and, at least at the time, more memorable work.

And it was work—sometimes hard work. A theme that emerged over and over as I researched and wrote this book was the chasm between fandom and the people who make movies. It's especially stark for *Clue*. Since the film flopped on release, there was no celebratory moment for the cast and crew. There were no victory laps on late-night talk shows, let alone box office bonanzas or industry recognition at awards shows. Perhaps if there had been, perhaps if *Clue* had been a major hit, the experience might have imprinted itself more deeply on the memories of the cast and Lynn.

Lynn was one who went on to other projects, back in his native England. For me, as a fan of *Clue*, to interview Lynn, even just over email, was to feel a bit self-conscious. I am bursting with questions about the most minute details, but Lynn, always polite and generous, answers even some of the broadest queries with the reminder that all of this took place decades ago, and he can't really remember. To fans who obsess over every detail of movies they love, the response might be disappointing, even disingenuous. How can a director who worked on a film so transformative in their lives not remember the experience?

But Lynn isn't dodging questions. *Clue* was, for him, a work for hire. It was not a passion project he had labored on for years. After principal photography, he had to edit *Clue* while commuting between Los Angeles and London as he worked on the follow-up to *Yes Minister*, titled *Yes, Prime Minister*. He was juggling a lot. When Lynn says he can't remember the fourth ending, fans wonder how that's possible. But until recently, he didn't even have a copy of the script with the fourth ending. He remains, he told me, "astonished" that so many people know the movie by heart and love it so much.

Kellye Nakahara, who played the cook, spoke on the *M*A*S*H Matters* podcast in 2019 with her *M*A*S*H* costar Jeff Maxwell about the inevitable gap between fans and stars. The people who work on a show or a movie can't, she believed, "have the same emotional connection" to that movie or show that the fans do.[3] *Clue* was a job for these people, and at times a very tedious one. There were fifty-nine days of principal photography, and the movie, with all three endings, runs for just over ninety-three minutes (without the end credits). That averages out to a little more than a minute and a half of final footage per shooting day. Eight or ten or twelve hours (or more) of work to get around ninety seconds of usable footage. The story of the cast and crew shooting pool in the billiard room points to a mundane reality: there's an awful lot of waiting around on a film set.

Fandom is a strange thing. We are obsessed with the money surrounding movies—how much they cost, how much they make, which box office records they break—and entertainment headlines routinely blare how many millions a big movie star was paid or how much a film went over budget. But we're also often in denial that money is at the heart of it all. These movies and TV shows can come to mean a lot to us. Was it really all just to satisfy shareholders and get a producer a new Ferrari? *Clue*, like the countless movies that came before and have come after, was made with the hope that it would turn a tidy profit for its makers and for Paramount Pictures. The board game, as an existing property, was referenced often in marketing materials, all to entice

---

3 Nakahara, interview with Maxwell and Patrick, 32:20.

people who played the game to flock to theaters. When they didn't, it almost ended its director's Hollywood career. The movie business is a business, and it's a tough one. While *Clue* had a remarkably smooth production, I try to balance the realities of filmmaking against the love fans have for the movie.

Knowing that those fans can quote the movie by heart influenced how I wanted to tell the story. Most production histories follow a film's shooting schedule, jumping around the movie's timeline based on location and actor availability. But I decided early on to walk fans through *Clue* as it unfolded, annotating everything from set design to lighting, from script evolution to deleted scenes. I also did not want to jump right into every detail at the beginning. *Clue* is different from most films in that it takes place almost entirely in one location, with almost everyone in the cast introduced in the first five minutes. Even though we glimpse the kitchen shortly after Wadsworth arrives at the mansion, I wait until all of the characters are in there to talk about some of the details in that room. In other words, hang in there—I'll get to everything. That's especially true for the endings. While I nod to who did what, when, and how throughout the book, I hold off until Chapter 8 to examine the four solutions in detail, occasionally jumping back in the film to look at how each was produced.

For those readers who haven't seen *Clue* for a while, here's a recap. Spoilers follow, so now is your chance to put the book down and watch the movie again.

Six guests have received a strange letter summoning them to dinner at a mansion in New England in 1954. The letter assigns each an alias, the only name they are to use for the night: Colonel Mustard, Professor Plum, Mr. Green, Mrs. Peacock, Miss Scarlet, and Mrs. White. Upon reaching the mansion, each encounters a butler (Wadsworth), a maid (Yvette), and a cook (Mrs. Ho).

Dinner is served. They eat mostly in uncomfortable silence, unsure why they are there and growing impatient at the lack of answers. Finally, another guest arrives: the menacing Mr. Boddy. It is only after dinner, as the guests gather in the study, that Wadsworth finally explains: the six guests are being blackmailed by Boddy. Wadsworth, who was himself a victim of Boddy's blackmail when he worked for him, has decided to put a stop to it. But Boddy has other plans. He hands the guests six gifts, all weapons: a dagger, a lead pipe, a rope, a wrench, a candlestick, and a revolver. After the guests unwrap the weapons, Boddy explains that unless one of them kills Wadsworth, their secrets will be exposed, humiliating them and placing them in legal jeopardy.

Mr. Boddy shuts off the lights in the study to give someone a chance to kill Wadsworth anonymously, but the blackmailer has miscalculated badly. Instead, when the lights come back on, it's Boddy who lies on the floor, "apparently dead," in the words of the butler. But he is only the first victim. Soon, the guests find the cook murdered in the kitchen. They're baffled, wondering why anyone would kill a harmless cook. Just as Wadsworth, Yvette, and the six guests/suspects debate what their next steps should be, the doorbell rings. A man known only as the Motorist stands in the rain, explaining that his car has broken down and he needs to use the phone.

Wadsworth shows the Motorist to the lounge, but locks him inside the room. The rest of the group decides to split up into pairs to search the house for the killer. But within minutes, the Motorist is murdered, interrupting the search and causing panic among the guests before a police officer arrives unexpectedly. He has found the Motorist's abandoned car down the road and wants to know what is going on, especially given how suspicious everyone is acting.

Wadsworth shows the Cop to the library and, just as he did with the Motorist in the lounge, locks him inside. The group splits up again, determined to finish their search and learn if the murderer is hiding or one of them is the guilty party. But just after they separate, someone shuts off the power to the mansion. Three more murders happen in quick succession: Yvette is strangled with the rope, the Cop is bashed over the head with the lead pipe, and a Singing Telegram Girl who arrived just seconds earlier is shot at the front door before she can deliver her message.

Wadsworth turns the power back on, and the six guests slowly emerge from different rooms in the house. They discover the bodies, no longer shocked but now resigned to what has happened. There have been six murders: Mr. Boddy, the Cook, the Motorist, the Cop, Yvette, and the Singing Telegram Girl. Wadsworth stuns the guests when he announces he knows who did it and he's going to show them how it was done.

He says that he has to walk them "through the events of the evening step-by-step." He begins reenacting what happened, much to the guests' bewilderment. He tells them that the six murder victims weren't there by chance, but were invited because they were Mr. Boddy's informers, the sources of his blackmail intel, and each of them knew one of the suspects. The Cook had worked for Mrs. Peacock; the Motorist was Colonel Mustard's driver in World War II; Yvette had worked for Miss Scarlet in her cathouse and also had affairs with Colonel Mustard and Mrs. White's husband; Professor Plum had a sexual relationship with the Singing Telegram Girl, a former psychiatric patient. In other words, all of the guests had a reason to kill at least one of the victims. Wadsworth also reveals the presence of two secret passages that the killer used to sneak around the mansion, plus additional details of how the murders were committed.

The butler, as part of his reenactment, switches off the electricity. When he turns it back on, one of four solutions is revealed. This was *Clue*'s gimmick: it had four different endings, each triggered when Wadsworth turns the light back on. Producers planned to show a different solution in different theaters, labeled ending A, B, C, or D. This, producers hoped, would encourage viewers to see the movie more than once.

Here's whodunit:

In one ending, Mrs. Peacock killed everyone.

In another, everyone but Mr. Green killed someone.

In yet another, Miss Scarlet ordered Yvette to kill Mr. Boddy and the Cook before Scarlet herself killed the remaining four victims (including Yvette).

Finally, in an ending that was cut after test screenings, Wadsworth killed everyone.

The killers' motives vary, and as we will see, some solutions hold up over time better than others, but these are the basics of what you need to know before we dive into *Clue*.

This book is not based on interviews, though I reached out to all of the surviving cast members and some of the crew, and a few graciously and patiently answered my questions, including Lynn. But like all of us when recounting some event from our past, the cast has defaulted to sharing the same anecdotes, and a few of their memories contradict the written record. It's inevitable with the passage of time—some things stand out, some moments make for better stories, and many details slip away. I've prioritized manuscripts and contemporaneous reports from 1985 over memories shared some thirty years later. By way of example, John Landis remembered in the *Buzzfeed* oral history that Tom Stoppard worked on *Clue* for a year; it was actually less than two months, though the two corresponded for about six months.

As a historian who usually writes about people long deceased, I am also aware that here I'm writing mostly about people who were still alive in 2023. If any of them perchance read this book, I hope they'll find I've done them justice and accurately represented their experience. I'd make a terrible celebrity, because the thought of having other people write and talk about what I think, what I believe, what I did, what I'm going to do—it all sounds exhausting. I've also tried to ask myself, "Would I say this if they were standing right in front of me?" Fortunately, there were no horrific scandals on *Clue* that forced me into the uncomfortable position of having to ask embarrassing questions.

Records documenting the production of *Clue* were much more robust than I imagined. The Margaret Herrick Library in Los Angeles has wonderful material, including nearly every draft of the script by both Manzi and Lynn, plus Debra Hill's delightful 1980 treatment. It also has a casting notebook that was a joy to look through. Seeing "Weird Al" Yankovic's name on a list of possible Mr. Boddys made my heart skip a few beats. In the John Landis papers held at the library are other materials—press kits, invitations to the premiere, and a transcript of his animated pitch given to Tom Stoppard. The Stoppard papers at the Harry Ransom Center in Austin house Landis and Stoppard's correspondence. UCLA's special collections had copies of script drafts that were not available at the Herrick Library.

Other useful sources were newspaper and trade reports. The first public notice of *Clue* was in the *Hollywood Reporter* in October 1980, when Debra Hill still envisioned Detective Parker solving a murder with the help of a giant board outlining the rooms of Boddy Mansion.

Notices a few months later begin to mention Landis's involvement. By early 1985, after *Clue* was officially greenlit, newspapers and the trades were mentioning the movie nearly every week. Most of these were small notices, but they all help trace the story. Paramount Pictures marketed *Clue* aggressively, and the Friday before filming began, it invited reporters from around the country to the massive mansion set on Stage 18. In the summer of 1985, lengthy reports began to pop up in publications like the *New York Times* and the *San Francisco Examiner*. A story in *The Guardian of London* took on the angle of Lynn the Brit making his way in Hollywood. One of the densest sources was an article in *American Cinematographer* in January 1986. Coauthored by Paramount Pictures's press liaison, Saul Kahan, it is therefore a sympathetic report filled with insider information, including an in-depth interview with director of photography Victor Kemper. A copy of the complete shot list, likely kept by script supervisor Doris Grau, made its way into my hands, allowing me to see exactly how many takes there were of each scene, when they were filmed, and what was cut.

Finally, there was Lynn's audio commentary, which most fans still don't know exists. Before anyone grabs their Blu-ray to find it or rushes off to buy another one, save your time and money: it's not there. Instead, writer, director, and *Clue* fan Josh Brandon reached out to Lynn to record it, and the commentary became an episode of Kevin Smith's *Smodcast* podcast. It's available only via a paid subscription to Smith's website. Brandon kindly spoke with me about the experience of reaching out to Lynn and recording the commentary.

Despite all of these marvelous sources, sorting out Hollywood fact from fiction can be daunting. There are millions of dollars on the line when it comes to a movie, and studios, producers, directors, and actors are well practiced at promotion, marketing, and slapping the best face on even the most dire production. The ever-present tug of showmanship renders benign information or story loaded with hyperbole. Lynn, a newcomer to Hollywood when he wrote and directed *Clue*, quickly learned that the only acceptable adjective to describe anything was "great!"[4] Well, maybe not the only acceptable; there was also "stupendous," "terrific," "brilliant" . . .

Given *Clue*'s planned four-ending mystery, red herrings (not of the communist variety, thankfully) were planted in the press. Just as one newspaper reported on the multiple endings, another would quote producer Debra Hill insisting that it wasn't true. Other outlets said that multiple endings were being filmed to keep even the cast in the dark, but only one would be used. These kinds of contradictions recur often enough to make it clear that this was a strategy employed by Hill, Lynn, and Paramount Pictures, not sloppy reporting.

Although it did go nine days over schedule, causing the budget to climb by almost half a million dollars, the *Clue* production suffered no catastrophes that required smoothing over in the press. It was, with only a few hiccups, a remarkably drama-free production. Lynn is the polar opposite of the egomaniacal director screaming that an actor has ruined his flawless work of art. While juicy tales of drug-fueled productions and intense personality conflicts often dominate film histories, this book is free of them. The people who worked on *Clue* appear to have been thoroughly professional; they got along well, and they all worked hard to make a good movie. This is all the more remarkable given the ensemble nature of the film. All of it shows in the end product, and in some ways, it's just as newsworthy as the gossip that often accompanies big productions.

As a historian, I'm used to documenting nearly every claim I make in a book, with footnotes peppering every page. It is drilled into you early: say the sky is blue and you best have a citation for it. But I have taken a different route in this book; I didn't want the documentation to get in the way of the story. Instead, I have a list of sources I relied on in the back of the book. I do footnote direct quotes.

One last note on what this book is and what it is not: in today's geek culture, there is something of an obsession with canon—what counts and what doesn't in the mythology of a book, movie, or TV series. With ever-growing access to content and creators, fans parse even the

---

4 Lynn, *Comedy Rules*, 135.

most benign comments, determined to mine deeper and deeper in the hope of uncovering a rare gem. Is an off-the-cuff remark at Comic-Con by the screenwriter canon? What about a paragraph on a now-defunct promotional website run by the studio? How about a tweet by a cast member? Is something canon simply because the creator says it is, or do fans have a say?

If such things seem trivial, ask a *Star Wars* fan about Disney declaring books written before it bought the franchise from LucasFilm no longer canon. Or tell a Harry Potter devotee that the stage play *Harry Potter and the Cursed Child* is definitely canon. They might politely agree with you; more likely you'll get an earful. Fans can be more than a little intense about their mythology; their passion can be a beautiful thing, but it's not without its dark side, as evidenced by the toxicity stirred up when casting is more inclusive than some fans believe the source material warrants.

I do not put *Clue* to the canon test. It seems absurd to hold a movie made in 1985 up to today's geek standards. No one who worked on the film imagined that fans would be scanning a high-definition Blu-ray frame by frame for the most minuscule of details. I'm much more interested in writing about how *Clue* was made, and I approach it hoping to understand what the filmmakers were trying to do. Unless I think it's an interesting aside, I won't be pointing out most continuity errors, lists of which are available online for just about every movie ever made. Lynn, alongside Landis and Hill, wanted *Clue* to be a funny and scary mystery. Each viewer can decide for themselves whether they succeeded, but that is how I approach the movie. I am a fan who loves *Clue*, but I am not uncritical. I think some aspects of the movie (the comedy) work better than others (the mystery), and I talk about why.

I couldn't have told this story without the help of some wonderful people. I am always grateful to archivists and librarians, without whom none of my work would be possible. My deepest thanks to Genevieve Maxwell of the Academy of Motion Picture Arts and Sciences's Margaret Herrick Library, who helped me find material and much of that material remotely during the COVID pandemic. I learned early on in our correspondence not to write her on her day off because she would respond anyway. My thanks also to Cristina Meisner of the Harry Ransom Center at the University of Texas at Austin. I am indebted to the unfailing patience of Edda Manriquez and Taylor Morales of the Academy of Motion Picture Arts and Sciences's film archive; both answered my questions over a period of several months. I'm grateful to Patricia Svoboda of the Smithsonian National Portrait Gallery for her help in identifying some of the paintings in the film. My thanks to Tyne Lowe, archivist at the Browne Popular Culture Library at Bowling Green State University, for hunting down *Clue* materials from the Michael McDowell collection.

One effect of getting older is believing that anything that happened during your lifetime, by definition of you being alive for it, is modern. I assumed that video from the 1980s would be a breeze to find—surely it would be on YouTube or other popular sites. Instead, I was shocked to learn how much is gone. My thanks therefore to Don Giller, the foremost archiver of David Letterman episodes, who provided me with clips from the show, including Martin Mull's appearance promoting *Clue*, within minutes of me reaching out to him. I am also grateful to Jane Klain and the staff of the Paley Center, who located a tape of Madeline Kahn's appearance on *The Tonight Show Starring Johnny Carson*.

My thanks to Brett Vickerman, who reached out with scans of records that would have been otherwise unavailable to me until the academy library reopened for in-person research, which would not happen for another year and a half. Brett's thoughtfulness allowed me to get to work much earlier than I would have been able to otherwise. My appreciation also to Jim McCarthy, who believed in this project long before almost anyone else. His encouragement meant a great deal to me.

When I reached out to Jonathan Lynn, I did so hesitantly, wondering how he might respond to a random person asking about a movie he had made nearly four decades earlier. I expected to hear from an assistant; instead I heard from him. He could have ignored this stranger popping up in his email, but he took the time to answer my questions, always patient and generous with his responses. I am grateful to him—for *Clue*, *Greedy*, *My Cousin Vinny*, *Yes Minister*, and more, and especially for his kindness to me.

It was a joy to speak with Colleen Camp, who quoted effortlessly from a dozen different movies and shared with me her thought process on approaching Yvette. My thanks to Josh Brandon, who spoke to me about his love of *Clue* since childhood and his experience recording the audio commentary with Lynn. Josh wrote for the criminally underappreciated series *Houdini & Doyle*, and it was a delight talking with him. I was saddened to learn of the passing of Kellye Nakahara in 2020, and I am grateful to her husband, David Wallett, and her daughter, Lani Coleman, for taking the time to speak with me. While we talked mostly about *Clue*, I couldn't help myself and also asked about *M*A*S*H*. They graciously shared memories and details about Kellye's background. While I did not get a chance to speak to other cast members, I remain grateful to them for sharing their experiences on *Clue* in other venues. Speaking of which . . .

If you haven't seen Jeff Smith's *Who Done It? The Clue Documentary*, I hope you'll remedy that immediately. Meeting Jeff has been one of the highlights of working on this book. He helped me understand more about what went on when *Clue* was being made, and traveling to see him screen the documentary allowed me to meet other fans and share in the fun that this movie has brought to all of us.

I am indebted to those who read parts or all of the manuscript as I worked, tweaked, and refined; their feedback was invaluable. My thanks to Scot Denhalter, Dallas Robbins, Jimmy Hatch, and especially the careful eyes of Lincoln Peterson. I am grateful to David Bushman and Scott Ryan of Fayetteville Mafia Press for taking this project on and for their help in crafting a better book.

Most importantly, to my wife, Joy, who upon hearing that I had decided to write a book about *Clue* did not ask me if I had lost my mind. Instead, she willingly shared her husband with this movie and was unfailingly supportive every step of the way. She has read this book more than once, offering praise, criticism, corrections, and, most of all, encouragement. She makes me feel lucky every single day.

Lastly, while this might feel perfunctory, it must be said because it's true: while these people helped me, the final work is mine, and mine alone, and I am therefore the one responsible for any errors.

# PART I
# MYSTERIES AND MOVIES

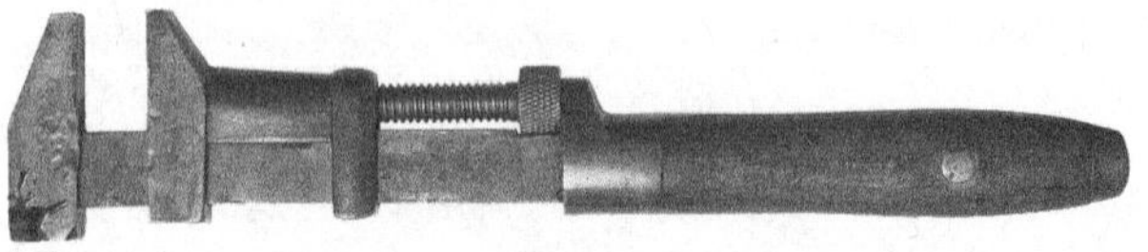

# 1. MURDER MANIA

"A whodunit is such an intrinsically ridiculous genre."
-Jonathan Lynn[1]

*Clue* debuted in American theaters on December 13, 1985. Thirty-six years before that, the board game Cluedo went on sale in England (now is your chance to marvel that Clue has existed as a movie longer than as just a board game). Twenty-eight years before Cluedo was introduced to the public, Agatha Christie published her first book, *The Mysterious Affair at Styles*. Thirty-three years before that novel introduced the world to Hercule Poirot, Sherlock Holmes solved the murder of two Mormon elders in *A Study in Scarlet*. Travel back in time another nineteen years to 1868 and there's Wilkie Collins's *The Moonstone*, often thought of as the first full-length detective novel. From there it's just another twenty-seven years to what is widely recognized as the first work of detective fiction, Edgar Allan Poe's short story "The Murders in the Rue Morgue," published in 1841.

Claiming that anything in literature, art, or pop culture is the first is oversimplifying at best and is never quite so easy to verify. So it goes with Poe and "The Murders in the Rue Morgue." Some historians argue that written detective fiction existed many hundreds of years ago, in

1 Brandon and Lynn, "*Clue*: The Director's Commentary Track," 1:05:35.

works ranging from *One Thousand and One Nights* to Chinese crime fiction from the Ming Dynasty.

The detective introduced in "The Murders in the Rue Morgue" displays many of the traits that would become so well-known, to the point of parody, in the world of mystery fiction. Poe's amateur sleuth, C. Auguste Dupin, is an odd fellow. First and foremost, he is an amateur. He comes from a prominent family but finds himself in less-than-ideal circumstances in Paris. He is rooming with an unnamed man who also serves as the story's narrator. If a roommate sharing the adventures of a detective not employed by the police rings a bell, it's because that same trope plays out in the stories of Sherlock Holmes. But long before Holmes dazzled Watson with abilities so stunning he seemed to be able to read minds, Dupin used similar abilities to shock his own, anonymous sidekick, who asks Dupin how he "should know what I was thinking?"[1]

It was Dupin's clever wits, not luck or intuition, that worked out devilishly intractable puzzles. This might seem obvious to modern readers accustomed to brilliant detectives after 180 years of mysteries, but it was new in 1841. Dupin did not tap into the supernatural but instead relied on powers of observation that led him to unshakable conclusions in "The Murders in the Rue Morgue" and in two other Poe stories—conclusions that always turned out to be right.

These characteristics—the use of brains and logic over intuition and luck, the ability to shock others by knowing things that by all appearances they couldn't possibly know, and the ability to spot the clues that really matter—became the foundation of dozens of famous detectives and hundreds of imitators. Edgar Allan Poe birthed a new genre. It didn't flourish overnight; it would take nearly twenty years for Émile Gaboriau to create Monsieur Lecoq, who appeared in *L'Affaire Lerouge* (1866). Collins's *The Moonstone*, published two years later, is often forgotten except among fans of mystery. But as time passed, what came to be known as the cozy mystery would thrive. Rigid definitions are a fool's errand when it comes to sorting out the many subgenres

---

1 Poe, "Murders in the Rue Morgue."

of crime fiction, but cozy mysteries tend to focus on the puzzle of whodunit, often in an exotic or charming locale. There is little violence in a cozy mystery, and the suspense is at a minimum. Often, but not always, the sleuth investigating the mystery is an amateur rather than a police officer or professional detective.

In 1887 the world's best-known detective made his debut, and would only further endear readers to mysteries. Sherlock Holmes got his start in a very different genre, however: anti-polygamy publications about Mormons in the American West. These stories, often published as cheap paperbacks, portrayed virtuous young women who had been tricked, threatened, or even kidnapped into marrying a Mormon polygamist. The reality of Latter-day Saint plural marriage was usually more mundane than the salacious treatment it received in the press, both in the United States and Great Britain, but stories of young women escaping or being rescued from the throes of polygamy titillated Victorian audiences. In *A Study in Scarlet*, Holmes solves the crime and then vanishes halfway through the book and the rest of the story is a flashback of events in Utah.

Five years after he wrote *A Study in Scarlet*, Sir Arthur Conan Doyle put Holmes in two short stories and submitted them to the *Strand Magazine*. These stories, "A Scandal in Bohemia" and "The Red-Headed League," made Holmes a phenomenal success and sparked unprecedented interest in detective fiction. Holmes straddled the line between amateur and professional; he often helped the police, but he wasn't one of them. Doyle gave him the label of "consulting detective."

Holmes's popularity sprang from deep wells of evolving Victorian sensibility in Britain. That someone could coldly evaluate a scene and know with certainty what happened comforted a people confronted with urban decay, crime, and violence. In 1888, a real murderer evaded police after hacking several women to death. Jack the Ripper is as synonymous with gaslit streets and hansom cabs as Sherlock Holmes is. The Ripper killed at least five women; he may have killed more. To this day, no one knows his identity, despite an entire industry of books, articles, websites, and documentaries that insist otherwise. He terrified London's East End as the Whitechapel Murderer, but he was far from the only danger Londoners read about in their newspapers.

In the same issue of *Lloyd's Weekly London* that reported on the Ripper with "Tragedy in Whitechapel: A Woman Stabbed in 39 Places," readers saw headlines that could double as titles of Holmes stories: "The Chloroform Mystery," "Seduction by a Magistrate," "The Railway Robberies at Plymouth," "The Lewisham Poisoning Case," and "Murderers' Mementoes."[2]

What appealed to readers in 1891 still appeals to readers today. Crime is chaotic and disorienting. It upsets our expectations of how the world is supposed to work. The detective, through powers of observation and deduction, imposes order and restores our sense of security. If they are able to solve the crime without moving from their proverbial armchair, then it is all the more comforting. To read or watch a cozy mystery is to spend most of one's time wondering what happened. Perhaps we're even confused. We look forward to seeing things resolved, order restored.

After Sherlock Holmes came an era so rampant with brilliant investigators (and teeming with bad knockoffs) that it has come to be known as the Golden Age of Detective Fiction, roughly defined as occurring between the two world wars, though again, rigid definitions are impossible. One of the better-known authors of the era, G. K. Chesterton, published his first Father Brown story four years before the assassination of Archduke Ferdinand in 1914 plunged the world into a war unlike any other before it. Other Golden Age writers are also well-known to mystery aficionados, including Agatha Christie, Dorothy L. Sayers, Anthony Berkeley, and Henry Wade. While the Brits dominated this period, Americans had their say. Ellery Queen (a pseudonym for two cousins, Frederic Dannay and Manfred B. Lee) wrote dense puzzles, famous for adding a "Note to the Reader" explaining that all the clues had been revealed and that they have all the information needed to solve the mystery. John Dickson Carr was the master of the locked-room murder—there's a dead body, a locked door, and no way in or out. Dashiell Hammett and Raymond Chandler wrote hardboiled stories, different from the prim-and-proper

---

2 *Lloyd's Weekly London Newspaper*, Aug. 12, 1888.

mysteries of other writers. Their books were short on whodunits but full of colorful characters and still driven by a central mystery. The detectives, unlike those in cozy mysteries, were morally complex and often found themselves on the wrong side of the law.

If Sherlock Holmes is the epitome of the detective, Dame Agatha Christie is the personification of the cozy mystery author. Christie published *The Mysterious Affair at Styles* in 1920, featuring her first detective, Hercule Poirot, the Belgian with the egg-shaped head full of "little grey cells" that he put to work solving a myriad of puzzles. Christie also created Miss Jane Marple, an amateur sleuth who leveraged her lifelong observations of human nature to solve crimes. A handful of Christie's books had standalone detectives who appeared only once, and one of her most famous works, *And Then There Were None*, had no detective at all.

Christie's novels contained all the elements of what readers came to recognize as the quintessential detective story: the unlikable murder victim, usually killed off before readers could find a reason to care about them; the closed circle of suspects, all of whom had a motive to kill; a remote location—an island, a country house, a stranded train, a ship on the Nile—that makes the likelihood of an intruder next to impossible; the detective, often summoned before the murder under suspicious circumstances or invited, much to the consternation of the murderer, as a guest, or who finds some other reason to be included in the closed circle; red herrings and misdirection; large clues that turn out to be meaningless and small details that explain everything; and the dénouement, or ending—the detective gathers all of the suspects and walks through all the events, explains the red herrings, and exposes the murderer.

*Clue* follows all of these tropes, and is itself a cozy mystery. Mr. Boddy, the victim, is a despised blackmailer. All of the guests—trapped as they are in an isolated mansion during a storm—have a reason to kill him. It will take an amateur detective, Wadsworth, the butler, to solve the mystery, though not before explaining the red herrings and misdirection.

It was only a matter of time before the cozy mystery, so familiar to the public and often formulaic, would make the jump to games. Once again, it was a Brit who took the leap. Anthony Pratt lived with his wife in Birmingham during World War II, and they knew a couple who had invented a board game called Buccaneer and sold the idea to Waddingtons toys. Waddingtons had licensed Monopoly from the States; now it was time to return the favor, this time with Clue.

Pratt spent some years developing what would become Clue. He would later recall that as kids, "we would play a stupid game called Murder, where guests crept up on each other in corridors, and the victim would shriek and fall to the floor."[3] It is difficult for Americans to appreciate what it means to live in a war zone. While the United States sacrificed tremendously during World War II (including over four hundred thousand military personnel who perished in combat), its struggle cannot compare to the nightly bombing raids Britain endured. Pratt remembered that even the simple fun of their murder game was ruined when "came the war and the blackout and it all went, 'Pouf!' Overnight, all the fun ended."[4] Pratt applied for a patent in 1944 for a game set in a country house named Tudor Close. The manor had ten rooms, including a gun room, and characters named Mr. Black, Mr. Brown, Mr. Gold, Nurse White, Colonel Yellow, and Mrs. Silver. The weapons originally included a syringe, poison, an ax, and a bomb. The bomb seemed a bit excessive, and it was dropped as changes were made. The first Waddingtons-licensed games appeared in 1949, though a shortage of materials after the war meant it was not widely produced until 1950. Waddingtons quickly gave US manufacturer Parker Brothers the rights to produce it in America, and the game first appeared there months before they were on shelves in England, retailing for $2.98. In Britain, the game was called Cluedo, a portmanteau of clue and *ludo*, Latin for "I play." In the US, it was Clue: The Great Detective Game. In the first retail version, the suspects were Colonel Mustard, Professor Plum, Mr. Green, Miss Scarlet, Mrs. White, and Mrs. Peacock. The weapons were a revolver, a rope, a lead pipe, a wrench, a dagger, and a candlestick. The nine rooms in the

---

3 Summerscale, "Jack Mustard."

4 Summerscale.

mansion that players could visit were the hall, lounge, dining room, kitchen, ballroom, conservatory (a music room, not a greenhouse), billiard room, library, and study.

Parker Brothers was initially squeamish about selling a game where the victim could have been shot, stabbed, strangled, or bludgeoned to death, and it took some coaxing to get the company to do it. Board game historian Tristan Donovan writes that Parker Brothers even refused to announce the game's launch, "concerned about being associated with a game about murder."[5] One curious change from the British version reflected Americans' growing sensitivities around religion in the postwar era, as they sought to distinguish themselves from godless communism. Cluedo's Reverend Green became Mr. Green in the US version; a man of God could hardly be a suspect in a murder. These American sensitivities were also reflected in film, where the production code said that "ministers of religion . . . should not be used as comic characters or as villains."[6]

Cluedo was at once a symbol of the success of the cozy mystery and an indictment of it. The game worked well. It was fun and popular. But what did it say about a genre that could be boiled down to a simple board game that managed to recreate much of the formula of a detective story? There was a closed circle of six suspects, stuck in a mansion together. There was the little-known and little-cared-for victim, Mr. Boddy. Pratt initially had characters hunting clues by visiting each room, where the cards were placed. He later switched to a format that has remained unchanged since 1949: the cards are passed around and players interrogate one another, much like a detective might. Hunting clues, Pratt understood, is less a part of detective fiction than interviewing suspects and trying to spot deception. The game even has a dénouement, as one player guesses who did it, with what weapon, and in which room.

It seems likely that one of Christie's Miss Marple books, *The Body in the Library* (1942), was an inspiration for the game. The story

---

5 Donovan, *It's All a Game*, chap. 8.

6 "Motion Picture Production Code."

begins with a colonel, his wife, and the body of one Ruby Keene. The colors ruby and scarlet may not be identical, but they also may not be coincidence. The criticisms of the cozy mystery aren't without merit: Christie and other authors, cranking out one book after another, would sometimes resort to silly, even offensive stereotypes to create their characters, some of whom might resemble a plastic game token more than a real person.

In the mid-1990s, Waddingtons sought out Anthony Pratt, hoping to celebrate the fiftieth anniversary of Cluedo and no doubt to sell a few more games. But the company discovered he had died in 1994 after spending his last few years in a nursing home suffering from Alzheimer's. While Pratt made some money from Cluedo in its first few years of release, in 1953 he gave up any international royalties for £5,000, the equivalent of nearly $200,000 in 2023. While it wasn't an insignificant sum, Parker Brothers made millions off of the game before the company was purchased by Hasbro in 1991. Pratt's daughter said her parents "were rather bitter about it," while taking care to note that Cluedo was not the focus of their life.[7] When word of his death spread, news outlets seemed unable to help themselves with such headlines such as "In the Ground, of Natural Causes, Cluedo's Inventor, Anthony Pratt."[8]

The formulaic nature of cozy mysteries, with its rules, idiosyncrasies, and recycled plots, led almost at once to another subgenre: the mystery-comedy parody. Some of the first spoofs took aim at Sherlock Holmes as early as the 1890s. Most parodies were short stories published in magazines or newspapers, but over time there were plays, movies, television shows, and even musicals.

By 1980, when the first public notices appeared that *Clue* was being turned into a movie, comedy was all over the map. Consider that after *The Empire Strikes Back*, the five top-grossing movies of the year were comedies—and none of them looked a thing like the others: *9 to 5*, about secretaries who were fed up with their abusive, creepy boss; *Stir*

---

7 Treneman, "Mr. Pratt, in the Old People's Home."

8 Boseley, "In the Ground, of Natural Causes."

*Crazy*, with Gene Wilder and Richard Pryor seemingly ad-libbing their way through a prison comedy; *Airplane!*, the absurd, whacky, slapstick disaster-movie parody that is still quoted almost as much as *Clue*; *Any Which Way You Can*, an action sequel to *Every Which Way But Loose* (1978) starring Clint Eastwood as a boxer with a pet orangutan named Clyde; and *Private Benjamin*, with Goldie Hawn joining the Army and battling sexism, her own insecurities, and a brutal drill sergeant played by Eileen Brennan. *Caddyshack* was another 1980 movie, and while it didn't garner too much notice then, many critics now rate it among the greatest comedies of all time. After a decade of political upheaval and blows to the national ego, Americans, it seemed, were ready to laugh at anything, including murder.

The modern mystery parody got a significant boost from would-be *Clue* screenwriter Tom Stoppard. His 1968 play, *The Real Inspector Hound*, was a send-up of Agatha Christie's *The Mousetrap*. Stoppard's *Hound* is a hilariously clever play within a play, unfolding as two critics watch the performance of a whodunit that takes place in an isolated manor house. Like many parodies, *Inspector Hound* takes aim at the broader genre by focusing on the best-known examples. Christie's *Mousetrap*, the longest-running play of all time, is better than Stoppard's spoof implies, but the point is well-taken—manor house mysteries are ripe for the plucking.

Several direct film parodies of detective stories appeared throughout the 1970s and 1980s. The best known is Neil Simon's *Murder by Death* (1976), which features riffs on Hercule Poirot, Sam Spade, Miss Marple, Nick and Nora Charles, and Charlie Chan and boasts an absurd performance by Truman Capote. It was followed by another Simon parody, *The Cheap Detective* (1978). In 1980, Don Knotts and Tim Conway spoofed Holmes and Watson in their last comedic outing together in *The Private Eyes*. That same year came *The Man with Bogart's Face*, about a man so obsessed with Humphrey Bogart that he goes by Sam Marlowe and has plastic surgery to resemble the Hollywood icon. A year later, Peter Ustinov, who had played Poirot in *Death on the Nile* (1978), appeared in *Charlie Chan and the Curse of the Dragon Queen*. In 1982, Steve Martin starred in Carl Reiner's *Dead Men Don't Wear Plaid*. Seven months after *Clue* premiered, *Haunted Honeymoon*

(1986), with husband-and-wife duo Gene Wilder and Gilda Radner, opened. Another writer–director had been trying to develop his own comedy–mystery since the early '70s, titled *Radioland Murders*, but he'd been consumed by another project, called *Star Wars*. George Lucas finally produced *Radioland Murders* in 1994; it was a critical and commercial bomb, and unlike *Clue*, it thus far has not found new life as a cult classic.

*Clue* is most often compared to *Murder by Death*, directed by Robert Moore. It's easy to understand why: guests are invited to a mysterious mansion, a murder takes place, and they have to solve the crime. It, like *Clue*, stars Eileen Brennan. But *Clue* director Jonathan Lynn believed, not incorrectly, that *Murder by Death* had no interest in a sensical plot. Even as *Clue* was being filmed, reporters asked Lynn how his movie differed from Simon's parody. Lynn, bristling somewhat at the question, repeatedly insisted that *Clue*, unlike *Murder by Death*, had a real mystery to solve, and he went to pains to explain that his movie was a comedy, not a parody. He and producer Debra Hill often said that audiences could solve the murder sitting in their seats. Simon's movie, by contrast, existed solely to parody the genre, and by the end of the film, nothing makes sense—which is the whole point. Simon believed that mystery writers cheated and so devising an airtight plot was a useless endeavor, especially if the goal was to poke fun at all the stereotypes of the genre.

But while *Murder by Death* still has a lot of fans who, like fans of *Clue*, discovered it as kids, it doesn't hold up quite as well. Today *Murder by Death* is perhaps best remembered for Peter Sellers's unfortunate yellow-face portrayal of Sidney Wang. *The Cheap Detective* brought back director Moore and a sizable chunk of the actors from *Murder by Death*. Peter Falk starred alongside Brennan, James Coco, and James Cromwell. The movie bursts at the seams with recognizable faces, so many that it's tempting to play six degrees of *Clue*. Madeline Kahn, brilliant as always, turns up. So does *M*A*S*H* star David Ogden Stiers, who was a finalist for the role of Colonel Mustard. *The Cheap Detective* is primarily a parody of *The Maltese Falcon* and *Casablanca*, even replicating lines of dialogue verbatim. It is more lighthearted than *Murder by Death* and is genuinely funny, but it lacks the repeat watchability of *Clue*.

*The Private Eyes* and *Haunted Honeymoon* also have something in common with *Clue*: kids love all three, even if adults (at first) don't. The films have moments that can seem scary for kids but then quickly retreat into comedy, often slapstick or silly, deflating the tension. All three are period pieces in the style of manor house mysteries. They have secret passages, power outages, butlers, cooks, and maids. They have dead bodies that go missing only to turn up again at inopportune times. All three are closed-circle mysteries with endings that at least make some attempt at plausibility, especially in comparison with *Murder by Death*. In *The Private Eyes*, Conway and Knotts are, respectively, Inspector Winship and Doctor Tart. Each is a buffoon, but Conway takes on the role of the dumber of the two as they try to solve the murder of a wealthy couple and bodies pile up around them. *Haunted Honeymoon*, like *Radioland Murders*, takes place in the golden age of radio. Radner and Wilder play radio stars set to be married at Wilder's family home, a spooky country manor complete with a werewolf, disfigured zombielike monsters, and a murderer using the confusion for his own purposes. Neither *Haunted Honeymoon* nor *The Private Eyes* impressed critics, and while both have their fans today, they can hardly be considered cult favorites.

Box office success eluded most of the whodunit parodies made in the 1970s and 'eighties. But a talented young producer thought she could make a murder-mystery spoof audiences wanted to see. She would take an existing, well-known property and license it to create her movie—and it would have everything. It would be a tightly woven narrative with plenty of comedy but also a whodunit audiences would care about—part homage, part spoof, part mystery, part thriller, and part throwback. They would get so wrapped up in the story, she thought, they would yell out solutions to the murder at the screen. And so, in 1980, Debra Hill picked up the phone and called Parker Brothers.

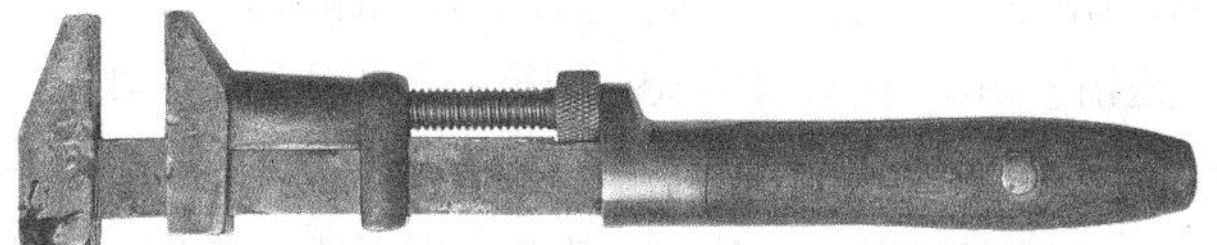

# 2. "IT WAS ALL MY IDEA"

"It was my favorite game because it really made you think."
-Debra Hill[1]

Movies are a collaborative process, no matter how much devotees might revere the fabled auteur, the director visionary who brings cinema to life. A lot of people worked on *Clue*, from the cast and the director to the boom mic operators and the construction crew. But it would not have existed at all if it were not for one woman: producer Debra Hill.

Nearly every article mentioning Hill says she was born in Haddonfield, New Jersey, on November 10, 1950. They have the date right, but the location wrong. The confusion is understandable—Hill's family later moved to Haddonfield, and she used the same name for the town terrorized by Michael Myers in *Halloween*, only relocated on celluloid from New Jersey to Illinois. Hill was born across the Delaware River from Haddonfield in Philadelphia; then, a year later, her family moved to New York City. When she was eight years old, she was given a toy movie camera, and she got to work making her first pictures. By the time the family settled in Detroit, when Hill was thirteen, there had been other homes in other towns. Her brother, Bob, later remembered that during one house-hunting trip, his parents dropped him and Debra off at a nearby movie theater where they watched *Gone with the Wind.*

1 Farber, "Off the Board, onto the Screen."

It must've been terribly boring for poor Bob, since he remembered that they watched it four times—a sixteen-hour endeavor. By the time the family made their way to Haddonfield, Debra was in high school.

Bouncing from neighborhood to neighborhood, saying goodbye to friends, walking into new schools time after time—this is the stuff that makes people who they are. Hill, instead of walling herself off and shying away from attention, stood front and center and forced people to take stock of her. They all found out the same thing: she was nice, fun, smart, and tough, and she meant business.

After graduating from high school, she made her way back across the river to Philadelphia, where she attended Temple University. Hill received a bachelor's degree in sociology, but she already knew she wanted to make movies. She took several film classes at Temple, all while her parents discouraged her from majoring in cinema, believing, like nearly every parent of every child who wants to be in show business, that she wouldn't find work. But she did, initially in public relations working on documentaries around New York City. The experience was invaluable, as she learned how to make movies. "On documentaries, you have a small enough crew that you do everything," she recalled.[2] Hill learned editing and screenwriting and how to work a camera.

But even with experience under her belt, she wasn't ready to move to Hollywood just yet. Instead she became a flight attendant, eager to see the world. When she quickly tired of being "a waitress in the sky," she settled in Jamaica.[3] She worked as a bartender, dated a jazz musician, and wrote liner notes for his records. Other artists noticed, and she penned their liner notes too. Hill could write, and people paid attention. She was invited to *Playboy* magazine headquarters in Chicago for a job interview. She flew back to the East Coast, jumped in a car, and drove to the Windy City. Once there, Hill decided the job wasn't for her, and soon she was back in her car, heading for San Francisco. She was twenty-three years old.

Hill was relentless, whether appeasing her wanderlust or carving out

---

2 Applebaum, "Working with Numbers," 20.

3 McFadden, *Real Woman*, 19.

her own space in the male-dominated entertainment industry. When she got her first job, working on *The Streets of San Francisco*, in 1974, men called her "Honey" and assumed she was there to type, style hair, or fetch coffee. Her true job was script supervisor. She spent the next eighteen months working on low-budget films, officially as a script supervisor, unofficially doing anything that needed to be done. Her life changed, even if she didn't realize it at the time, when she was hired by John Carpenter for *Assault on Precinct 13* (1976). Carpenter immediately recognized Hill's talents, and he started giving her more work and consulting her on bigger and bigger decisions.

Hill and Carpenter began dating, and with $300,000 and nothing more than an idea from their financier about babysitters being terrorized, they set out to make their next picture. Together they wrote *Halloween*, a movie that has spawned countless sequels, reboots, and knockoffs. It took them less than three weeks to write the script and twenty days to shoot the movie. The story takes place in Haddonfield, Illinois, around—when else?—Halloween. But Hill and Carpenter filmed in Southern California with a budget so small they had to pick up the fake leaves they had scattered to make it look like autumn so they could be reused in other scenes. In one or two wide shots, palm trees, definitely not native to Illinois, appear in the background.

It didn't matter. Neither did the initial unenthusiastic reviews. *Halloween* was a massive hit, cementing Carpenter's career as a director and launching Hill's as a producer. In today's world of tentpole movies (including, ironically, the *Halloween* sequels) movies opening on thousands of screens as studios hope to recoup most of their budget in the first weekend or two, it might be hard to appreciate the staying power popular movies once had. *Star Wars*, which opened in May 1977, was still playing in some theaters in the United States a year later. When *Clue* premiered in December 1985, it was competing against—and was outperformed by—another movie starring Christopher Lloyd, *Back to the Future*, which had bowed six months earlier.

*Halloween* became one of the most successful independent films of all time. It opened in only a handful of theaters in October 1978. But over time and through word of mouth (there was little in the way of a promotional budget to speak of), *Halloween* caught on. Well into

1979, the movie was still chugging along at the box office.

It was after the success of her first big hit that Hill had the idea to make a whodunit. She reached out to Parker Brothers, a board game manufacturer in Salem, Massachusetts. She was going to license Clue, because she felt that "the easiest way to sell the idea" of her own whodunit "would be through these characters."[4] After all, everyone already knew who Colonel Mustard, Professor Plum, and Mrs. Peacock were, and she had liked playing the game as a kid.

The first public notice that Clue was being made into a movie appeared in the *Hollywood Reporter* in October 1980. She and Carpenter were still producing and still dating, and the notice said they were making *Clue* together. Once Carpenter and Hill parted ways, he was no longer mentioned in reports. According to Hill, they had dated for seven years, but even after they broke up as a couple, they remained friends. They made *The Fog* (1980), and investors begged them to make *Halloween II* (1981). But while most of Hollywood may have seen Hill as the producer of horror movies, she had something entirely different in mind.

Hill would spend the rest of her life as a producer. Profiles of her in newspapers and magazines inevitably report on how she challenged Hollywood stereotypes of women, only for reporters to reinforce those stereotypes on the next page. They seemed unable to talk about her work without delving into personal matters like when she would decide to have a family, all with the moldy scent of "Can today's modern woman really have it all?" The point is obvious, but still worth making: reporters never ask men how they manage to work in movies, date girlfriends or have wives (or sometimes both), raise children, and live out their existence beyond the nuclear family. Hill wanted a family and she wanted to work—and that very notion seemed to baffle some people. She told one reporter she had "a need for a child that I don't know how to satisfy."[5] She wanted to write, and she wanted a partner who understood her passion for film. But she never married and never

4 Rico, "Miss Scarlet Did It."

5 Rosenfield, "5 Films, 5 Hits."

had children. She died in 2005 from colon cancer at the age of fifty-four.

Hill considered herself a storyteller. While many Hollywood producers see themselves as wheelers and dealers, hopscotching from one lunch to another, Hill loved being on set and making movies. Before they got to know her, men who worked for her on movies would wonder what kind of woman she was: mouthy broad or pushover. She was never so easy to pigeonhole into such binary, misogynistic thinking. She would arrive on set, hands on her hips, "like Peter Pan arriving in Neverland,"[6] staring down the latest problem. She learned early that crews would eye her a little warily, wondering if she was "nice," the way women were expected to be. Hill made sure the crew saw that she was in charge. She was plenty nice, but at the end of the day, "They see I mean business."[7] Her friend Jeffrey Kramer (the Motorist in *Clue*) called her "a force of nature, a ball of fire."[8]

Her licensing agreement with Parker Brothers showcases her shrewd negotiating skills. She persuaded the company to waive any upfront fee in exchange for a share of profits. The family-friendly board game maker had a few requests of its own, however. Parker Brothers insisted on no profanity—an unintentional throwback to the Golden Age of Detective Fiction: murder was fine, but swear words? Absolutely not. Parker Brothers also wanted all marketing materials to include the registered trademark symbol after the word "Clue." Even today, long after Parker Brothers was bought by Hasbro, the DVD, Blu-ray, and digital versions of *Clue* all sport a tiny ® at the end of the title. Parker Brothers also asked for final script approval, and got it. But if any of that was complicated, Hill didn't let on. She would later say acquiring the rights wasn't a problem.

The first ideas for how a *Clue* movie might look come from Hill's August 1980 one-and-a-half-page treatment—and it is delightfully good fun. Her vision pops off the page, and it is hard not to wish this

6 Ryzik, "Overlooked No More."

7 Rosenfield.

8 Smith, *Who Done It?*, 53:55.

movie could have been made too. Hill foresaw a bumbling newbie, Detective Parker, called to the scene of a crime at a mansion. Mr. Boddy lies dead, and only one of six people could have done it. There's Colonel Mustard, an oddball who collects, of all things, candlesticks. Miss Scarlet is "a woman of questionable background."[9] Professor Plum is a criminologist anxious to devise the perfect crime. Mrs. Peacock is a socialite, and Mrs. White and Mr. Green are the maid and the butler.

Detective Parker, unsure of how to handle all of this, is thrown by all the clues. He draws a huge floor plan of the mansion on a blackboard and places color-coded markers to signify where each suspect was when Boddy was killed, adding marks for the weapons for good measure. But Parker is baffled when someone breaks into his office and moves it all around. The clues, just as in the game, don't stay put.

From the beginning, Hill wanted an "intricately woven" whodunit in the spirit of Agatha Christie and Ellery Queen. She also wanted the movie to be fun. Her first line describes *Clue* as "a comedy spoof." At different points in the film she envisioned the on-screen action freezing as an old-timey radio voice boomed out possible solutions: "Was it Mrs. Peacock in the pantry with the wrench?" The audience, following along and hopefully spotting the well-placed clues, would yell back, "No!" Hill's plans would be at least partially fulfilled thirty-five years later when, at midnight anniversary screenings of *Clue*, audiences quoted dialogue at the screen.

Although Hill unequivocally wrote about "the film" in her treatment, for a short time she envisioned a stage play for the board game in its first incarnation. It is not a coincidence that so many writers considered for *Clue*, including two who worked on it separately for several months, were playwrights. *Clue*'s roots are deeply entwined with the theater, and the final movie itself resembles something of a play. It's easy to picture its mansion set converted for the stage, since most of the action takes place in only a handful of rooms. It unfolds in real time, over one night, meaning costume changes might not even be needed. Jonathan Lynn, though directing his first film, was a master of the stage who

---

9 All quotes here are from Hill, "Clue," treatment.

had directed shows for the West End and Broadway. Theater had long been home to whodunits, mysteries, and mystery parodies. Only after *Clue* transformed from flop to cult classic would it come full circle and finally be adapted for the stage.

Hill flew to London several times trying to bring her idea to life. She wanted to hire British playwright Alan Ayckbourn, a master of farce with works such as *Absurd Person Singular* and *How the Other Half Loves*. Negotiations made it far enough along that Ayckbourn was mentioned as *Clue*'s first writer in some of the earliest reports about the movie. It was also in England that Hill met with a crackerjack young director named John Landis, who, over the course of twenty-three months, had made two of the highest-grossing comedies of all time: *Animal House* and *The Blues Brothers*. Hill hired Landis to direct *Clue* in early 1981, when he was in the middle of making *An American Werewolf in London*. By that summer her plans were coming together: Ayckbourn would write a play, it would debut on London's West End, and then Landis would adapt the play into a movie.

John Landis was born in Chicago in August 1950, but his family relocated to Los Angeles just a few months later. From an early age, he was obsessed with movies and fantasy. Disneyland had opened just a few weeks before he turned five, and his family went nearly once a year, long before season passes made routine visits commonplace. For decades he has told the same story about when he knew he wanted to work in movies. He was eight years old and riveted by *The 7th Voyage of Sinbad* (1958). He asked his mother, "Who makes movies?" When she told him it was the director, "ever since that day, being a director has been my burning ambition."[10]

Five years after the family moved to Los Angeles, Landis's father died suddenly of an aneurysm. It upended their lives, but he was fortunate to have a wealthy uncle who was "very glamorous to me."[11] After his mother remarried, he lived what he's described as a solidly middle-class American lifestyle. But it was still a lifestyle surrounded by moviedom,

---

10 Thomas, "John Landis Always Wanted to Direct."

11 Vallan, *John Landis*, 38.

the kind no kid in Iowa or Montana or West Virginia was experiencing. His sister went to school with Liza Minnelli, and once the two became friends, Judy Garland would stop by the Landis house to pick her up. After his parents enrolled him in a private high school, Landis also became friends with kids whose parents worked in films. He was close to Peter Bernstein, the son of composer Elmer Bernstein, who once took both boys to see the Beatles at the Hollywood Bowl. But when his parents could no longer afford the tuition, he was kicked out of his private high school. Instead of bothering to enroll back in a public school, Landis got to work.

He landed a job in the mailroom at 20th Century Fox. Landis's experience there was like something straight out of its own movie, a dream too good to be true for a kid who loved cinema and wanted to be a director. He met actors like Donald Sutherland and Richard Burton and directors like George Cukor. He wandered the backlot in awe, seeing people in costumes from different productions. "You know when you watch old movies about Hollywood studios, they show the lot and you see Indians and space men and showgirls? It was just like that," he remembered.[12]

But Landis had arrived at a time when things were collapsing for the old studios. Massive conglomerates or wealthy investors were buying up these once-unstoppable behemoths. People who had worked in the studio system since the 1930s were laid off or forced to retire. Some studios changed hands more than once. While this shakeup helped create Hollywood's second golden age in the 1970s, it was chaos for the people who worked at the studios. Landis left the mailroom at Fox and in 1969 ended up in what was then Yugoslavia working as a gofer on *Kelly's Heroes* (1970), an action comedy about American soldiers stealing Nazi gold during World War II, with an all-star cast including Sutherland, Clint Eastwood, and Don Rickles. Landis fetched coffee and performed odd tasks before making his way to Spain, where he worked on spaghetti westerns, sometimes as a stuntman.

When he finally returned to Los Angeles, after nearly two years in

12 Vallan, 39.

Europe, he had visions of making his own movie. He poured his energy into *Schlock*, which he shot in 1971 but couldn't get released until 1973, after showing clips on *The Tonight Show Starring Johnny Carson*. Landis calls the comedy, about a prehistoric ape-man terrorizing a California town, a "terrible movie," but it has since gained a small cult following.[13] Critic Charles Johnson of the *Sacramento Bee* said he was relieved that after seeing brilliant film after brilliant film from people half his age (like George Lucas and Francis Ford Coppola), twenty-three-year-old, "hard-working, intelligent John Landis" can make a lousy movie.[14]

But Landis had already met people he would later work with on his bigger hits. Sutherland would appear in *Animal House*, and Elmer Bernstein would score it. Rick Baker, makeup artist extraordinaire, had one of his first jobs working on *Schlock*. In the mid-1970s, with sketch comedy booming, Landis got a call from David Zucker, Jim Abrahams, and Jerry Zucker. They had created an act called the Kentucky Fried Theater that they wanted to turn into a movie. After being roundly rejected in Hollywood, they had decided to make it on their own, and *Schlock* had convinced them Landis might be the right director for it.

He was. The *Kentucky Fried Movie* banked $7 million at the box office and was made for around $650,000. After that success, he was hired to direct *Animal House*, and its stratospheric success cemented Landis's career. Profile after profile of the new Hollywood wunderkind marveled at his off-the-charts energy. But Landis was more than a barrage of energy. He seemed to have an innate sense of what would work and what audiences wanted to see without pandering or dumbing down material. When he was brought on board to direct *Animal House*, every character in the script was an unlikable slob. It was Landis who created protagonists and antagonists; he said the audience needed someone to root for. If anyone could turn a thirty-year-old board game with a bunch of suspected murderers into a funny movie, it was Landis. Once more, he got to work.

Sometime after Hill wrote her treatment and developed her plans

---

13 Vallan, 50.

14 Johnson, "'Schlock' Really Is."

for a stage play followed by a movie, a new idea bubbled to the surface. If the board game had multiple endings, why couldn't the play and the film? It was an ingenious way to invigorate a stage play, and it remained faithful to the game. Six suspects, six weapons, and nine rooms can have up to 324 variations. While the multiple endings of the movie struck critics as gimmicky, it's hard to imagine a play not energized by all the possibilities. Every actor gets a chance to be the one whodunit, and it keeps the cast on their toes. It also seems likely to bring people back for more. There's an intimacy theater offers that is absent from films. What fun might it be to see sweet Mrs. Peacock horrified by the murder one night, only to learn on another night that this time she's the ruthless killer?

Writers of whodunits produced during the 1970s and eighties were striving to keep their work relevant by adding multiple twists to keep audiences on their toes, with varying degrees of success. *The Last of Sheila* (1973), a film written by Stephen Sondheim and Anthony Perkins, seems to resolve everything before taking an unexpected turn. Plays-turned-films *Sleuth* and *Deathtrap* piled twists upon twists. *The Mystery of Edwin Drood*, a 1985 Broadway musical by Rupert Holmes, based on Charles Dickens's unfinished novel, perhaps came closest to Hill's vision of multiple endings. Audiences attending the musical would cast votes to determine who the murderer was. The votes not only affected whodunit, but could change which cast member sang certain numbers. While different ideas for *Clue* would come and go, the multiple endings stuck, and today it's one of the first things people remember about the movie.

As fun as Hill's initial treatment might be, none of it was used. Landis quickly came up with his own story. His outline, preserved in a transcript of his pitch to potential writers, makes it clear how much of the plot of *Clue* originated with him. While some of his ideas were abandoned, others appear in the finished film nearly unchanged.[15]

Landis wanted to disconnect the film from the game. He reasoned

---

15 The summary and all of the quoted material is from Landis and Stoppard, "Transcript of Conversation between John Landis and Tom Stoppard," Feb. 7, 1983, in Stoppard and Landis Correspondence. Emphases are in original.

that anyone seeing the movie had to understand it whether they had played the game or not. He began with the guests eating dinner with Mr. Boddy, who, unlike in the game, is very much alive at the start of the picture. He wanted the action to take place in real time, over two hours or so, which he admitted was "setting up a tremendous problem," since it would make writing the movie that much more difficult. He explained the requirements—they needed all six suspects, all six weapons, and all nine rooms—and then said that "the big thing to surmount . . . is *why* it was done." The motive was no part of the game at all, but it "is so important to the film." Landis added two more characters, a "saucy French maid" named Yvette and a butler he called Cleese, since he kept thinking of Monty Python alum John Cleese for the role.

The guests, all unknown to each other, gather at Mr. Boddy's house, "maybe in Palm Beach, Florida," in 1954. Landis wanted to set the film in the early '50s because he believed "nobody has really done" a mystery film in that time period. The first scene would be dinner, and all the guests are there because of a connection to Mr. Boddy. Scarlet could be Mr. Boddy's fiancée, and White his mistress. Landis's pitch is peppered with words and phrases like "maybe," "who knows," and "perhaps." But as he ramps up, the story begins to unfold more clearly and more frenetically. Mrs. Peacock, Mr. Boddy's first wife, is now married to a US senator. Professor Plum is a gambling addict, complete with a racing form in his checkered-coat pocket. He's also a bookie who owes Mr. Boddy a lot of money—or perhaps it's Boddy who owes him; Landis isn't sure. Colonel Mustard and Boddy could have been war profiteers together. Regardless, "they're all connected somehow."

There's a terrific storm outside, and dinner is an uncomfortable affair. Yvette is outlandishly dressed, and it's clear she's having sex with at least a few of the men seated at the table. She has a terrible French accent, and all of the characters feel awkward, unsure of what is going on. They "adjourn to the conservatory or the lounge," where Mr. Boddy tells Cleese to distribute some gifts. Boddy leaves, and the guests unwrap the gifts, revealing a different weapon within each one. The alarmed guests begin haranguing the butler for information, asking what's going on and why Mr. Boddy has left. Cleese leaves to fetch Boddy and stumbles upon him "in a sexually compromising situation with Yvette." Landis is open to ideas, but he's also clear on some things that he wants for the movie. "I really want to play this as farce, and you'll see that what I want to do is start off at a fairly sedate level and escalate to total lunacy playing and running around and lots of screaming and doors slamming."

Mr. Boddy returns after his rendezvous with Yvette, or all the guests go find him, holding their weapons (Landis tells it both ways), and as Boddy's pouring a brandy, the lights go out. There's a gunshot, a scream, and confused noises until the lights come back on, only to reveal Mr. Boddy lying dead on the floor. Butler Cleese reads a letter from a large envelope that says "To be read aloud in case of my untimely demise." Boddy tells them all from the grave, "If you're hearing this, I'm dead, and one or more persons in this room has reason to kill me." He goes on to say he wants to know, by midnight, who it was. Unless they solve the crime, however, Boddy's attorney will make public all of their worst secrets. Cleese reveals evidence from the envelope, "ghastly secrets" indeed. There's a photograph of Senator Peacock dressed as a Nazi and standing above Yvette, bound to a chair. There's a pornographic reel of Miss Scarlet. Landis leaves us to guess at the other terrible secrets. Boddy ends his letter with a postscript: "Mr. Green is innocent." Everyone immediately turns to face Green, who yells out desperately, "I didn't do it!!!"

Landis believed that because there were so many characters, it should be easy for one to slip away to commit a murder. With film, "you can be very selective with the camera." Everything will be structured, Landis explains, to allow audiences to spot what is going on. After the guests' initial panic at being exposed subsides, they examine Mr. Boddy. There is no gunshot wound, no stab wound, no rope burns, no blunt-force trauma. They have no idea how he died. Miss Scarlet drinks Boddy's brandy, and the others suggest that perhaps it's poisoned. She screams and screams until she realizes she's not going to die. It's then that the guests remember that there's someone else in the house: the cook. They race to find her, and when they do, she has a knife in her back. Unsure what to do, they put the cook's corpse next to Mr. Boddy and begin arguing. Just then, the doorbell rings. A man has arrived claiming that his car has broken down, and he asks to use the phone.

Colonel Mustard suggests they split up to search the house, and everyone vies to be Mr. Green's partner, since Boddy has cleared him of suspicion. As they search the house, there's a cut to the motorist. He's on the phone saying something "innocuous, but it could mean something later." As he speaks, the "wrench comes into frame" and the motorist is killed. The guests quickly find him after stumbling on a secret passage, and sheer panic ensues. There have been three murders. None of the main characters from the game has been killed; none can be eliminated as a suspect.

As they all continue to panic, terrified that their lives will be over if their secrets get out, the bell rings again. This time it's a police officer checking on the motorist's car. Each of the guests contradicts the others as they try to explain to the cop what has happened. They don't trust one another, and "the paranoia increases with the rate of death." The cop, repeating the earlier scene with the motorist, asks to use the phone. The suspects split up again to keep searching, and just as in the final film, the cop and Yvette are murdered. It's clear that Yvette knows her killer, as she drops her heavy French accent for the first time to ask the unseen person, "How's it going? What do you think?"

With the murder count up to five, "hysteria has now set in." No one has seen the gun, and the guests all wonder who has it. Cleese says the murderer has it, and he knows what happened. Landis says Cleese will repeat "the entire movie" in a "tour de force" performance. At this point, the movie has run about eighty minutes. It's as Cleese reenacts the entire movie at high speed that the multiple endings come into play.

Initially, Landis wanted to have all of the solutions in the same showing of the movie, one after another. He settled on four endings, each about five minutes long, so that they could all fit on one two thousand-foot reel when the film was shipped to theaters. Although Landis would say he needed a writer to figure out who did it, he did have some ideas for the endings. He wanted Mrs. Peacock to be the murderer in one because she was a Communist who had married a US senator and in the age of McCarthyism couldn't afford to let her secret get out. In another ending, the butler would have done it. But no matter who killed whom, he was adamant that "the one constant I want to keep is that Mr. Green is innocent. It's just odd, I don't know why." The final screenplay would need enough variables to create the four endings, and doing so would be an enormous challenge.

Landis would conclude his pitch with an extended complaint that making the movie work would be next to impossible, since "all the classic whodunits cheat outrageously." He seems almost resentful that successful authors like Christie crafted clever mysteries, arguing that "they cheat, they lie, they're really outrageous." He would argue that translating the whodunit to film is much more difficult than writing a mystery novel because filmmakers don't have the luxury of the "literary conceit" that novelists have.

Hill liked Landis's ideas, and she quickly pitched them to PolyGram Pictures, which agreed to produce; Universal Studios would distribute the movie. Over the next four years, more producers and studios would hop on. Watching the opening of *Clue*, most viewers won't pick up on the list of people and companies credited with making the film, accustomed as they are to seeing names pop up that they've never heard of. Everyone knows Paramount and its famous mountain logo, but Peter Guber? Jon Peters? George Folsey Jr.? The names go by, but it's more interesting to watch Wadsworth's car wind its way up the drive to Hill House (named for the producer and not Shirley Jackson's *The Haunting of Hill House*). Still, those names are a reminder of the kinds of deals often needed to get a movie made.

There's a reason most movies today are produced by megacorporations: they have a built-in infrastructure and ecosystem, and they have money. If Disney loses $50 million on a movie, that's not exactly great for business, but investors know they'll make it up in a few months with the next Marvel or Star Wars picture. Besides, there's still a cruise line, a theme park, a streaming service, and more toys, T-shirts, and games than you can fathom to add to the bottom line. But most companies aren't Disney, and even those with a string of blockbusters can go bankrupt if a few of its movies bomb in the same year.

*Clue* was on shaky ground, but it never collapsed. It took Hill nearly six years to see the film produced and released to theaters. In that time, it wound its way through the tangled web of Hollywood dealmaking the way so many films of that era did, adding an executive producer here, dropping a writer there. Hill's deals with PolyGram Pictures to produce and Universal Studios to distribute seemed simple enough, but time would reveal them as anything but.

By October 1980, when the deals were announced, PolyGram had two hotshot producers, Jon Peters and Peter Guber. Hill, the storyteller who wanted to be a writer and who loved to be on set solving problems, needed money to make *Clue*, and PolyGram was becoming famous for throwing money around as if it literally grew on trees. According to the duo's biographers, entertainment journalists Kim Masters and Nancy Griffin, Guber and Peters were mostly interested in fame and money. They rarely visited the sets of the films they produced (Steven Spielberg banned them from the set of *The Color Purple*), unless it meant a trip to an exotic locale.[16] The late 1960s and the seventies ushered in the second golden age of Hollywood, a time when experimentation and innovation were encouraged, but in the eighties, when Ronald Reagan was in the White House, the renewed obsession with huge profits once again discouraged risk-taking. Producer Don Simpson (*Flashdance, Top Gun, Beverly Hills Cop*) wrote, in a memo outlining Paramount Pictures's corporate ethos, "The pursuit of making money is the only reason to make movies. We have no obligation to make history. We have no obligation to make art."[17] Gordon Gekko was talking about Wall Street when he said "greed is good," but he might as well have been talking about coke-fueled Hollywood.

Bill Tennant left his post as president of PolyGram Pictures in 1980 after his own drug addiction caught up with him, clearing the way for Guber and Peters to run the company. They put out a string of movies that lost money at the box office, and executives at the company's European headquarters began to panic. Lynda Obst, a friend and mentee of Debra Hill's and a successful producer in her own right, left PolyGram to work with Mary Tyler Moore. Others also jumped

---

16 Griffin and Masters, *Hit and Run.*

17 Rule, "Son of a Pitch."

ship. By 1982, Peters and Guber were no longer at PolyGram, but they took with them the rights to movies they'd already begun to develop, including *Clue*. Since it had originated with PolyGram, however, that company still had its own claim. Landis also brought in his longtime producing partner, George Folsey Jr.

Universal had its own issues. The studio had supported Hill's plans under president Ned Tanen, who had worked directly with Landis at Universal when they released *Animal House*. Tanen had overseen some staggering moneymakers at the studio, from *Jaws* to *E.T. the Extra-Terrestrial*. But Tanen resigned in December 1982, and Universal dropped *Clue* six months later. Tanen went on to produce *Sixteen Candles* and *The Breakfast Club*. In October 1984, he got back his title as president of motion pictures, but this time at Paramount, where he quickly greenlit *Clue*.

And so it was that *Clue* ended up presented by Paramount Pictures as a Guber–Peters production in association with PolyGram Pictures and Debra Hill Productions, executive produced by Jon Peters, Peter Guber, John Landis, and George Folsey Jr. Each would add to the movie in his own way, but the hunt for a writer continued to be the work of Hill and Landis.

Hill's initial idea for a play had by now fizzled out, and attention turned to getting *Clue* made as a movie. She hired Warren Manzi to write the screenplay. Manzi is rarely mentioned in *Clue* retrospectives, but he, apart from Jonathan Lynn, got farther than any other writer, finishing two separate screenplays over two years, each very different from the other.

Manzi was born in New Hampshire and raised in Massachusetts. He attended Catholic schools before graduating from the Yale School of Drama with a master's degree. His first big break was as an understudy in *Amadeus*, then showing on Broadway. He was twenty-five. Ian McKellan starred as Salieri, and Manzi understudied another British actor, playing the role of Mozart: Tim Curry. It was during this time that Manzi began writing the play he would become best known for, the mystery thriller *Perfect Crime*. Manzi rewrote and tinkered with the play for years, even after it opened in 1987. He trimmed its runtime and tightened the plot after some critics complained that it was confusing.

It became the longest-running play in New York history and was the first to reopen after the COVID-19 pandemic.

Manzi remained invested in the success of his play even as he continued to write. He married in 1995, but his wife died shortly after their wedding. Devastated, he moved back to Massachusetts to care for his aging mother, to whom he had dedicated *Perfect Crime*. After she died in 2003, Manzi stayed and focused on his writing instead of returning to New York. He died in 2016 of pneumonia at the age of sixty. Between 1981 and 1983, he wrote *Perfect Crime* and two drafts of *Clue*, all while performing on Broadway.

His first draft of "Clue: A Mystery, Based on the Parker Brothers Board Game," was finished in 1981.[18] Because the screenplay was incorrectly formatted, lacking slug lines (EXT. PARKING GARAGE—DAY . . . ) and other standard requirements for Hollywood scripts, he had to revise the draft, which he did, submitting it at the end of March 1982. Manzi's first version is radically different from Jonathan Lynn's or even John Landis's. Rather than trying to recreate the game with a body in a mansion and six suspects, Manzi cleverly incorporates the game into real life. A serial killer is sending the cards from the Clue board game to a mystery writer named Charlie. Charlie, who uses the absurd nom de plume H. Lawrence Grith-style, has no idea what to make of the first three cards or why they were sent to him: Colonel Mustard, the wrench, the library. But when a retired Army colonel named James Mustard is lured to the main branch of the New York Public Library and killed with a wrench, Charlie realizes that he's being pulled into a dangerous game of cat and mouse.

The story is a direct homage to Agatha Christie's *The ABC Murders*, one of her more famous Hercule Poirot novels. Lest anyone think Manzi is ripping Christie off, he includes a scene in which Charlie's publisher, Sheila, is reading the book, winking at those audience members who are in the know. Just like Christie's book, Manzi's story features a man trying to cover up one murder by pretending to be a serial killer who is choosing his victims based on their name. Charlie's

18 Manzi, "Clue," preliminary screenplay, 1981.

daughter, Agatha (named for Christie herself), is a nine-year-old prodigy whom kids would likely have loved to see on-screen. Agatha is cunning and brave, and she outsmarts adults more than once. But Agatha comes off as unrealistic—she has her own credit cards and thinks nothing of hopping on a plane alone. The resolution of the story is also far-fetched. Who is the murderer? The vice president of the United States, who has created this elaborate scheme to make it seem as if the president's murder (foiled by Charlie, Sheila, and Agatha) was only one of many deaths perpetrated by a serial killer.

There were other problems too. Hill expected *Clue* to be a family film, and Manzi included a gay sex scene that would have earned the movie an instant R rating. But it's not hard to see how a second draft could have resolved these issues. Manzi could have toned down the sex scene (*Deathtrap*, rated PG, features its two male stars kissing passionately); made Agatha a little older, eliminating the silliness of a nine-year-old jetting around the country; and reworked the resolution, which would have been tricky but not impossible. Manzi's first draft has Hill's handwritten notes scribbled in the margins, and it is clear that at least for a time, she was open to his ideas. But *The ABC Murders* homage was ultimately dropped, and Manzi went back to the drawing board.

His second attempt at a *Clue* screenplay is dated August 1983 and weighs in at 138 pages including architectural drawings of the mansion. This time Manzi followed Landis's basic outline; there's a butler named Cleese, Mr. Boddy gives the weapons as gifts before he's caught having sex with Yvette (another scene that would have been far too graphic for the family film Parker Brothers was expecting), and the cook, the cop, and the motorist are all killed off. Manzi's second screenplay also embraced Landis's idea of having events unfold in real time, but still, it had only one ending and one murderer. This story, like his first version, is clever but wildly improbable. Arthur Boddy is a billionaire genius architect who designs a house that appears to defy the very laws of physics, and he wants to show it off. In the library, characters can't be heard, even if screaming at the top of their lungs, since libraries are supposed to be quiet; the lounge makes its occupants feel heavier, to coax them to sit or lie down; the ballroom begins playing music whenever anyone enters; and the conservatory, filled with exotic plants, emits pleasant aromas when visitors step inside.

The guests are gathered for dinner when Miss Lola Scarlet, Boddy's fiancée, excuses herself to use the bathroom. Yvette, the maid, with her outlandish outfit and outlandish accent, serves dessert. When dinner is over, the guests are dispatched throughout the mansion to collect their gifts; each is stashed in a different room. It is all a ploy for Boddy to show off his magnificent home. After he is killed, the guests split up and search the mansion for Yvette, who has vanished and is suspected of the gruesome murder. In the end, they solve the mystery together: Miss Scarlet pretended to be Yvette and double-crossed Boddy, murdering him for his money. Scarlet reveals that she and Boddy had secretly wed weeks before. She drops the bombshell that the mansion is set to explode, and the guests manage to get out just before the building is consumed "in a flurry of blue and white flame."[19]

The story is convoluted and a little silly, but with flashes of cleverness in the mystery and lively dialogue. It is also funny and relentlessly adult, with a sex scene, profanity, and Boddy's graphic murder (he is killed with a seven-inch knife, plunged into his skull). It needed work but could have been crafted into a usable screenplay. Cutting the profanity would have been easy, and the sex scene, though integral to the plot, could have been shot in a way to garner a PG rating. The violence could have been toned down; Boddy could have been stabbed in the chest or the stomach, with minimal blood loss. But Hill ultimately passed on Manzi's second screenplay as well.

The exact reasons why Manzi's screenplays were not used are lost to time, but a few possibilities suggest themselves. His first story made no attempt to mimic the game—a mansion, Mr. Boddy, the weapons, and the rooms all are either absent or reimagined. The candlestick murder takes place at the Baseball Hall of Fame in Cooperstown, New York, where a massive sign that says Candlestick Park, home at the time to the San Francisco Giants, falls on a victim. Ingenious in its way, but not exactly what Parker Brothers was hoping for to promote its board

19 Manzi, "Clue," first-draft screenplay, Aug. 1983, 126.

game. Manzi also seemed entirely unconcerned with concocting four different endings; both screenplays have only one. He also ignored Parker Brothers's insistence on a family film. At the time, there was no PG-13 rating to breach the gap between family and R-rated films. At least some of the murders in Manzi's second screenplay are violent enough to have complicated any attempt at a PG rating. The stories are often unbelievable, even for Hollywood. A young girl who flies around the country on her own? An architect so brilliant he devises a mansion that seems to defy the laws of physics?

Although Manzi's screenplays were never used, they were submitted to the Writers Guild of America in 1985 as part of the standard arbitration process to see if he should receive credit as a writer. He did not, and it's not hard to see why. Anything in Manzi's screenplays that ended up in the final film were taken from Landis's original story pitch. With another writer not panning out, Hill and Landis kept looking. They hit on what must have felt like a sure thing.

If Manzi's career was just getting started in the early eighties, Tom Stoppard was already thought of as one of the world's finest living playwrights. His *Rosencrantz and Guildenstern Are Dead* (1966) regularly appears on lists of the greatest plays of the modern era. He followed it up with *The Real Inspector Hound*, a one-act parody of country-house mysteries. It's funny as a spoof, but two-thirds of the way in, the play takes a mind-bending turn that might explain Stoppard's later struggles to write *Clue*: it's hard to imagine topping the creativity of *Inspector Hound*. Even as he was being wooed to write *Clue*, his play *The Real Thing* was earning top notices; it would win the Tony Award for Best Play.

Stoppard was born on July 3, 1937, in Czechoslovakia as Tomáš Sträussler, to Moravian Jews. Two years later, his family fled the Nazi occupation to Singapore, where they lived until that British colony was attacked in 1942. His father stayed behind as an army volunteer while Stoppard, his brother, and his mother narrowly escaped to India. He never saw his father again. It would be nearly sixty years before he learned that his dad had died when a ship he was on was bombed and sank. Stoppard's paternal grandparents died in a Jewish ghetto in Latvia; his maternal grandparents died at Auschwitz. Some members of his family survived the war; most did not.

In India, Stoppard's mother met an English soldier named Kenneth Stoppard. The two married and moved to England, and Tomáš Sträussler became Tom Stoppard. In his early years, he did not identify as Czech or give much thought to his ancestry, but in the words of his biographer, "the luck of the draw, the road not taken, the alternative possible path to the one chosen . . . came to haunt him as an adult."[20] His family's identity as Eastern European Jews would come to influence much of his work.

Stoppard began his career as a journalist, and he worked for the BBC writing radio plays. Throughout the 1970s he also wrote teleplays and screenplays. He would later work on the scripts for *Brazil* and *Indiana Jones and the Last Crusade* and as a script doctor or adviser on many more films. He liked movies but was ambivalent about writing them, even calling it "junk food." He did it, he said, because he was well paid, but he regarded the film business as a "different moral universe."[21]

Stoppard was wooed by Landis to write the screenplay for *Clue* in October 1982. Their correspondence—the over-the-top Hollywood insider and the unfailingly polite Brit—is something to behold. Landis writes on TWA stationery midflight or on elegant hotel letterhead from Saint Martin in the Caribbean. His letters burst with enthusiasm and charm, and he signs each one "John!" Landis had read *The Real Thing* weeks before its premiere in London, and in one letter he tells Stoppard what he thought of it for a few pages before getting to his real purpose: "Somehow I must convince you how marvelous it would be for you to write 'Clue.'" Landis dangles money and the challenge of writing the movie in front of Stoppard before asking, "How can I seduce you?" He admits he "selfishly" wants to work with Stoppard.[22]

Landis's entreaties worked, and Stoppard agreed to meet with him in early 1983. Universal Studios was still on board to produce (that would change soon), and excited at the prospect of having Stoppard

20 Lee, *Tom Stoppard*, 24.

21 Lee, 429.

22 Landis to Stoppard, Oct. 24, 1982, in Stoppard and Landis Correspondence.

write it, Universal Executive Vice President Sean Daniel sent Stoppard a telegram introducing himself. He asked Stoppard to let him know if he "can be of any assistance."[23] Stoppard flew from London to New York on Friday, February 4, 1983, and stayed at the five-star St. Regis Hotel at Universal's considerable expense. They were determined to charm him into taking the job.

Stoppard and Landis met over the weekend for a lengthy brainstorming session where Landis gave Stoppard his pitch. It was essentially the same pitch he had given Manzi and would give Jonathan Lynn a year later, though it's unknown if Landis jumped on furniture and bounced around the room with Stoppard as he would with Lynn. It's interesting to wonder what Stoppard thought when Landis got to the part about a bound Yvette cowering beneath Senator Peacock in a Nazi uniform, given that members of his family had been killed by the Germans in World War II.

Stoppard mostly listened, but he did have a handful of questions and ideas of his own. "I decided Scarlet sounds like the mistress and White like the fiancée" of Mr. Boddy. Landis liked the idea, and he always allowed for plenty of malleability in the story he pitched to writers. But most of what Tom Stoppard thought of this whirlwind pitch is unknown. Throughout the nine-page, single-spaced transcript, he says fewer than fifty words. It is all Landis explaining the plot of the film, throwing out ideas on the fly, sometimes losing his place and backtracking. But whatever Stoppard thought, he accepted the job to write *Clue*. He and Landis agreed that he would turn in a first draft in twelve weeks.

Except he couldn't.

Adam Vary, in his oral history of *Clue*, concludes that Stoppard's failure to write the screenplay "must have been quite painful." Vary had reached out to Stoppard, who responded that he remembered Landis but not *Clue*. "I've never heard of *Clue*."[24] Stoppard's denials might seem farfetched, but for such a prolific writer, it's certainly possible

23 Sean Daniel to Tom Stoppard, Jan. 22, 1983, in Stoppard and Landis Correspondence.

24 Vary, "Something Terrible Has Happened Here."

that he wouldn't remember a job he officially had for less than two months and that he never finished. Whatever he remembers (or doesn't remember) about *Clue*, Stoppard did seem pained at the time by his inability to complete his draft.

Within a few weeks of their meeting, Landis got word, probably from Stoppard himself, that things were not going well. Landis, puzzled, told him in a letter from Saint Martin, "Your fears are not entirely clear to me," and he wondered if Stoppard thought himself above the material. Perhaps *Clue* might be too commercial? Can it become "Kafka meets the 3 Stooges?" In the next line, Landis dismissed his own idea, blaming its strangeness on the Caribbean's "tropical sun." Then he pleaded with Stoppard to "stop fucking around and write something wonderful!" He felt he needed to play the role of the tough Hollywood producer and asked if the shtick worked. "Have the clouds parted?" He tried to give Stoppard the leeway he needed, asking if the movie ought to be set somewhere other than Florida. England, perhaps? Even Paris or Hong Kong? But Landis's good-natured ribbing didn't work.[25]

Stoppard wrote Landis halfway into his twelve-week deadline. He was having "considerable trouble with it." He hadn't made much progress, and "much worse, I don't really like what I have done." Throughout the letter, Stoppard sounds terribly apologetic. He didn't know, he said, how to make something fresh out of such an old genre as a whodunit. The whole point of the board game was to provide a stock situation with "stock characters"—the very thing they wanted to avoid for the movie. He couldn't even write a proper parody because "the parody is almost as familiar as the parodied."[26]

In the end, he could not come up with a logical puzzle, to say nothing of four logical puzzles, for Landis and Hill's dream of four different endings. During their New York meetings, Stoppard reminded him, he had expressed some concern about all of this, but he ultimately felt "there was a good chance of solving the problems simply by working

25 Landis to Stoppard, Mar. 6, 1983, in Stoppard and Landis Correspondence.

26 Stoppard to Landis, Mar. 22, 1983, in Stoppard and Landis Correspondence.

on them." That didn't happen, and Stoppard believed it was "unfair" to Landis and the other producers for him "to stagger on." He hoped Universal had a precedent for a writer dropping out, because "I sure haven't."

"This is the very first time I haven't completed something I started, in or out of contract," he wrote.[27] He ends the letter asking Landis to forgive him. Landis would remember years later that Stoppard also enclosed a check for the full amount he was paid.

Landis tried to salvage the situation. He spoke to both Stoppard and Stoppard's agent on the telephone and told them "everything will be alright." He wrote Stoppard and enclosed a pen he had bought for him, though he acknowledged his dog and his daughter had gotten to it first, so "I'm afraid it's not too pristine." Stoppard responded to Landis's letter, but not for a month, and whatever he said has not survived. Regardless, he was done with *Clue*, and Landis and Hill were back at square one. They needed a writer. And what's more, perhaps in part because of Stoppard's withdrawal, Universal had pulled out as well. *Clue* was officially in development hell.

Hill and Landis had several separate projects they were juggling while they struggled to get *Clue* off the ground. For Hill, it was *Halloween III: Season of the Witch* (1982) and the adaptation of Stephen King's novel *The Dead Zone* (1983). Hill had little enthusiasm left for the Halloween series, but she and John Carpenter agreed to return to the third installment only if it took a new creative direction. It did—by eliminating Michael Myers, the villain from the first two films. Critics were . . . well . . . critical, but *Season of the Witch* made enough money at the box office to justify still more sequels, though without Hill's involvement.

Hill was hired by *Halloween II* and *Halloween III* producer Dino De Laurentiis to work on *The Dead Zone*, and it paid off. Hill teamed up with director David Cronenberg and writer Jeffrey Boam to revise the script over three intense days. *The Dead Zone* was a bigger success than *Season of the Witch,* both critically and commercially. It premiered in

27 Stoppard to Landis, Mar. 22, 1983, in Stoppard and Landis Correspondence.

October 1983, and afterward Hill could finally return her attention to getting *Clue* made.

Landis was busier. After *An American Werewolf in London* (1981), he juggled several projects, including *Twilight Zone: The Movie* (1983), *Trading Places* (1983), and the music video for Michael Jackson's "Thriller," all while still pitching *Clue* to writers. Landis, perhaps Hollywood's most in-demand comedy director at the time, was enjoying a career that would have seemed unfathomable to him a decade before. But the young directors who had taken cinema by storm in the 1970s were, in the words of Steven Spielberg, about to "grow up a little more."[28]

*Twilight Zone: The Movie* was cooked up at Warner Bros. after the studio had obtained the rights from the widow of Rod Serling, creator of the television show. Anxious to work with Spielberg, the hottest commodity in Hollywood, Warners pitched the idea to him, and he responded with unbridled enthusiasm. Spielberg grew up watching *The Twilight Zone*, and his first movie job, in 1969, was directing a segment of Serling's new anthology series, *Night Gallery*. Spielberg approached Landis, a friend, to produce the movie with him, and each would direct one of the four storylines.

Landis's segment was about a vile racist named Bill Connor. Connor found himself moving through the Twilight Zone as a Jew in Nazi-occupied France, a Black man about to be lynched by the Klan in the American South, and a Vietnamese man hunted by US soldiers during the Vietnam War. Vic Morrow played Connor, who was supposed to finish his trip through time back with the Nazis, where he was loaded onto a train with Jews to be sent off to death at a concentration camp. But the studio found the ending too bleak, so a scene was written with Connor rescuing two Vietnamese children from a firefight as he's pursued by the soldiers, an act apparently redeemable enough for Hollywood after the character's lifetime of bigotry.

The Asian child actors, Renee Shin-Yi Chen and Myca Dinh Le, had been hired under the table to circumvent California labor laws,

28 Pollock, "Spielberg Philosophical."

which would have prevented the children from working in the early-morning hours required by the shoot. On the last day of filming, July 23, 1982, at 2:20 a.m., Landis yelled "Action!" Morrow, carrying the two children under his arm, made his way across the Santa Clara River, which was doubling for an unnamed river in Vietnam. A helicopter was to pursue him as pyrotechnics exploded around the actors. But one of the explosions caused something to hit the tail of the chopper, and it spun out of control. The main rotor blades came down at an angle, decapitating Morrow and one of the kids, while the other child was crushed to death by the helicopter as both of the children's parents looked on.

Had the crash happened a few seconds later, or a few feet in one direction or another, Morrow and the children would've had a terrible scare, but nothing more. Instead, a domino effect of one accident after another killed three people on a film set, and all of it was recorded by six different cameras. Landis and others would be sued by multiple relatives of Morrow and the children, but it was Warner Bros. that would pay millions in attorneys' fees and legal settlements. Five people working on the set that night, including Landis, were charged with involuntary manslaughter. In a high-profile criminal trial, Landis, George Folsey Jr., and the other crew members were all found not guilty in May 1987, nearly five years after the accident.

Decades later, it's difficult to fully comprehend the roots of the tragedy. Reams of newspaper articles, court records, two books, and a television documentary have told the story over and over again. What most frequently emerges is a picture of a brash young director known as a "screamer," too caught up in his own ego to listen to crew members who expressed safety concerns.[29] That image has been reinforced by Landis's refusal, with rare exceptions, to speak about it. When he does, he acknowledges the tragedy, and it's clear he was, and remains, deeply shaken by it. But he also remains defensive, arguing that people made him a scapegoat.

The deaths reverberated throughout Hollywood, and they would

29 Bailey, "Twilight Zone."

indirectly affect *Clue.* Jonathan Lynn wondered if one reason why Landis switched from directing *Clue* to directing *Spies Like Us* was a financial one. He thought that Landis perhaps "needed to do bigger and more expensive films because his trial was coming up and he needed to make a lot of money for his defense."[30]

After the accident, Landis threw himself into his work. He pushed forward on *Twilight Zone*, filmed *Trading Places*, directed the "Thriller" music video, and continued looking for writers for *Clue*. It's difficult to reconstruct an exact timeline of which other writers were approached and when. Manzi and Stoppard worked on *Clue* at the same time, though neither likely knew it. There's also Hollywood showmanship to consider. While Hill or Landis probably would not have told a reporter that a famous author was writing the movie without at least having approached them, a name in a newspaper article doesn't guarantee that the author worked on *Clue.* Some of the writers reported in the press between 1981 and 1984 to be working on the *Clue* screenplay may have signed a contract, they may have sketched out some ideas, they may have even completed a draft. Or they may have had a brief telephone conversation and expressed some mild interest in working on the movie, with nothing more coming of it.

In addition to Alan Ayckbourn, Warren Manzi, and Tom Stoppard, renowned mystery writer P. D. James was approached. So was Simon Raven, an accomplished Brit who had written, in addition to his ten-novel series, *Alms for Oblivion*, several plays and had worked on a James Bond script. Stephen Sondheim and Anthony Perkins also were offered a writing deal, but Landis later remembered that they "asked for some outrageous amount of money," and the studio said no. Landis couldn't believe the refusal, but in fairness, Perkins's only credited screenplay was *The Last of Sheila*, which he cowrote with Sondheim. Finally, there was John Cleese. He turned them down, but he had another writer in mind the producers ought to look into. He wasn't well known outside of Britain, though he had a popular hit there called *Yes Minister*.

Jonathan Lynn was going to rescue *Clue.*

---

30 Lynn, interview with *Movies and Stuff.*

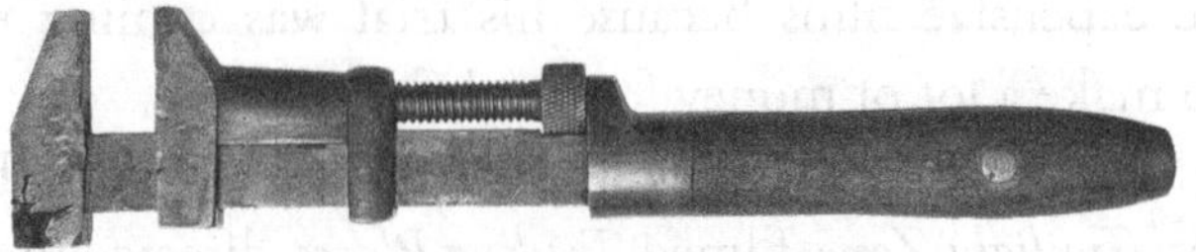

# 3. SUSPECTS

"I thought this was the dumbest thing I've ever heard."
-Jonathan Lynn[1]

Jonathan Lynn has told the story of how he came to write *Clue* many times. He detailed it in his own book, *Comedy Rules*. He was interviewed about it in 1985 while filming the movie. He's talked about it on podcasts and radio shows. He's retold it for retrospective articles celebrating *Clue*'s popularity today. He repeated it for the audio commentary he recorded with Josh Brandon in 2017. He most recently shared it for Jeff Smith's 2022 documentary, *Who Done It?* Given that this story has been told over some thirty-plus years, it's remarkably consistent. Lynn's whirlwind experience of being courted by Hollywood, complete with riding around in private cars, staying at the famed Chateau Marmont hotel, meeting Michael Jackson, and eating oceans of sushi seems to have seared itself into his brain. Though Lynn often responds "I can't remember" when asked about other details around *Clue*, he does remember how he was hired to write it.

It started in London in October 1983, with Peter Guber. At John Cleese's suggestion, *Clue*'s producers had decided to approach Lynn to write the screenplay. When his agent suggested that Lynn meet with Guber, Lynn sighed, "Must I?"[2] He agreed to meet for breakfast in the

1 Lynn, interview with *Movies and Stuff*.

2 Stanley, "*Clue* The Movie."

London hotel where Guber was staying, and after a few minutes, the energetic Hollywood producer dove into business. Lynn was perfect for *Clue*, he insisted. But soon Guber was up, running to another table, and his assistant sat down to finish the conversation. Guber had made appointments with three different writers for three different projects that same morning, and he was bouncing around trying to speak with all of them. After the meeting, Lynn told his agent, "These people are insane, they want me to write something called *Clue*, they've never read any of my work, we'll never hear from them again."[3]

Lynn did hear from them. They wanted him to fly to Los Angeles to meet with John Landis and Debra Hill. He thought the idea of basing a movie on a board game was utterly absurd, but, he says, he accepted because he wanted to fly first-class. He had also just finished the third series of *Yes Minister*, so he had a rare bit of free time. What was the harm in hearing Landis out? He landed at LAX and was whisked away to the Chateau Marmont off of Sunset Boulevard. The Marmont was where stars—real stars—had stayed for over fifty years. But when Lynn arrived, it was far from its old Hollywood glamour days, when Greta Garbo and Errol Flynn were among those signing the guest register. Now it was famous for being the place where John Belushi had died of a drug overdose.

Lynn had not brought his driver's license and hadn't thought to rent a car. London, with its double-decker buses and the Tube, is a walkable city; Los Angeles is not. With no car, he was a "virtual prisoner" at the Marmont.[4] There was, according to Lynn, no real restaurant to speak of at the hotel, a "terrible, rundown, old place."[5] He met Landis the next day at the postproduction studio where Landis was finishing up the "Thriller" music video. As Landis fussed over the mixing board and Lynn stood around, a "nice-looking kid" wandered in and asked everyone if they'd like some pizza.[6] He soon learned that the kid was

---

3 Bygrave, "The Man Whodunnit."

4 Lynn, *Comedy Rules*, 133.

5 Wixsom, "Communism Was a Red Herring."

6 Lynn, *Comedy Rules*, 134.

Michael Jackson. This was Michael Jackson when he was the most popular singer in the world, long before that reputation would be soiled, if not entirely shattered, by accusations of child molestation and rape. Landis was too busy with the video, so there was no talk of *Clue*, and Lynn was whisked back to the Marmont. He went for a walk on Sunset Boulevard, which was then "a bunch of one-story wooden shops that looked like expensive shacks."[7] Dinner was with someone he had never met before from Peter Guber and John Peters' company. Assigned by her boss to feed Lynn, she took him for sushi, which he'd never eaten before. He was not a fan. The whole experience was surreal and disorienting.

Finally, on day three, Lynn went to Landis's office to hear his pitch alongside Hill. This was Landis's famous pitch, the same one he had given to Manzi, Stoppard, and others, where he bounced off the walls, "careening around the office, jumping up and down on the furniture."[8] Lynn sat stunned by Landis's energy. In perhaps the best-known moment of this story among *Clue* fans, when Landis finished, Lynn, with barely baited breath, asked, "Who did it?" to which Landis replied, "I don't know, that's why I need a writer!"[9]

Back to the Chateau Marmont Lynn went, bewildered and ready to leave. Entranced as he was by Landis and his unbridled energy, he had zeroed in at once on the problem. Clue was a game with no story. These people at Boddy mansion were colors; they weren't characters. Suspected murderers named White and Green and Mustard don't just show up at a house together. Even in the Golden Age of Detective Fiction that would have been stretching it, to say nothing of 1983. Once more he phoned his agent, saying that "these people are mad, can I come home now?"[10] Once more his agent suggested that he hang in there and see where this all goes. Lynn was already in LA; why not sketch out a few ideas and see what they think? He took his agent's

7 Alter, "*Clue* at 35."

8 Vary, "Something Terrible Has Happened Here."

9 Lynn, *Comedy Rules*, 136.

10 Wixsom, "Communism Was a Red Herring."

advice and scribbled out two or three pages of notes, but not before being taken out to dinner by Landis and his wife—for sushi.

The following day, back in Landis's office—somehow staring down yet another spread of sushi that Landis had ordered—Lynn began pitching his own take. Landis, unable to help himself, jumped up and began riffing on these new ideas until Lynn interrupted and told him it was his turn to talk. Lynn got through his few "feeble" thoughts, and then Landis suggested a few more.[11] Lynn didn't realize it, but in that moment, his *Clue* was born. There were only some vague notions about how this might go—barely ideas, barely anything. But it was the germ of a screenplay. Landis glimpsed it through his round spectacles and asked Lynn to write the script; Lynn was "both pleased and horrified."[12] He accepted, even though he knew he "was at least the fifth writer to attempt it," reasoning that "there could be no great disgrace in failing if several distinguished predecessors had also failed."[13] He was also offered "a lot of money," something the BBC was not able to offer him, despite the accolades and stellar notices for *Yes Minister*.[14] That night, his last in Hollywood, Lynn was once again treated to dinner, this time by Hill. She took him to another sushi joint, but he "demanded a steak."[15] His bizarre Hollywood experience was over. The next day, he was on a plane home to London.

What were the ideas that Lynn managed to dream up to get the job, inchoate though they were? The people at the house were all connected, according to Landis. Why couldn't their names be aliases, Lynn reasoned, because they were being blackmailed? And why were they being blackmailed? Lynn didn't have a lot of experience with US history, but he had, in his youth in England, a connection to one particularly ugly episode of the American past: the Hollywood blacklist and the Red Scare.

---

11 Lynn, *Comedy Rules*, 137.

12 Lynn, 138.

13 Darling, "Clue," 26; Bygrave, "The Man Whodunnit."

14 Bygrave, "The Man Whodunnit."

15 Lynn, *Comedy Rules*, 138.

Lynn entered the world with, quite literally, a bang. He was born in the middle of a bombing raid at the height of World War II on April 3, 1943. His father, Robin Lynn, was a Jewish doctor who followed news and politics obsessively. He read the details coming out of Germany in the mid-1930s with growing alarm, and he came to believe war was inevitable. In 1936 he moved his family to Bath, hoping it would be far enough out of the way that it might escape the Luftwaffe's attention. It didn't.

The war was a daily reality for Britain that transformed the nation's way of life, including bombings, rationing, and blackouts. In 1940, Lynn's father was one of a dozen people fined for accidentally leaving two lights on in his office during a blackout.

The extended Lynn family was full of doctors, and it was assumed that Jonathan would follow in a similarly respectable profession. After the war, as Britain got back to rebuilding its battered nation, he attended Kingswood School, three years senior to another Kingswood student, Tim Curry. The main Kingswood building looks as if it comes straight out of a cozy mystery, and British TV series have used it for location filming. Lynn was the only Jewish boy at Kingswood, and it must have been lonely. In one interview he refers to his "school friends," catches himself, and then calls them "school acquaintances."[16] While Lynn, like his classmates, watched *The Phil Silvers Show*, *I Married Jane*, *The Jack Benny Program*, and the occasional episode of *I Love Lucy*, he paid special attention to the credits, eager to see who wrote them. If Landis was drawn to know who made the movies he saw, Lynn was drawn to know who wrote the TV shows he watched.

After finishing at Kingswood in the early 1960s, Lynn went to Pembroke College at Cambridge to study law. He had no interest in being a doctor, joking that "they say a lawyer is a Jewish boy who can't stand the sight of blood."[17] His parents, much like Hill's, did not want him to go into show business. Decades later, when he'd already had a successful career, his mother called him after he directed a play that

---

16 Lynn, interview with Gottfriend and Santopadre.

17 Lynn.

flopped and said, "You know, you can still go back to the law."[18] Even before he wanted to be a writer, Lynn desperately wanted to act, and ironically it was his mother who helped fuel the dream. She loved the theater, and she and her son traveled often to nearby Bristol, where he saw the giants of the British stage: Peter O'Toole, John Gielgud, Laurence Olivier, Ralph Richardson, and countless others.

As a child, Lynn had learned to play the drums, and at Pembroke he joined the Footlights band, the theater club at Cambridge. He overcame some initial stage fright to perform in a handful of plays. At the Footlights he also met John Cleese, Graham Chapman, and Eric Idle, three comedians who would, by the end of the decade, go on to form Monty Python with Terry Gilliam, Michael Palin, and Terry Jones. Cleese, Chapman, Idle, and others would create their first hit at the Footlights, a sketch comedy show they dubbed *The Cambridge Circus*. They invited Lynn to join, and the show opened in London's West End in July 1963. It was such a hit that it moved to New York; Lynn deadpanned in a 1984 interview that his first real acting job was on Broadway and that he's "been going steadily down hill ever since."[19]

It was a head-spinning time. He got the call to join *The Cambridge Circus* the same week he graduated from Pembroke; he has never practiced so much as a minute of law. Before the show opened on Broadway, the producers wanted to preview it for test audiences—in New Zealand. Lynn literally traveled around the globe, from the UK to New Zealand and then to the United States. The show debuted in New York in October 1964 to excellent reviews in all but one newspaper, the one that mattered most: the *New York Times*. But even the paper of record saw the potential: "These young performers . . . are so appealing one wishes that the level of their material was consistently higher."[20] After the *Circus* opened, they were invited to perform on *The Ed Sullivan Show*, one of the biggest TV programs in the country. Lynn was twenty-one years old. But while *The Cambridge Circus* didn't

---

18 Lynn.

19 Lynn, interview with Plomley.

20 Taubman, "Theater."

bomb, there were too many empty seats, and it closed after twenty-three performances, a few weeks after it had opened. It continued for a few more months off-Broadway and in some regional theaters before disbanding.

Lynn's gift for comedy might have seemed obvious to those around him, but it wasn't to him. While the other members of the *Circus* knew they wanted to be comedians, Lynn took acting classes in New York and later said he had a "very inflated idea" about where his life was headed, dreaming of being "the next Alec Guinness or something."[21] Like so many young, talented people trying to find their footing, he took jobs when he could. He returned to England and got work in regional theaters, sold records at Selfridges department store, and played drums at a few jazz clubs. In 1967, he was in the original West End production of *Fiddler on the Roof*. It wasn't all work; he also married his girlfriend, Rita Merkelis, a psychoanalyst. Two years later he played Hitler in *Comedy of the Changing Years*, reportedly making him the first Jew to portray the Führer. He had also slowly moved into television, acting in roles here and there while juggling theater parts.

It was in the 1970s that Lynn began writing for TV. He had finally landed a semiregular role, on *Doctor in the House*, a comedy about medical students that spawned six more series over the next two decades. He and fellow *Doctor* actor George Layton decided to take a swing at writing an episode for the sequel, *Doctor at Large*, and it was accepted. He went on to write episodes for *On the Buses*, *My Name Is Harry Worth*, and three more *Doctor* series. He had some wild ideas as he tried to push these shows in new directions. Lynn wanted one episode of *On the Buses*, a blue-collar show about bus drivers chatting up ladies and clashing with their boss, to play off of the huge spike in airplane hijackings at the time by featuring a bus-jacking. The idea was politely declined.

Sitcom writing can be its own kind of drudgery. Lynn was forced to Goldilocks his way into scripts that weren't too different, weren't too repetitive, but just right. The struggles of writing for television sent

21 Lynn, interview with Gottfried and Santopadre.

Lynn into a depression that "took hold and sapped my energy, closing down my brain."[22]

He pushed through and developed his own TV show with Layton, called *My Brother's Keeper*, a series about twins, one a cop, the other a criminal. Even that simple scenario was too much for TV executives, who were convinced the criminal wouldn't be likable or funny enough, so the character morphed into a radical college student. Layton played the police officer, Lynn the student. The show ran from 1975 to 1976 and did well both in ratings and among critics but did not garner a second season. Lynn was thirty-two years old with a wife and two children to support. He continued working in theater alongside his television writing and acting, occasionally directing a show or appearing in a role.

After *My Brother's Keeper* concluded, he was tapped as director of the Cambridge Theatre Company (CTC). Lynn drew upon ten years of experience and contacts within the British stage to direct some marvelous productions, including *The Glass Menagerie*, *Songbook*, and *The Unvarnished Truth*. Lynn's shows frequently ended up playing in the West End. *Songbook* was especially celebrated, running for over two hundred performances and winning the Olivier Award for Best New Musical before moving to Broadway under the new title *The Moony Shapiro Songbook*. But in one of those curious showbiz twists, it bombed in New York and played only one night before closing, despite good notices for the lead actor, a young Jeff Goldblum. But by the time *Songbook* had opened on Broadway in 1981, Lynn had another hit TV show on his hands.

He had met Anthony Jay some years earlier when Lynn was acting in training videos. Jay told Lynn he had an idea for a political comedy about civil servants in the British government. Lynn "thought it sounded boring," and Jay's suggestion came just as Lynn was exhausted writing sitcoms, so he passed.[23] But as he was directing hits for the CTC, he came to miss writing. He phoned Jay and asked if he was still

22 Lynn, *Comedy Rules*, 71.

23 Lynn, 83.

interested in writing the TV series.

Lynn grasped something at a young age that seems to escape many of us until we are much older: that the people in charge—in charge of government, in charge of massive corporations, in charge of nearly anything—are often self-important buffoons who have no more idea what they are doing than the rest of us. At Pembroke College, as a member of the Cambridge Union Society debate club, he watched young men act as if they were sitting in Parliament. They would pompously stroll to the podium, some of them still teenagers, ready to argue away the world's problems. Much to his horror, in twenty years some of those same men actually had become members of Parliament, still trying to argue away the world's problems. Politicians, he would say decades later, "inspired me with contempt and a desire to ridicule them at every possible occasion."[24] He is not brave, he says, but is "reckless and opinionated and I find it terribly hard to keep my mouth shut."[25]

They came up with a fictitious Administrative Affairs Department, ostensibly run by Minister Jim Hacker but really run by Hacker's permanent secretary, Sir Humphrey Appleby. Appleby's job is to protect the status quo at all costs. When Hacker, eager to enact change in his new job, suggests reforms, Sir Humphrey delivers long-winded, circular speeches, appearing to be sound and reasonable while actually managing to say nothing at all.

*Yes Minister* manages to be scathing and dark without feeling dour. There are jokes about war and annihilation, about Irish and Scottish sovereignty, and about British imperialism, all playing out against a laugh track. It performs a masterful high-wire act, balancing nihilism and overwrought horror as it exposes the boundless amorality of the people who run the world. Viewers will be immediately reminded of HBO's *Veep*, starring Julia Louis-Dreyfus and created by Armando Iannucci, who cites *Yes Minister* as a direct influence on the series.

Lynn and Jay's studious avoidance of the partisan makes the series's popularity all the more remarkable. Although it aired during Margaret

---

24 Lynn, interview with Gottfried and Santopadre.

25 Lynn, *Comedy Rules*, 32.

Thatcher's tenure as prime minister, it was written before she took office, when James Callaghan held the office. Lynn and Jay took aim at government and bureaucracy broadly, writing about bribery, public relations, and pandering to voters. The two friends were themselves politically divided; Jay was a staunch conservative, Lynn a more liberal soul. But that didn't affect their writing; Lynn called it "the best working relationship I have ever had."

*Yes Minister* is one of the main reasons Lynn was hired to write *Clue*, and fans of the latter will recognize a lot of similarities to the movie in the series despite their ostensibly very different topics. Wordplay and rapid-fire dialogue abound in *Yes Minister*. A handful of jokes from the series even turn up in *Clue*, including this one:

"Can you keep a secret?" Sir Humphrey asks Hacker.

"Yes."

"So can I."

Sir Humphrey also tells the minister that he doesn't need any of his help to make a fool of himself—a line given to Colonel Mustard when speaking to Wadsworth. Lynn often has a remarkably dry sense of humor. As he's being interviewed on the radio or for podcasts, he will say something funny, but there's always a beat as the interviewer has to process what they just heard before they burst out laughing. For Lynn, comedy is a serious business, one he's spent countless hours thinking and writing about. Many of his thoughts on farce and humor, recorded in *Comedy Rules*, feature prominently in *Clue*. One rule insists that "if you start with an absurd premise, you must follow it through with total logic." *Clue* plays it straight because it has to in order for audiences to believe the characters. A good farce, Lynn writes, "is usually about serious people doing—and trying to cover up—desperate things that would be horribly embarrassing if they were discovered. They do them because their demons drive them, and they try to cover them up in order to maintain their dignity. Thus the logic of their actions, and their lies, forces them to behave in what appears to be a ridiculous way." It's a perfect summary of *Clue*, as the characters, dressed in evening gowns and suits, run around a mansion, crashing into each other and throwing dead bodies into the study.

While *Yes Minister* was garnering critical acclaim and laughs, Lynn knew from personal experience that politicians aren't always funny—they can be menacing. It seems someone in the British government wasn't so enamored with *Yes Minister*, and Lynn was interviewed by the Whitehall police force after the series aired. Then his taxes were mysteriously audited. But it was his friendship with victims of US government persecution that gave him the central idea for *Clue*, which is what led Landis to offer him the job of writing the movie in fall 1983.

After Lynn returned to England in the mid-1960s, following his stint in *The Cambridge Circus*, he met Donald Ogden Stewart. Stewart was a screenwriter, and not one who toiled away on unproduced scripts. He had written *Holiday* (1938), *Love Affair* (1939), and *The Philadelphia Story* (1940), all massive hits with some of the biggest stars in Hollywood. He wrote at least two dozen other screenplays as a cog in the studio system machine, usually for MGM but also for Paramount and RKO. Stewart was also a fierce political activist. When, in 1937, producer Hal Roach entered into a partnership with Italy's fascist dictator, Benito Mussolini, complete with a lavish party at Roach's home, Stewart joined Charlie Chaplin and others in signing a letter of condemnation. Stewart was president of the Hollywood Anti-Nazi League, and at one meeting he made the mistake of admitting he was a Communist.

After World War II, the Red Scare seized America by the throat. In 1950, Stewart was blacklisted, and the following year he and his wife, Ella Winter, moved to London. They would live there for the rest of their lives, dying three days apart in 1980. Lynn met Stewart and Winter when he was getting his start as an actor. He was invited to their home for the weekend tea parties that the couple hosted for other American expats. Among the guests were Charlie Chaplin and Dalton Trumbo, other victims of anti-communist hysteria. From them and other visitors at Stewart and Winter's home, Lynn heard the stories of the House Un-American Activities Committee firsthand. Some fifteen years later, when Landis pitched the story to him and said he wanted it set in the 1950s, Lynn realized the Clue game tokens—which he had lamented were nothing more than colors—could be real people. They could be blackmail victims, terrified of being branded un-American at the height of the Red Scare if their secrets got out. Lynn would later add that golden age detective mysteries were too absurd to pull off in the modern era, so he agreed with Landis that the film had to take place in the past.

Lynn soon realized it would be unlike any other project he had worked on. It was "very strange," because the actual writing went quickly, but he had to sit and work out the plot for months at a time.[26] He went everywhere with a notebook so that he could jot down ideas, and he kept a board with notes pinned to it to keep track of the dizzying mystery. After he wrote the first act in a week, he sat with the plot for another three months.[27] The process repeated itself, and he wrote most of the final act, with all four endings, on his flight from London to LA to turn in the script. In all, he believed, the first draft took about six months, but only three weeks were spent putting words to page.

What was Lynn trying to accomplish as he wrote *Clue*? He told a reporter in 1985 that his "single guiding light was that our film was not to be a parody."[28] He could spoof aspects of old country-house mysteries, but a parody, he feared, would be too much like *Murder by Death*: funny, but with no plot to speak of. He believed the movie needed to instill fear in audiences to work. "It may be funny to the audience, but it's deadly serious to the characters. [It's] the worst day of their lives."[29] He was determined to tell a real story with a real mystery amid the comedy rather than cobbling together a pastiche of Golden Age Detective Fiction tropes. He also had Hill and Landis to consider. They had been trying for three years before they hired him to get *Clue* made, and they had definite notions about what they wanted it to look like. It had to have four endings, and each ending had to work on its own. It should be scary, yes, but also funny. There were seven main characters, and each needed to have roughly the same number of lines lest it seem that some of the actors were being neglected.

---

26 Lynn, interview with *Movies and Stuff*.

27 Lynn.

28 Farber, "Off the Board."

29 Stanley, "Clue."

Lynn's first attempt at the screenplay set the story down so closely to the final film that later drafts changed little, a rarity in Hollywood. Whole sections of dialogue and action are unchanged, and most scenes remain the same. He would go on to write at least five versions. The first two, close as they are to the movie, were preliminary drafts from early 1984. The third version was the one he considered the official "first draft," and he labeled it as such on the title page and dated it May 4, 1984. The second draft was finished a month later, on June 4, 1984, with only the barest of edits. In fact, to write the second draft, Lynn photocopied the first draft and retyped only a handful of pages or used Wite-Out to delete a few lines. Some of these changes included switching from Lynn's British English to American English, so a torch Colonel Mustard grabs in the first draft becomes a flashlight in the second, for example.

After the second draft, Lynn spent another six months working on the screenplay. The third draft, finished in early January 1985, had the most changes. This was the version that would finally be greenlit, a few weeks later, by the studio and the producers; subsequent edits to the script were labeled revisions and printed on different-colored paper, since production was moving forward with the third draft as the foundation of the film. I'll highlight most of the changes made for each draft during our walk through the movie in later chapters, but a few stand out. The early drafts are darker and include more references to communism, McCarthyism, and the Red Scare. There's more profanity—Wadsworth complains when he ends up "in the fucking shower."[30] They have more sexual innuendo—when Mrs. White asks how they can stop the police from coming, Miss Scarlet replies that "they never come when you want them, only when you don't."[31] These earlier drafts also have more tension and fear. Some of that tension was jettisoned for the third and final draft, which introduced more slapstick and humor— such as when Wadsworth commands the dogs to "sit!" and Mr. Green quickly shuffles backward to the bench. Lynn

---

30 Lynn, "Clue," undated preliminary draft.

31 Lynn, "Clue," first-draft screenplay, 46.

also swapped a phony security guard in the first two drafts for the dogs, to convince the guests they were trapped in the house. He switched the locale from Florida to an unnamed New England state. Lastly, he rewrote what was then "ending C"—the much-rumored deleted ending, indicating that it was not working as well as the others.

At long last, Hill and Landis had their screenplay. *Clue* had been dropped in 1983 by Universal, after President Ned Tanen left; now, in January 1985, it was picked up by Paramount, where Tanen had been hired to run the motion picture division. However, Lynn was unknown to the studio executives, and his screenplay was handed to Paramount script reader Julie Lantz to write a summary and provide Tanen and head of production Dawn Steel with feedback. On January 18, Lantz rendered her verdict: "The set-up, the pace, and the humor all work well here."[32] Lantz identified no major red flags, only a handful of suggestions. Why, for example, was Professor Plum able to be blackmailed if he'd lost his license and had to get another job, which seems like a rather public scandal? She suggested adding some details that would explain how Plum was able to escape notice for his dalliances. She also worried that the four endings "sort of bleed into one another."[33] Lantz liked the ending with Miss Scarlet as the culprit best. She found it "clever, very twisty," and she loved the final line, "Frankly, Scarlet, I don't give a damn" (Lynn hadn't yet added the 1+2+2+1 scene).[34] Lantz acknowledged that her concerns were all minor, and the heads of Paramount were ready to move forward. After struggling through development hell for years, *Clue* was back on track. Now the movie needed a cast and crew.

Landis had dropped out of the director's chair to make *Spies Like Us*, and Lynn signed on for that role in addition to writing. Lynn would later wonder if Landis took on the bigger project, with bigger stars, because he needed money for his defense in the upcoming *Twilight*

---

32 Julie Lantz, screenplay summary to Dawn Steel, Jan. 18, 1985, in Paramount Pictures, *Clue* Development File.

33 Lantz to Steel.

34 Lantz to Steel; Lynn, "Clue" third-draft screenplay, 125(D).

*Zone* trial. But Landis remained as an executive producer. The film's caravan of producers and executive producers could be a blessing and a curse. While it meant that there were more people who had to approve decisions, it also meant more people could work the phones and hire crew members. Hill recruited casting directors Jane Jenkins and Janet Hirshenson, whom she had worked with on *The Dead Zone*. The duo, well-known today for casting everything from *Home Alone* (1990)to *Harry Potter and the Sorcerer's Stone* (2001), had worked on only a handful of films when they were hired for *Clue*.

On January 23, 1985, Hirshenson and Jenkins sent their first list of possibilities to Hill, Peter Guber, and Lynn. Suggestions for Wadsworth included Bill Cosby and Bill Murray, both with dollar signs penciled next to their names, signaling that they would likely be too expensive. *Clue* wasn't exactly a cheap film; the initial budget was $8 million, a respectable amount for the era but not a sum reserved for blockbusters. At each end of the scale, *Once Bitten*, a vampire teen sex comedy starring Lauren Hutton and a young Jim Carrey, had a $3 million budget; *Back to the Future*'s budget was closer to $19 million. Movies like *Witness* and *Beverly Hills Cop*, with their big-name stars, had budgets of around $13 million. But *Clue*, as an ensemble comedy, was different, with no fewer than seven people sharing top billing—the actors who portrayed the six guests plus Wadsworth. Whoever was cast as Yvette and Mr. Boddy would also be credited in the opening titles; everyone else, from the Motorist to Mrs. Ho, would be added to the end credits. Hill was also insistent that all seven stars be given equal pay and equal perks. Everything down to their trailers would be the same. Hill's idea led to a cooperative environment, with egos set aside to make the best possible movie, but it made casting major stars, accustomed to being paid gobs of money, difficult.

The producers budgeted a $100,000 salary for each of the seven main leads for fifty days of work. They would end up getting a little more when the film ran over schedule, but it was not the kind of money that would land an Eddie Murphy or a Chevy Chase, though both were still listed as suggestions. The casting notebook is filled with the names of recognizable stars, some with lines through their name when a producer said no. Actors on whom the producers were particularly keen got a star by their names. As the process moved forward and the casting directors reached out to the actors' agents, they scribbled notes next to the names in pencil. An NI meant the actor was not interested; an NA meant not available due to other projects (or that they weren't interested but their agents, not wanting to alienate anyone, made up excuses).[35] At the bottom of each character list were a few names added in pencil, as ideas came and went.

How about Steve Martin or Robin Williams for Wadsworth? Not available. Ditto Michael Caine. Tim Curry appears on the list alongside Tom Hanks. Ned Tanen suggested Anthony Perkins; he loved the idea of "Norman Bates as the Butler."[36] Danny DeVito wasn't available for Mr. Boddy, and Mr. T has a line through his name. Peter Boyle, Howard Hesseman, and Mel Brooks are listed, but Lee Ving isn't. George Carlin and John Candy were suggested for Colonel Mustard. A note jotted down next to Candy's name by one of the producers reads "not funny." Michael McKean's name first appears under Professor Plum. David Letterman's name is struck through; Mick Jagger's is not. More than a few singers were suggested. It was the eighties, and Paramount wanted to turn rock stars into movie stars to drum up ticket sales. David Lee Roth's name is under Jagger's, and David Bowie shows up elsewhere on the list. What about Billy Crystal, Louie Anderson, or Judge Reinhold for Mr. Green?

Lucille Ball is crossed off for Mrs. Peacock; Joan Rivers is penciled in. Another singer, Tina Turner, tops the list for Miss Scarlet; Cher and Sigourney Weaver are also mentioned. Mrs. White has several big early-eighties stars on her list: Kathleen Turner, Karen Allen, and Shelley Duvall, among others. Colleen Camp appears under Yvette, along with Demi Moore, Sheena Easton, and Melanie Griffith. Someone wisely crossed out Jennifer Jason Leigh's name; she is Vic Morrow's daughter, and after the *Twilight Zone* accident, it's hard to imagine she'd want to work on a movie produced by Landis. Only a few names appear under Mrs. Ho, the cook, including Yoko Ono and Rhea Perlman. A note

---

35 Casting Company, Casting Notebook.

36 Ned Tanen to Jonathan Lynn, Jan. 15, 1985, in Casting Company, Casting Notebook.

suggests that a man could play the cook instead of a woman, and Pat Morita, still in the glow of the success of *The Karate Kid* (1984), had his agent inquire about the part. The Motorist, the Singing Telegram Girl, and the Evangelist were all envisioned as cameo roles, and names like Fred Astaire, John Houseman, Elvis Costello, Madonna, and Whoopi Goldberg were suggested. Madonna would come up again later as a possibility for Yvette.

Several names turn up repeatedly, so it becomes clear who, at least in the producers' minds, were the frontrunners. They aggressively pursued Dabney Coleman for Colonel Mustard. Coleman was on a roll—he'd starred in *9 to 5*, *On Golden Pond*, *Tootsie*, and *WarGames* in the previous four years. Martin Mull was also a popular choice for Mustard. Harry Anderson, fresh off of his newfound *Night Court* TV fame, was the leading contender for Mr. Green. Tim Curry also remained a top possibility for Mr. Green. Christopher Lloyd's name shows up more than anyone else's, mentioned as a potential Wadsworth, Professor Plum, or Mr. Green. Lloyd would end up being a charmed casting choice, even apart from his skill as an actor. While *Clue* was trying to find guests to populate its murder mystery, Lloyd was in the middle of filming *Back to the Future*. A few months later, while *Clue* was two months into its own shoot, *Back to the Future* would open to massive receipts and more than one review that said Lloyd's performance stole the show. When he signed on to be Professor Plum, *Clue* producers had landed a household name; they just didn't know it yet.

Lloyd was born in 1938 in Connecticut. He got his acting start on the stage, and he's continued performing in plays; well into his eighties, he was onstage as King Lear in the Berkshires in 2021. His first film role was *One Flew over the Cuckoo's Nest* (1975). He continued to act in movies, but until *Back to the Future*, his best known role was Reverend Jim in the TV series *Taxi*. He won two Emmys for the part. Lloyd doesn't do many interviews, though when he does he is thoughtful and chooses his words deliberately. He, in his own words, likes to "stick to myself a lot,"[37] and he doesn't like to be presumptuous with other

37 Itzkoff, "Surprise of a Salesman."

people's time, something introverts will recognize in themselves. But while filming *Clue*, he would spend time hanging out with the rest of the cast, "game for anything," in the words of Lesley Ann Warren.[38] He often attends fan conventions, signing autographs and doing meet and greets. A few weeks after being officially cast in *Clue*, he would wrap shooting on *Back to the Future*, in which he plays a frantic, frenzied mad scientist. A month later, in *Clue*, he was giving a subtle performance as a pervert and a creep, showing off his range in two movies in a single year.

Carrie Fisher appears early on the casting lists and is immediately zeroed in on for either Miss Scarlet or Mrs. White. She was born in 1952 to stars Eddie Fisher and Debbie Reynolds. As a child, she loved books and was sneeringly called the Bookworm by her family. She would join her mom onstage in the musical *Irene* in 1973, then she had a small part in *Shampoo* (1975) before *Star Wars* rocketed her to fame. She would be *Clue*'s biggest coup as the instantly recognizable Princess Leia. In 1985, George Lucas's space adventure remained immeasurably popular; *Return of the Jedi* topped the box office in 1983, and when it was rereleased in 1985, it would gross another $11.2 million at the domestic box office. *Star Wars* had been released on VHS for the rental market, and it aired on network TV for the first time in February 1984. At every turn in the casting process, things would go smoothly with Fisher. She wanted the role, and the producers wanted her for it.

If only Mrs. Peacock were so simple. The names Carol Burnett, Mary Tyler Moore, and Lily Tomlin were suggested—among a dozen more—for the corrupt senator's wife. Those three stuck as casting went on, but little was done to secure any of them for the part, since the producers were divided on who would be the best choice. Six days after Hirshenson and Jenkins sent their initial lists of ideas to Lynn and the producers, they followed up on January 29, 1985. The duo had been busy phoning agents to learn who was and who wasn't available. The list was trimmed and a few other names added. A note says Landis would speak to Eddie Murphy after Murphy said he was not

38 Ivie, "Lesley Ann Warren."

interested. Several prominent names had NR added—"not right"—including Cosby, Murray, and Richard Pryor. Fisher, Lloyd, Coleman, and Anderson had all emerged as favorites. Michael McKean seemed a good fit for a couple of roles, and Wallace Shawn shot to the top of the list for Professor Plum. But as meetings were scheduled with actors, other names vanished as performers balked at accepting salaries lower than they were accustomed to. Other stars, such as Peter Boyle and Candace Bergen, wanted upfront offers before they even met with anyone.

On February 5, Lynn and Hill sat with Hirshenson and Jenkins to further narrow the list. At this point, some of the characters, like Wadsworth, had only a few names remaining (in the butler's case, they were Tim Conti, John Lithgow, and Rowan Atkinson). Lesley Ann Warren was now a top pick for Mrs. White. Anthony Perkins headed the list for Mr. Boddy. Pamela Stephenson, a *Saturday Night Live* cast member, was the favorite for Yvette. Other notes began to be added by the names, like "we like, she likes," indicating the production team and the star were in agreement this might be a good match. Jamie Lee Curtis passed for Miss Scarlet, and Carrie Fisher, now at the top of the list, had a star next to her name.

The next day, Lynn and Hill, sometimes joined by Guber, began meeting with the interested actors. Their first appointment was at 1:00 p.m. with McKean for the role of Mr. Green. They talked to Shelley Duvall about Mrs. White and Dabney Coleman for Colonel Mustard. *M*A*S*H* star David Ogden Stiers had become another popular choice for Mustard, and the group saw both him and Martin Mull on February 7. They met with Lloyd about Mr. Green after canceling an earlier meeting with him to discuss the role of Mr. Boddy. They saw both Fisher and Warren on February 8. That same morning, a casting call was issued for the Cop, the Evangelist, the Motorist, Mrs. Ho, the Singing Telegram Girl, and a handful of police and FBI agents who would run in at the end of the film and say a few lines (later cut). On February 10, Lynn and Hill flew to New York, where they met with actors who lived there. They saw Billy Crystal for Mr. Green and Charles Grodin for Colonel Mustard. They also saw Phoebe Cates for Yvette and Madeline Kahn and Jane Curtin for Mrs. Peacock.

Lynn was working closely with producers on casting, and he would tell reporters a few months later that he had a lot of freedom in his choices. As an outsider he also benefited from not knowing anyone personally. He was at least somewhat familiar with Kahn, since he'd seen her in Mel Brooks's *Blazing Saddles* and *Young Frankenstein*. He may have recognized other names, and he would later say that he took "a crash course in American actors" by watching as many movies and TV shows as he could.[39] But there were no favors to repay, no grudges to interfere, no loyalties to sway him one way or another. All of the actors would come in for a meeting, and then the top contenders would be screen-tested, at least according to Lynn (some of the actors later remembered not having screen tests or even reading for the part).

By February 12, some decisions, while not yet final, were becoming apparent. Lloyd now had the "he likes, we like" note next to his name for Professor Plum. Coleman and Grodin had passed on Colonel Mustard, and Mull, now the favorite, had the same note as Lloyd next to his name. Mull came to comedy and acting via a much different route from his costars. He was born in Chicago, spent most of his childhood in Ohio, and moved to Connecticut with his family when he was fifteen. His mother acted in local theater, and his father was an electronics whiz who, according to Mull, built his family's first TV set. Mull's family helped him learn comedy early; he remembers growing up with them "was a series of one-liners."[40] He went to art school in 1961. He is a painter and a musician, and he's had solo shows at art galleries across the United States. In the beginning, as he struggled to find work, he played guitar at various gigs and then "started to write the odd song here and there."[41] Not being a great singer (in his own estimation), he made the songs funny, with long asides to the audience, and a career was born.

Mull started releasing comedy records, and he would later be nominated for a Grammy for his album *Sex and Violins*. His brand of

39 Stanley, "'Clue' The Movie."

40 Ely, "Martin Mull."

41 Wojciechowski, "FOX's *Dads* Star Martin Mull."

humor was, and remains, almost impossible to pin down, a blend of silly, edgy, dry, and, in the words of different reporters, "irreverent," "subdued," "bizarre," and "cerebral."[42] No matter how absurd Mull's lines or how wacky the plot, he always plays it straight. In 1975, he met with Norman Lear hoping to write for his new syndicated soap opera satire, *Mary Hartman, Mary Hartman*. He was turned down, but six months later he got an acting job on the show instead, playing Garth Gimble. When Gimble was killed off, impaled by an aluminum Christmas tree, Mull returned as his twin brother, Barth Gimble. He starred in two spinoffs of *Mary Hartman* called *Fernwood 2 Night* and *America 2-Night*. By the 1980s, Mull had largely stopped appearing on television and was acting in movies. Before *Clue*, his most visible movie role was in *Mr. Mom* (1982) alongside Michael Keaton, Teri Garr, and Christopher Lloyd.

Despite their initial enthusiasm for Harry Anderson as Mr. Green, Lynn and Hill decided after meeting with him that he wasn't right for the part. But a star appears next to Michael McKean's name along with the now-familiar line "we like, he likes." McKean had earned rave reviews as David St. Hubbins in *This Is Spinal Tap* a year earlier, though it took audiences a few years to catch up and turn *Spinal Tap* into the revered comedy classic it is today. He was also credited as a writer on the heavily improvised film.

McKean was born in New York in 1947 and grew up on Long Island. His dad, a massive jazz fan, worked as a copywriter for Decca, RCA Victor, and Columbia Records. His mother was a stay-at-home mom until she began working in McKean's high school office, and she then became the school librarian. McKean says that "we are who we are because of whom and where we are from."[43] His parents were loving and supportive and took him to the theater from an early age. He has written that their love of movies and music left him in "awe of creative people." Like Mull, he learned to play the guitar and was a versatile performer. He attended New York University, where he met

42 Shales, "Mull's Life after Death"; Alterman, "Martin Mull's Fabulous Furniture"; Ely, "Martin Mull."
43 McKean, "Biographical Snippet."

Christopher Guest, whom he would go on to work with on a number of projects. He also went to Carnegie Mellon, where he met David Lander. After college, McKean and Lander joined the Credibility Gap, a comedy group in Los Angeles. They performed on radio and in the occasional club. McKean and Lander would create Lenny and Squiggy, a pair of delusional doofus roommates, on the TV series *Laverne & Shirley*, They proved extremely popular, giving McKean's career a nice boost, and he went on to appear in a handful of films and other TV series before starring in *Spinal Tap*.

Lynn and the producers of *Clue* had all but settled on Lloyd for Professor Plum, Mull for Colonel Mustard, Fisher for Miss Scarlet, and McKean for Mr. Green. Warren wasn't yet a lock for Mrs. White, but she was close. Perkins had passed on Mr. Boddy, leaving that role up in the air. Auditions were still ongoing for the Evangelist, the Cop, Mrs. Ho, and the Motorist. Casting Wadsworth and Mrs. Peacock was proving most troublesome. The producers thought perhaps an old Hollywood star might be right for Peacock. As written by Lynn, she was a perpetually scandalized society dame. They might even be able to afford a big-name actor, since in youth-obsessed showbiz, the older an actor got, the less in demand she became. Film roles dried up, and some of the most glamorous women of the big screen in the 1950s were now popping up on television in guest spots for *Fantasy Island* or *Murder, She Wrote*. Perhaps, the producers thought, they could sign Ava Gardner, Janet Leigh, Doris Day, or Elizabeth Taylor.

Taylor was interested, but only in playing Miss Scarlet, and nothing came of the other names suggested for Peacock. And then, out of nowhere, Pamela Stephenson dropped out as Yvette. She hadn't been officially cast yet, but she was everyone's favorite choice. It was back to the drawing board, and another list of names was quickly cranked out. Colleen Camp wasn't on it, but Christie Brinkley, Madonna, and Nicolette Sheridan were. On February 27, Lynn and Hill heard Sheridan, Pia Zadora, and Olivia Newton-John read for Yvette.

By March 1985, Mull, McKean, Fisher, and Lloyd had all officially signed on. *Clue* had its Colonel Mustard, Mr. Green, Miss Scarlet, and Professor Plum. Soon, Warren was offered the role of Mrs. White. Until Warren's selection, everyone cast in *Clue* had started in theater or television in the 1970s, then made the jump to movies in the early eighties. By contrast, Warren had been acting on stage, in television, and in movies for two decades. She'd been nominated for four Golden Globes and an Oscar and had worked relentlessly, appearing in over thirty TV series, miniseries, and made-for-TV movies, and nine films. She was born in New York City in 1946, and by the time she was six, she was taking dance lessons. She attended New York's High School of Music and Art and was acting on Broadway when she was sixteen. In 1965, she played Cinderella in CBS's television production of the Rodgers and Hammerstein musical. The broadcast dominated the ratings and was rerun several times over the next ten years. It made Warren a household name. She was first nominated for a Golden Globe in 1971 for her role in *Mission: Impossible.* She won the Globe in 1978 for the miniseries *79 Park Avenue.* In 1983, she was nominated for the Best Supporting Actress Oscar for playing Norma Cassidy in *Victor/Victoria.* On the way to *Clue* she'd been Lois Lane, worked with Walt Disney, and starred with nearly every major Hollywood actor imaginable.

Casting progress had been made, but the producers were still looking for Mr. Boddy, hopeful of snagging Peter Boyle. Boyle would make it far enough along in negotiations that his name appeared the next month in a cast list published by *Variety.* A new list of possibilities for Mr. Boddy drawn up on March 18 suggested Christopher Lee and, perhaps the strangest casting idea of all, "Weird Al" Yankovic. On March 21, more people read for parts, including Kellye Nakahara for the role of Mrs. Ho and Jane Wiedlin, rhythm guitarist for the Go-Go's, for Yvette. Next to her name are the initials NR, for "not right." Principal photography was scheduled to begin two months later, on Monday, May 20, pushed back a week from the original start date of May 13. There were contracts to draw up, lawyers to review them, costumes to size, lines to memorize, characters to develop, and rehearsals to conduct. Time was running out, and the producers had no Yvette, no Mr. Boddy, no Motorist, no Cop, no Evangelist, no Singing Telegram Girl, and no cook, but at least they were getting closer to their Wadsworth.

Lynn thought Rowan Atkinson would be excellent for the role, but he wasn't well-known outside of England, and the producers weren't sold. Instead, the team circled back to a name on the very first list put together by casting directors Hirshenson and Jenkins: Tim Curry. Curry had also been suggested for other roles and had been on the producers' radar since the production began. He was born in 1946 in Cheshire, England, but his family moved frequently, and by the time he was six months old, they had relocated to Hong Kong. After his father died of a stroke, Curry got a scholarship to Kingswood School in Bath, where he first met Lynn. Lynn was also familiar with Curry's work on the British stage, where he had performed in at least a dozen shows before immortalizing the role of Dr. Frank-N-Furter in *The Rocky Horror Show*. He'd also starred in Tom Stoppard's *Travesties*, was nominated for a Tony Award for his turn as Mozart in *Amadeus*, and was then nominated for an Olivier Award for *The Pirates of Penzance*. Curry had acted in a handful of movies, including *Rocky Horror*, and now he would fill *Clue*'s most demanding part.

Things were also looking better for most of the smaller roles. Nakahara's reading was excellent, so she was quickly cast as Mrs. Ho. Nakahara was born in 1948 in Hawaii to a Japanese mother and American father. Her grandfather Buntaro Nakahara had moved from Japan and started a fishing business in Hawaii. But after Pearl Harbor was bombed in 1941, he was forced into an internment camp in New Mexico. He died there, and his family never knew exactly what happened. When Kellye Nakahara was still a teenager, she moved to California to be an artist and an actor. She got a role as an extra on *M*A*S*H*, where, she would later say, she tried to put herself "in every scene, and no one told me to get out."[44] She appeared, whether credited or not, in nearly every episode of the series as, appropriately, Nurse Kellye.

Producers thought Wiedlin wasn't right for Yvette, but a singer seemed an obvious choice for the Singing Telegram Girl, and Wiedlin got the part. She was the youngest credited cast member on *Clue*, born in Wisconsin in 1958. Her family moved to Los Angeles when she

44 Carmel, "Kellye Nakahara."

was young, and she called her childhood "idyllic."[45] Wiedlin got into LA's punk rock scene and, in the late 1970s, formed the Go-Go's with Belinda Carlisle. The band transitioned to pop and new wave and became a huge success. Tension among the band members prompted Wiedlin to leave in 1984 for a solo and acting career. *Clue* was her first feature film.

On March 26, Tim Reid read for the role of the Cop. Reid had been on TV screens for years, well-known as Venus Flytrap on *WKRP in Cincinnati*. In 1985, he was playing Lieutenant "Downtown" Brown on *Simon & Simon*. Lynn and Hill were impressed. They offered him the role; Reid accepted. Two days after Reid met with producers, a blonde actress strolled into her audition for Yvette wearing a full French maid uniform and speaking with an outlandish French accent. She was the last person to read for the day; Lynn and Hill had already auditioned some impressive actors in the previous two hours: Kelly Preston, Pam Dawber, and Heather Locklear. But Colleen Camp's audaciousness bowled them over. She was their Yvette.

Camp was born in San Francisco in 1953. To put herself through college, she got a job working as a bird trainer in the daily bird show at the now-defunct Busch Gardens theme park in Van Nuys. She was great with the animals, but thanks to their sharp claws and beaks, she ended up with "scars all over me." When Camp appeared in a Busch Gardens TV special, an agent spotted her, and before she knew it, she was doing commercials and guest spots on TV shows. By the time she was in *Clue*, she had been in over forty television episodes and movies. Despite her work ethic and talent as an actor, Camp sometimes struggled to get roles that didn't involve her parading around in a bikini. In Francis Ford Coppola's *Apocalypse Now* (1979), she was a *Playboy* Playmate. An early profile of her by gossip columnist Earl Wilson is so fawning it borders on parody. She was "one of the most beautiful girls" he had ever seen. She was always "Colleen" and never Camp. After mentioning that she trained birds, he segued to "Colleen herself would be a bird in England where that means sexy chick," and he "confessed

45 Wiedlin, interview with Retro Junk.

a vast interest in bird girls." He instructed readers to "remember the name Colleen Camp" because "you'll be hearing about her." He was at least right about that.

The cast was set now with the exceptions of Mr. Boddy, Mrs. Peacock, the Evangelist, and the Motorist. On April 3, two men came in to read for the part of the hapless Motorist. Jeffrey Kramer had been in *Jaws* and *Jaws II* as Deputy Hendricks and was a friend of Hill's. He'd also had guest spots on *M*A*S*H*, *Laverne & Shirley*, *The Incredible Hulk*, and *Soap*. Kramer was born in 1945 and grew up in New Jersey. In 1979, he costarred in a sitcom about the return of Frankenstein's monster called *Struck by Lightning*. Critics hammered the writing and premise, but enjoyed Kramer and his costar, Jack Elam, lamenting that the material wasn't up to the standard of their performances. Ratings were poor, and CBS canceled it after just three episodes. Lee Ving also read for the Motorist, and while the role went to Kramer, Paramount exec Dawn Steel began pushing hard for Ving to play Mr. Boddy.

Ving was born Lee Capellaro in Philadelphia in 1950. He had appeared in a handful of films by the time he auditioned for *Clue*, but he was best known as the singer for the hardcore punk band Fear. More accurately, he was best known for one performance Fear gave on *Saturday Night Live* on Halloween night 1981. Former cast member John Belushi was a massive fan of the group, and he lobbied for it to be on the show, even agreeing to do a cameo as incentive. Word got out, and dozens of hardcore punk fans, including members of other bands, ended up at Rockefeller Center for the live show. What transpired, after host Donald Pleasence introduced them—"They look very frightening, but they're really nice people"—was the first mosh pit broadcast live on television.[46] Audience members swarmed the stage while Ving performed, and some leaped off the stage and into the crowd. The microphone fell forward; a screaming fan grabbed it and let the world know that "New York sucks!" Other reports say someone yelled "Fuck New York!" When a man brought a giant pumpkin onstage to smash, the show quickly cut to a commercial. Media coverage of Fear's

46 McCloskey, "The Life and Times of Philly Hardcore Pioneer Lee Ving."

appearance was typically overwrought, with much hand-wringing and pearl-clutching over how far society had fallen. The *New York Post* reported that the "riot" had caused some $200,000 in damage.[47] In actuality, it was forty dollars. Not $40,000, but forty.

Even though Paramount was anxious to make stars out of singers, Ving was a wild choice. He loved to taunt people from the stage, and he was accused of homophobia for shouting slurs at his crowds. He insisted it was all part of the act; Fear would "sometimes advocate the exact opposite of what we believe to show how ridiculous the idea is." Lynn wasn't sold. He didn't necessarily have a problem with Ving the punk rocker, though he wasn't much of a connoisseur himself. He simply felt that Ving wasn't right for the part. He had written Mr. Boddy as a truly odious, disgusting man, someone who "bites his nails and picks his teeth, nose, and other orifices."[48] Ving was performing shirtless on stage as women screamed for him. Lynn eventually agreed to cast Ving because the studio was pushing for him, and Lynn worried that he'd already said no to too many recommendations.

Two parts remained: Mrs. Peacock and the Evangelist. Even though he wouldn't be signed until the day filming began, Howard Hesseman was looking more and more likely as the Evangelist. Hesseman, who had portrayed deejay Dr. Johnny Fever on *WKRP in Cincinnati*, had been a real-life disk jockey in college, then joined the improv group the Committee in San Francisco. While not as well remembered today as the Groundlings or Second City, the Committee (named to mock the House Un-American Activities Committee) was a groundbreaking part of the counterculture comedy scene. Hesseman sometimes used the alias Don Sturdy, and his *Clue* contract lists both his name and Don Sturdy Enterprises. He would make $10,000 a week for two weeks of guaranteed work, but his contract stipulated that "producer will put to use all good faith efforts to accede to Player's request that no credit be accorded on screen."[49] It's not entirely clear why Hesseman didn't

---

47 Hilburn, "Fear."; "Fear Riot Leaves Saturday Night Glad to Be Alive."

48 Lynn, "Clue," shooting script, 19.

49 Paramount Pictures, Authorization for Engagement of Artist, Howard Hesseman, in Casting Company, Casting Notebook.

want credit, but a couple of possibilities suggest themselves. First, since the Evangelist was envisioned as a surprise cameo role, Hesseman may have been willing to play along. He was certainly a recognizable talent, and most adult viewers would've realized who he was. The no-credit arrangement also got him out of any prerelease publicity—he'd be free from interviews, talk show gigs, and press junkets. He was well paid for what ended up being seven days of actual shooting at the end of July.

Mrs. Peacock had perhaps been the toughest role to fill. Although Eileen Brennan's name had shown up early in Hirshenson and Jenkins's lists of possible actors, that was as far as it had gone. Brennan may have conjured up too many comparisons to *Murder by Death*, since she'd appeared in that (and in *The Cheap Detective*). She was born Verla Eileen Brennen in Los Angeles in 1932. She would later switch the last e in Brennen to an a and go by her middle name. Like so many of her costars, she got her start onstage, then quickly transitioned to movies. She had appeared in *The Last Picture Show* (1971), *The Sting* (1973), and *Daisy Miller* (1974), among other films. She'd popped up on the small screen as well, earning an Emmy nomination for her work on *Taxi*.

Even though Brennan had worked throughout the 1970s and had received critical acclaim (and an Oscar nomination) for her role as Captain Lewis in *Private Benjamin*, she had barely acted in the past two and a half years. On October 27, 1982, she had dinner with Goldie Hawn in Los Angeles. The two said goodnight, and Brennan turned to cross the street when she was hit by a speeding car. She was thrown into the air and landed on the hood of the car. The accident wrenched one of her eyes from its socket and fractured her skull, both of her legs, her pelvis, and several facial bones. She was rushed to the hospital, lucky to be alive. She would have multiple surgeries, including facial reconstruction. Her first acting work after the accident was an appearance on *The Love Boat*. She still had no feeling on the left side of her face. In September 1984, she entered the Betty Ford Center for an addiction to painkillers, another horrible side effect of the car accident. *Clue* would not only be her first movie since 1982, it would also demand that she run around a large mansion set, move quickly down stairs, feign getting smacked in the face, collapse onto couches and chairs, and fall to the ground. Brennan told the producers and Lynn that she was up for it. They had finally found their Mrs. Peacock.

Shortly after filming began, there would be one more casting decision. Tim Reid, who had accepted the role of the Cop, dropped out for unspecified reasons. Lynn and Hill quickly turned to Bill Henderson, a jazz musician, to replace him. Henderson had performed with Count Basie and Frank Sinatra, and he'd recorded several albums in the 1960s. He often performed at Playboy nightclubs, and it was there that he met Bill Cosby. Cosby encouraged Henderson to get into acting, and Henderson relocated to Los Angeles. In the 1970s, he had dozens of roles in television and movies. In 1985 alone, he had guest spots on two TV series, was in a made-for-TV movie, and appeared in *Clue* and *Fletch*. Henderson was signed on June 19, 1985, for $1,000 a day for fifteen days of guaranteed work. Nine days later, he was in front of the camera filming his first scenes, his arrival at the mansion.

Main casting had been underway since January 1985, and other crew members had been hired in the intervening months. A friend of Lynn's had suggested that John Morris compose the score. Lynn mailed him a copy of the script, and Morris agreed. Costume designer Michael Kaplan had worked on half a dozen titles before *Clue*, including *Blade Runner* (1982). He has since become one of the best known costume designers in Hollywood, often working with J. J. Abrams and David Fincher. Jeffrey Chernov, who had worked with Hill on *Halloween II* and *Halloween III*, was hired early as *Clue*'s production manager, responsible for overseeing the day-to-day below-line work. Director of photography Victor Kemper had been working in movies since the 1960s. He had photographed with directors such as Sidney Lumet, Irvin Kershner, Carl Reiner, Tim Burton, and Harold Ramis. He would be instrumental in helping first-time film director Lynn light and shoot *Clue*. The production design fell to John Lloyd (no relation to Christopher). He would be responsible for creating the look and feel of Hill House, alongside set decorator Tommy Roysden. These were just a handful of the people who would work, along with dozens of others, on *Clue*. Hill kindly suggested one more crew member: Lynn's young son Teddy, as a "production assistant."

At Paramount studios, a mansion had begun to rise on Stage 18.

Crew members were scouring the prop department for furniture to populate the set. Calls were placed to rent or borrow antiques from all over the country. Painters were getting to work, not just on the fake mansion but also on the pictures that would hang in the house. This was a period piece, set in 1954, and every decision had to be made with that in mind. Everything from the cars to the cleanser above the kitchen sink would need to be from the early 1950s. Near the main mansion set, on Stage 17, the upstairs rooms, the secret passages, and the cellar were being built. They needed a master bedroom with a master bath, a dressing room, a second bedroom, and a nursery. An attic positively teemed with junk, and a cellar was constructed with a boiler and stuffed with more junk. Lynn also needed a handful of exterior shots, so location scouting was conducted in search of a suitably windy road and an estate that could double for Hill House. Paramount's Stage 16 was filled with furniture and reserved for about ten days of rehearsals, a "rare luxury for a film."[50] Actors are paid for rehearsals, and they aren't cheap, but Lynn felt it was essential given the complexity of the plot and the ensemble nature of the film. Hill backed him up, and rehearsals were set for early May. *Clue* was ready to go.

Then Carrie Fisher overdosed on tranquilizers.

Fisher's entry into rehab is often shared by *Clue* fans as an amusing bit of movie trivia, but for Fisher's friend Carol Caldwell, it was terrifying. Caldwell found Fisher on the floor barely conscious and incoherent. She rushed Fisher to the hospital, where another friend, a doctor, told Caldwell she'd have to help him pump Fisher's stomach because if he asked a member of the hospital staff to help instead, "they will sell the story and it will be in the [*National*] *Enquirer* in the morning."[51] Fisher would recover from the overdose, but she would later say she had hit rock bottom. She was using cocaine, drinking, and taking prescription drugs. It was time to go to rehab. But what about *Clue*? She told Lynn and Hill that this was no problem at all—rehab would let her out to work on the movie during the day. If that sounded

50 Paramount Pictures, *Clue* press kits.

51 Weller, *Carrie Fisher*, 180.

fine to Lynn and Hill, Paramount's lawyers and insurance agents were less than thrilled, and they rejected Fisher for Scarlet. Lynn would later say he had no idea what to make of all of this. He was, after all, the outsider. He would come to suspect that both Hill and Steel also were using cocaine, joking in Jeff Smith's documentary that "everybody that I'd met in Hollywood seemed to have hay fever."[52]

Exactly what transpired over the next few frantic days at Paramount Pictures as Lynn and the producers scrambled to replace Fisher in that last week of April isn't well-documented. Fisher's name appears on a cast list on Friday, April 26, 1985, as Miss Scarlet, immediately below Lesley Ann Warren's name as Mrs. White. One week later, on May 3, Madeline Kahn was listed as Mrs. White, and Warren was now Miss Scarlet. Although the story of Fisher dropping out of *Clue* has been told and retold, almost no one seems to remember that Warren was already cast as Mrs. White. In an interview celebrating the thirty-fifth anniversary of *Clue*, Warren remembered being in Greece with her family when she got offered the role of Miss Scarlet. "It just somehow came to me. I didn't audition, I didn't meet the director, any of it. It just came to me as a straight offer, which was fabulous."[53] Warren had met with Lynn and the producers—but for the role of Mrs. White. For Smith's *Who Done It?* documentary, she did recall being offered Mrs. White, but still couldn't remember all of the details, including auditioning for the role. She's not alone in forgetting what exactly happened; Lynn remembers casting Warren only after Fisher dropped out.

Kahn had met with Lynn and Hill in New York for the role of Mrs. Peacock, with the note "poss" for possibility next to her name. Perhaps they remained unsure. But now, desperate, they reached out. She was available, and she agreed to be in the movie, transplanting herself from Manhattan to Los Angeles in a matter of days. Although the specific details of what happened when Fisher dropped out and Kahn stepped in remain murky, both Warren and Kahn would save the day, and

52 Smith, *Who Done It?*, 18:41.

53 Conway, "Lesley Ann Warren."

*Clue*'s budget, by keeping everything on track. Warren swapped roles less than a week before rehearsals were set to begin, with new lines to learn and an entirely new character to make her own. Kahn jumped into the role of Mrs. White with just as little time to prepare and would go on to deliver one of fans' favorite performances in the movie.

Kahn was born in Boston in 1943, but after her parents divorced, she and her mother moved to New York City, where she grew up. She began acting off-Broadway before getting her first Broadway role in *How Now, Dow Jones*. In the early 1970s, she exploded onto the movie scene, largely through her association with two directors, Peter Bogdanovich and Mel Brooks. She appeared in *What's Up Doc* in 1972, *Paper Moon* in 1973, and both *Blazing Saddles* and *Young Frankenstein* in 1974. She was nominated for the Oscar for Best Supporting Actress two years in a row for *Paper Moon* and *Blazing Saddles*. She hosted *Saturday Night Live* twice. By the time she was cast in *Clue*, she'd been nominated for four Golden Globes awards. She had less success on television; her sitcom, *Oh Madeline*, was canceled after a single season.

Kahn appears so effortlessly funny on any screen, big or small, that it gives people the wrong idea about her. She was, in the words of her biographer, "intensely private."[54] Eileen Brennan had grown especially close to Kahn when the two worked together on Bogdanovich's *At Long Last Love* (1975). They also both appeared in *The Cheap Detective*. But by the time they shot *Clue*, Kahn was aloof and struggled to know what to say to her old friend. Brennan summed her up: "She was a unique person and people wanted to love her and be with her, but that wasn't what she did."[55] Warren remembered that unlike most of the other cast members, Kahn would usually retreat to her trailer in between scenes. "I can't even really tell a joke," Khan insisted, and as much as she loved acting, she found "being funny very hard work."[56] On *The Tonight Show*, she would compare working on *Clue* to being a pastry chef: it might be fun for the people who get to devour her work,

54 Madison, *Madeline Kahn*, 3.

55 Madison, 222.

56 Specter, "Funny?"

but it isn't that much fun for her.

In early May, the cast gathered for the first time. There was a table read, and then Lynn screened *His Girl Friday* to give everyone an idea of what he was looking for. The movie, directed by Howard Hawks and starring Rosalind Russell and Cary Grant, is the quintessential screwball comedy, with witty banter that moves so quickly it can be easy to miss. Lynn knew how to work with casts and how to get excellent performances. He needed the actors to understand how the dialogue was supposed to sound. Brennan, at the end of the screening, stood up and said, "You can tell this was before the Method. They just talked!"[57] But everyone understood what Lynn wanted and rehearsals ran for the next two weeks.

On Friday, May 17, 1985, the cast donned Michael Kaplan's costumes. Producers Jon Peters and Peter Guber wandered the set in sport coats and sneakers while Hill checked that everything was in order. In the first major promotional push for the movie, the press was invited to Stage 18. Photographs were dutifully snapped and funny quips were dutifully issued. Mull told reporters he'd put on thirty pounds for the role and called it his "*Raging Bull*."[58] The event was not an in-depth look at the movie, but a reception to put everything in the best light after the Fisher fiasco. They were scheduled to shoot for fifty days in May, June, and July. Everything was ready.

On Monday, May 20, 1985, Paramount Pictures production #31840 began filming.

---

57 Camp, interview with the author.

58 Natale, "The Countdown to 'Clue,' the Movie."

# PART II
## *CLUE*

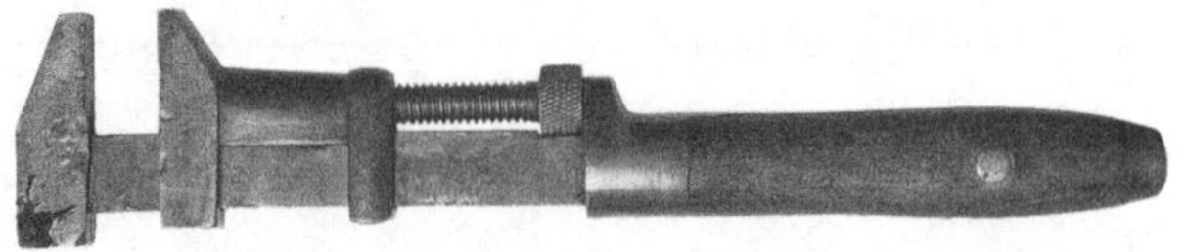

# 4. "GOOD EVENING, YOU ARE EAGERLY AWAITED"

"This opening joke is one I've always regretted."
-Jonathan Lynn[1]

*Clue* begins simply enough, with white titles against clouds, but it was already causing Jonathan Lynn headaches. He had decided in editing to scrap his original plan for the main titles: shots of the cook, Mrs. Ho, preparing dinner as she watched the Army–McCarthy hearings. Footage of Kellye Nakahara had been filmed in the middle of production—Mrs. Ho carrying pots to the stove, chopping vegetables, preparing appetizers, holding a sumptuous cake, and taking a cigarette break as she watched the hearings on the television. The idea isn't as odd as it might sound at first; it sets the stage for a group of people coming to dinner while it emphasizes the Red Scare and the threat of exposure that would drag the characters to this isolated mansion.

But Lynn decided he wanted something a tad more ominous than a cook making dinner in a charming white kitchen. *Clue* wasn't supposed to be just funny and mysterious. Since Debra Hill first envisioned it in 1980, it was supposed to be suspenseful. Lynn tried to come up with a new, clever opening sequence, but Paramount told him no—there wasn't enough money. He would later blame his first-time status

---

1 Brandon and Lynn, "*Clue*: The Director's Commentary," 39:20.

as a director on the foul-up, believing he should've sorted it all out long before filming began. Paramount executives suggested the white titles, but on a simple black background. Lynn instead searched stock footage for storm clouds. He found enough film to evoke the right mood, then put the remaining credits over the opening shots. He was quickly learning the Hollywood ropes; producers and studios would spend $1 million on an elaborate set but balk at something that hadn't been budgeted.

The titles were designed by Burke Mattsson and inspired by the font from the board game. Mattsson included small flourishes reminiscent of old movie posters such as those for *Dracula* (1931)—triangles instead of tittles (the dots over an *i* or a *j*) and angled diamond shapes on the letter *r* to add to the gothic feel. Such details might seem insignificant, but they contribute to the overall tone of the film. The title note that the seven principal cast members appear in alphabetical order derived from Hill's insistence that no one would have top billing and the actors would all be seen as equals.

Lynn, eager to convey the importance of creating suspense, spells out in the script how the score might sound, insisting the first music the audience hears be "urgent strings." He invokes Bernard Herrmann, who composed the score for Alfred Hitchcock's *Psycho* (1960), conjuring images of the famous shower scene when Janet Leigh is hacked to death. But *Clue* composer John Morris had something a little different in mind. His main title includes a few seconds of Lynn's "urgent strings," but they are followed by a synthesized beat, at once playful and mysterious. Morris was a master of musical contrasts, and he was well practiced from writing scores for the king of parody, Mel Brooks. When Lynn and Morris first met to discuss the score, Morris shared a few of his ideas on the piano, and Lynn, himself a musician, offered a few suggestions. Lynn wouldn't hear the full score until Morris conducted the recording sessions in October 1985, two months after principal photography had wrapped on August 12.

As the music swells, Wadsworth's car rolls into view, winding up a narrow road. The wind is picking up and is audible on the soundtrack. In the space of sixty seconds, the car travels through three different locations. The first is Franklin Canyon Drive in Los Angeles, just south of Upper Franklin Canyon Reservoir. Professor Plum will pick up Miss Scarlet on another stretch of the same road in a few minutes, at one of only two locations used in the entire film off the Paramount lot.

Cast and crew members often remember *Clue* being shot in continuity—that is, in the order the scenes unfold. It is true that the movie benefited from certain advantages that most other films don't have. The entire cast was contracted for the whole shoot, so devising complicated schedules around actor availability was not an issue. This also allowed for more in-depth rehearsals. And since all but a few minutes of footage would be shot on one set, juggling locations was not a problem. But while filming *Clue* did proceed more chronologically than most movies, it was not shot strictly in continuity. These opening exterior scenes were among the last filmed, shot on August 6 and 7, 1985, with production a week over schedule. Tim Curry completed two brief shots in the car as it was stopped, then a crew member, acting as Curry's double, drove the car while cameras rolled.

Wadsworth's introduction is intended to scream "Butler!" at the audience. Curry based his performance not on any real-life notion of what an English butler might be but on "a sort of film butler," he said, since "most people's ideas of butlers come from movies."[2] Lynn wanted to emphasize Wadsworth's status as a butler, and the production team obliged him. For Wadsworth's car, they picked a four-door 1948 Chevrolet Fleetline to show his lack of wealth and aversion to anything hip. As Wadsworth pulls up to a gate built by the set's construction crew, sharp-eyed viewers might notice the dings on the front bumper and the car's age, along with a 1955 Washington, DC, license plate. The crew had their work cut out for them hunting down period relics, and they did their research. In 1953, a year before the movie takes place, Washington switched from dating license plates in the year issued to the year they expired. The production team learned that and got the right plate, all without the benefit of a quick Google search.

Initially Wadsworth was to get out of his car and unchain the old, squeaky gates. In the script the home's ownership and history were

---

2 Mann, "Old Movies Clue Curry In."

vague to the point of being confusing. A press kit issued as Paramount ramped up marketing described it as a "long-deserted mansion," and in the screenplay, the front doors are said to be creaking.[3] But how then to explain the immaculate interior? The script seemed to want to have it both ways—a deserted, spooky house that is simultaneously sumptuous and ornately decorated. The contradiction may have worked on the written page, but as the production moved onto Paramount's Stage 18, it felt a little odd for Hill House to be abandoned. Production designer John Lloyd and his team, working with Lynn and Hill, opted for a luxurious main set over a cobwebbed, dusty house. The gates became key operated, the hinges on the front door were oiled, and the spookiness of the mansion was largely relegated to the cellar, the upstairs bedrooms, and the attic.

As for the home's owner, in each of Lynn's screenplay drafts and revisions, written between early 1984 and well into 1985, Wadsworth is asked who owns the mansion, and he responds, as he does in the film, that it belongs to a friend. Easily brushing aside who owns the home is a little convenient but entirely keeping within the spirit of the board game by making such details unimportant.

The script once again invokes *Psycho*, this time comparing the house to the Bates home. Lynn also writes that the mansion has the "soulless empty quality" of Xanadu in *Citizen Kane* (1941).[4] These exterior shots of Hill House also account for the bulk of *Clue*'s special effects. Albert Whitlock, the Academy Award-winning matte artist who had worked often with Hitchcock, came out of retirement to advise on the movie. Director of photography Victor Kemper recalled that he always enjoyed working with Whitlock, but in retirement "[he] was even more fun," since the famed effects guru "wasn't as intense."[5] Whitlock partnered with Illusion Arts, a special effects company owned by Syd Dutton and Bill Taylor, and relying on John Lloyd's design, the three created the eerie matte shots appearing in the film. In the final credits,

3 Paramount Pictures, *Clue*, press kits.

4 Lynn, "Clue," revised third draft, 1.

5 Kahan and Turner, "Clue is More Than a Game," 57.

Dutton is credited with the painting, Taylor with photographing it, and Whitlock as a "consultant." Taylor and Dutton began the effects work four days after principal photography wrapped on August 12 and worked on and off for the next three months, not finishing until November 22, just eighteen days before the film's premiere in New York and three weeks before *Clue*'s wide theatrical release.

*Clue* fans have been known to discuss the movie's anachronisms, continuity errors, and inconsistencies in online forums. One of the more common observations insists that the matte painting of Hill House does not match the interior layout of the mansion—not by a long shot. Today's geek culture prioritizes things like canon and world building. Entire websites carefully track minute details across film franchises like Harry Potter, Star Wars, and the Marvel Cinematic Universe. So demanding are fans—notably short for fanatic—of a consistent mythology that large franchises like Star Wars or the MCU employ people whose sole job is to ensure that a minor character detail or a plot development doesn't contradict anything from previous films, even those that are decades old. Fans have come to expect this, and there can be intense backlash if their expectations are not met.

Perhaps not surprisingly then, some devotees attempt to retroactively apply these obsessions to older films they love. But filmmakers, whether from 1945 or 1985, could hardly have foreseen the twenty-first century's world of on-demand films, streamable everywhere from the back seat of a car to a giant home movie theater. Entire podcasts and websites exist solely to examine single movies frame by frame, trying to deconstruct filmmakers' choices not from the perspective of the writers or the directors who want to tell a compelling story, but from the perspective of those fans who approach even the smallest details as integral to the production of a flawless whole.

The complaints about the matte painting not matching the set are technically right, but they ignore how well the painting contributes to the spirit of the film. Those exterior matte shots of Hill House appear for less than twenty seconds of total screen time, but Taylor and Dutton spent months getting it just right. They were designed and painted to create a sense of dread, and the artists succeeded; the house is at once beautiful and creepy. It worked so well that the painting, coupled with the lightning and thunder effects, terrified filmmaker Josh Brandon as a seven-year-old child and gave him nightmares. Brandon, who would later record an audio commentary with Lynn, said, "I'd wake up and go running into my parents room, and they said, 'You can't watch that movie anymore!'"[6]

As Wadsworth's car winds its way to the front of the house, the matte painting blends seamlessly with the second location in the film's opening minutes. While Hill House is a special effect and the gate was constructed by the crew in Franklin Canyon, the driveway and vine-covered retaining walls are real, belonging to a mansion in Pasadena, California. The production spent one day filming at the mansion on August 6, 1985, and also shot footage in the interior for the ballroom, which was the only room not replicated on the Paramount lot. The home, at 160 South San Rafael Drive, sometimes called the Max Busch house after one of its owners, was used for these exterior shots. The production added the gargoyles to the roof for the overhead shot of Wadsworth's car as it approaches. The mansion's driveway and front façade were replicated with admirable precision for the main *Clue* set on Stage 18. The old Chevy Fleetline moves across the screen from left to right, then doubles back in front of the house as it curves around the driveway, and with a single cut it has left Pasadena and arrived at the *Clue* mansion on the Paramount Studios lot. The rest of the movie, except for just over two minutes of footage in Franklin Canyon and fifty-five seconds in the ballroom of the Busch mansion, was shot on this single lot.

All of the following were copied from the Busch house: the brick walls on either side of the driveway that the car passes between, the stone balustrade with planters, the fountain in the driveway, and the garage Wadsworth parks in front of. The gargoyles on the brick walls, standing as sentinels over the house, are a creation of the production team, carved from Styrofoam. Fans still visit the house that inspired *Clue* and stand outside the gated driveway peeking in, but during a renovation in 2005, the Busch house caught fire and burned to

6 Brandon, interview with author.

the ground. Nearly two decades later, a new home was still under construction on the lot.

Movies are more accessible than ever before, and it's easy to forget what it takes to make them. Consider these details that unfold in the seventy seconds it takes for Wadsworth to exit his car, feed the dogs, and walk to the front door (stepping in dog feces along the way): a driver on the crew parks the car, then we cut to Curry exiting it as if he had been driving. Leaves are strewn about as the plants and trees rustle in the breeze. The wooden doghouse is worn and faded, and the metal hook that is bolted to the house to hold the dog chain is rusted. The stone balustrade is weather-beaten, and there are water stains below the planters. Decorative lamps illuminate the brick walkway and portico. As one of the dogs gnaws on his bone, we see a buildup of leaves and debris between the doghouse and the mansion. The brick, like the stone, is weathered and old. More leaves flutter across the screen as they drop from the nearby trees.

Every one of these flourishes was created by the production team inside a massive Hollywood soundstage. The wind was controlled by large fans, the leaves were scattered by crew members, and the porch lights were found at antique shops and in the Paramount prop department and drilled into the faux-brick facade—a facade constructed by a crew working on the set just weeks before filming began. This meticulous attention to detail is repeated in every room in the mansion. It is easy to take the magic of movies for granted, but producers, directors, set designers, matte painters, and countless others went to extraordinary lengths to make *Clue* feel real to its audience.

It's May 20, 1985, the first day of shooting. Curry getting out of the car and confronting the dogs are the first scenes filmed, including brief shots that were later cut of the dogs grabbing Wadsworth's coat and running off with it before he could shorten the chain and retrieve it. Lynn said shooting fell behind on day one because of the dogs, who, he joked in his deadpan British accent, did not understand continuity. Because of the difficulty in getting the animals to behave, more shots of the dogs (sans Curry) were taken on the last day of filming, August 12, and Curry did additional pickup shots on August 1.

As Wadsworth pushes open the front door, he is scraping the dog excrement off of his shoe. Decades later, Lynn would recall that he "always regretted" this joke but that "unfortunately I shot it in such a way that I couldn't remove it later."[7] The gag continues as Mrs. White, Colonel Mustard, and Yvette all pause in the next few minutes to smell their feet (shots of Mrs. Peacock sniffing around were filmed but cut in editing). Lynn says the gag was suggested by Dawn Steel. It doesn't appear in Lynn's first or second draft (the dogs didn't even exist until draft three). Lynn acknowledges that some people love the bit, but he feels it's out of sync with the rest of the film. He's right—*Clue* is more farcical and witty than puerile.

Wadsworth steps into the mansion and hangs his coat, hat, and umbrella in the hall closet. We're looking down the hall at him, taking in our first glimpse of the main floor of the mansion. Lynn wanted to avoid overt callouts to the game that would wink at the audience as if to say "Remember that game you played?" and instead let events unfold naturally. He keeps the camera on Wadsworth, and we will discover the house and its iconic rooms at the same time the characters do. In the hall we see paintings, hand-carved wood, gleaming marble, and soaring ceilings. One word repeatedly pops up in contemporaneous press reports about the set: lavish. The eighties was a decade of location shooting in Hollywood, and the set of *Clue* was something of an anomaly—a throwback to an earlier age. Paramount's Stage 18 once held the entire set of *Rear Window* (1954) and Norma Desmond's mansion in *Sunset Blvd.* (1950). Now it housed a new mansion.

The *Clue* set was decorated with everything from expensive (in some cases, very expensive) antiques to cheap props from the Paramount shop. Production designer John Lloyd and set decorator Tommy Roysden are responsible for the feel of the set. Lloyd led a team of people who worked with Hill and Lynn to create the film's gothic ambience. Cathryn Bangs, Les Gobruegge, William Major, Eugene Nollmann II, and Steven Schwartz are all credited as set designers, and they made everything from the glass panes in the front door to the carved nook for the old-fashioned doorbell look real. Roysden,

---

7 Brandon and Lynn, "*Clue*: Director's Commentary," 39:20–40:00.

alongside Ronald Jacobs, found the objects, large and small, that populate Hill House. Property master Horst Grandt and assistant Fred Throop were responsible for the items the characters handled, from Mrs. Ho's kitchen knife to the champagne flutes Yvette passed out.

Lloyd said the decision to build the giant set was made for the production team because they would "never find a house with the same layout as the game."[8] He initially envisioned the mansion as an English Tudor given the long history of manor house mysteries. But he went with American Victorian to keep the film rooted in the US. The house was built "to take a real beating," explained Lloyd, because it had to last the whole shoot.[9] Heavy lights, cameras, furniture—all of it would be dragged throughout the set at one time or another.

The words "New England" and the date "1954" appear on-screen. Setting the movie during the time of the Red Scare, meant everything from costumes to furniture to the kitchen supplies would need to be at least thirty years old. (It must've created déjà vu for Christopher Lloyd, who had traveled from the mid-1980s to the mid-1950s just a few months earlier while shooting his most famous role, Doc Brown in *Back to the Future*.)

One of the better decisions regarding set design was the parquet floor in the hall that resembles the Clue game board. Lynn's script originally had parquet flooring in a handful of other rooms, while the hall had "cold, grey" marble. The oak floor came later, and it was most likely a John Lloyd creation. The other rooms were given rugs and carpet.

Wadsworth walks purposefully through the hall, passing an eagle lectern on his left in front of the lounge. Set decorator Roysden said he "wanted an animalistic look" for the house.[10] While a handful of props, such as the gargoyles, stand out, most of the animals fade into the background, but look for them and it becomes apparent that they are everywhere—carved into furniture, mantels, staircases; sitting in glass

---

8 Haithman, "Clue's Played."

9 Kahan and Turner, "Clue is More Than a Game," 50.

10 Haithman, "Clue's Played."

cases; or, as we will see, standing in rooms, pretending to be something else. It's another subtle addition that adds to the sinister feel of the mansion. The massive painting hanging between the dining room and the lounge is from the Paramount prop department. Wadsworth passes it and glances into the dining room, ornately laid out for seven. He turns and makes his way to the library, as "Shake, Rattle and Roll" plays on the soundtrack.

Here, looking through a window, is our first glimpse of the library. Thanks to the temperamental dogs, shooting is already a day behind, and this was shot on May 22 instead of the twenty-first. Yvette is dancing to the music as she polishes glasses. In the foreground, on a table, is a "rare Hendell [Handel] eagle lamp," touted in promotional materials as worth $9,000.[11] Because most of the antiques were borrowed from private collections, museums, and estates, all were insured. Roysden shared his anxiety with reporters during production, explaining that "the furniture is being used so brutally here—it's been moved more times in a week than in its entire life." He gestured to a $35,000 rug "carelessly crumpled" in a corner to make way for cameras and lighting.[12]

The lyrics heard as Wadsworth enters the library fit perfectly with the sexual innuendo and double entendres in the rest of the film: "I'm like a one-eyed cat peepin' in a seafood store." Lynn later said he picked the music that was the least expensive to license. While cost was certainly a factor, he was working with a team of industry sound professionals who knew how to create the right mood with songs. The music also offers a lighthearted contrast to the formality of the mansion, keeping with the split personality of the film—murder and spookiness on the one hand and farce on the other and black humor. It's different from what Lynn originally envisioned. His first-draft screenplay created a more somber atmosphere for the beginning of the movie. Wadsworth is "grim and tense" when he enters the library, and there is no music.[13]

---

11 Thomas, "Whodunnit with All the Clues."

12 Haithman, "Clue's Played."

13 Lynn, "*Clue*," first draft, 2.

Instead, a frightened Yvette drops the glass she is polishing, and after it smashes on the floor, she apologizes.

In the final film, Wadsworth asks Yvette if everything is ready.

"*Oui, Monsieur.*"

"You have your, uh . . . instructions." It's here that a running gag is established, as Wadsworth pauses to glance down at Yvette's cleavage, something that nearly every other character will also do at one time or another. Is the joke a cheap laugh at a woman's expense or is it something else? Colleen Camp thought it was something else when she read the script. After taking the role of a *Playboy* bunny in *Apocalypse Now*, Camp began to criticize the use of nudity and the casting of women as mere eye candy in films. Instead of taking roles meant for a bombshell, she sought out parts that allowed her to be both funny and sexy—and her offers quickly dwindled.

"It got so I wasn't even considered for attractive, funny roles because I wasn't utilizing my physical appearance," Camp said. In *Clue*, she saw something more behind the skimpy French maid costume. She went to pains to stress that "there is no nudity or sex in the picture," insisted that "Yvette isn't a dumbbell," and believed the part wasn't exploitative.[14] Instead, Wadsworth's glance at her bosom hints at the role he intends for her. Yvette, who later drops her fake accent, is neither French nor a maid. But tonight she will play a floozy, there to throw the suspects off guard. Her presence will infuriate Mrs. White, titillate Colonel Mustard, and scare Miss Scarlet. It is a carefully designed act, one that only *Clue* loyalists will fully appreciate through repeated viewings. Camp was playing a character who was herself playing a part. Thirty-six years later, she remembers that this duplicity helped draw her to the role. "I've always liked roles where someone isn't what they seem." Camp is a walking encyclopedia of film history, and she explains her approach to Yvette with a spot-on impersonation of Marilyn Monroe in *Gentlemen Prefer Blondes* (1953): "I can be smart when it's important, but most men don't like it."[15]

---

14 Scott, "Actress Returns to Sex Symbol Role."

15 Camp, interview with author.

The books selected for inclusion in the library were mostly multivolume sets, which can often be bought at inexpensive prices in bookstores. This also allows for a uniformity in color, which is important because background colors, whether from books, paintings, and wallpaper can significantly affect how a shot is lit, framed, and filmed. As Yvette sniffs unpleasantly and checks her shoes, we see the couch and chair in the library, both with animals carved at the end of the armrests, continuing Roysden's animal decor.

Wadsworth exits and makes his way up the three steps, passing a large case filled with stuffed birds, and enters the bright kitchen. Mrs. Ho turns, with a massive chef's knife pointed at Wadsworth's throat. The moment, and a few ominous notes from composer John Morris, suggests menace, but also hints at the dangerous game Wadsworth is playing; the guests are not the only ones invited to Hill House tonight. Mr. Boddy's informers are there as well, and they, depending on which ending we might see, are working with Wadsworth—or Mr. Boddy.

"Dinner will be ready at 7:30" (moved up two hours from 9:30 p.m. in the script) is Mrs. Ho's only line in the movie, but Kellye Nakahara would be around for several weeks of filming, mostly playing a corpse. Her contract guaranteed her ten weeks of work, including at least three days of rehearsals. After rehearsals, she was scheduled to start May 21, 1985, for a flat fee of $30,000. This scene was shot primarily on June 5, the same day that footage was taken of the cook working in the kitchen for use in the opening credits, but the close-up of Wadsworth with the knife pointed at his face was shot on June 12.

The footage of Senator Joseph McCarthy on the television comes from June 9, 1954, on the thirtieth day of the Army–McCarthy hearings. It was earlier in that day's hearing that attorney Joseph Welch famously shamed McCarthy, "Have you no sense of decency, sir, at long last? Have you left no sense of decency?" The hearings were broadcast in their entirety on ABC and DuMont, and millions of Americans watched, if not the live proceedings then the weeknight news summaries on NBC or CBS. The hearings' appearance on the kitchen TV then is not a convenient plot device but a reflection of reality. *Clue* fans have been delighted to pinpoint the exact date the events of the film supposedly take place, though it seems likely that because this is the most famous day of the hearings, it was the easiest to obtain footage from. Other events in the movie—a terrible thunderstorm and a full moon, for example—don't align with the June 9 date.

The bell rings and Wadsworth passes yet another Styrofoam gargoyle, this one smaller and perched atop the end of the banister for the short set of stairs. The shot of Colonel Mustard's shadow and his hand reaching out to ring the bell happened because Lynn wanted a "sort of film noir" feel for the moment.[16] It's a nice shot, but the movie is edited at a fast clip, and such moments sometimes pass before the audience can spot them. Lynn would later suggest that perhaps the movie was cut a little too quickly.

A pair of growling dogs are making the colonel a little nervous; they will play an important, albeit inconsistent, role as the movie progresses. Lynn struggled with exactly how to make the guests feel trapped in the house, and only later did he settle on the dogs. Wadsworth interrupts Mustard's explanation of what his real name is, using the word "alias" instead of the word in the screenplay, "pseudonym." We will never learn any of the characters' names, and they never appear in any version of the script.

Martin Mull lightened the Mustard character in these opening moments from what was written in the screenplay. He was supposed to have a bit of an edge as he "eyes" Wadsworth "suspiciously" and "flinches" as the butler holds up his hand to prevent him from saying his real name. Instead, Mull is more genial and even respectful when he asks who Wadsworth is, rendering his character funny instead of off-putting. All of the actors would have to find a way to balance these two characteristics in portraying their characters. They are liars, cheaters, cads, and scoundrels; some are even murderers. How to make such a motley crew funny, even likable, despite their crimes? All of the actors took a different tack. Mull initially portrayed Mustard as nice enough, then leaned into his self-important buffoonery. During filming, he said that his character "could be in an intelligence contest all by himself and

16 Brandon and Lynn, "*Clue*: Director's Commentary," 41:15.

come in third."[17]

While the colonel is wearing a tan coat and a lighter-color hat, he quickly sheds them and is left with his brown suit. Lynn has said that people tell him the characters should have been dressed in the colors of their game tokens. In fact, Lynn went out of his way, working with costume designer Michael Kaplan, to ensure that the characters were not wearing the color of their tokens.

When Lynn first approached writing *Clue*, the challenge was obvious to him: These aren't characters at all; they're colors. That's what made him, like the writers who were approached earlier, skeptical initially about tackling the project. When he did agree to turn John Landis's ideas into a screenplay, he saw it as his primary responsibility to give each character a personality and a reason to appear at the mansion. He was insistent that dressing the characters in their colors would only reinforce their two-dimensional nature and distract the audience from the story, and it's hard to disagree. Instead, the production team decided to make each character's car the same color as their Clue game token. It might have been a perfect nod to the game, but the glimpses of the cars are so quick it's easy to miss. Had the fourth ending remained and another ending not been trimmed, audiences might have had more of a chance to notice the cars, but eagle-eyed fans have long spotted the in-joke and shared it widely on the internet.

As they did with Wadsworth's Chevy, the production team put more thought into each car than just their colors. Mustard is driving a yellow 1954 Cadillac Series 62 convertible, an expensive car for a man who is being blackmailed, hinting at his wealth. Wadsworth, in dialogue that was cut, later tells the other guests that Mustard buys a new car every year—a real luxury in 1954, before leases made getting newer models easy.

As Colonel Mustard and Wadsworth move across the parquet floor to the library, Mustard glances up at the chandelier—the same chandelier that later will nearly kill him—as the camera looks down at him. In the library, Wadsworth introduces Mustard to Yvette. He

---

17 Rico, "Miss Scarlet Did It?"

is clearly delighted by her but betrays no sign that he already knows her so intimately; she eyes him and slides her hand up the neck of the champagne bottle. These moments repeat throughout the movie; everyone there knows at least one other person who is present, and yet they almost always behave otherwise. This is, of course, partly because of Lynn's efforts not to give away too much. The script sometimes has details, both in direction and in dialogue—an extra line to acknowledge a previous relationship or a note that a character's eyes lingered on someone else, for example—that were cut in the final film, as a way of playing things close to the vest. But omitting these details also works as part of the story; these people are being blackmailed, they're terrified of their secrets getting out, and now they've been summoned to a mysterious house in the desperate hope that they might be able to put an end to their suffering. They are scared and on edge and are, with one notable exception, not about to reveal that they know any of the other characters.

We learn later that Wadsworth knows their connections, and so his instruction to Yvette to give Mustard anything he needs, "within reason, that is," fits nicely. But some critics, not knowing that background, found the film lacking, even childish, after one viewing. Wadsworth's "within reason" line, so dryly delivered it could be missed altogether, comes across as a dumb gag about a man grinning like an idiot at a sexy woman in a maid's costume. It's neither clever nor particularly funny. But when one understands Mustard and Yvette's messy history and how Miss Scarlet and Mrs. White factor in, the line gets laughs. It's this kind of moment that has made *Clue* a classic. Throughout the movie, jokes are set up to pay off later, and even then only after viewers have seen the film more than once, and perhaps several times. While fans today appreciate the layers of jokes that require multiple viewings, critics seeing it once in 1985 couldn't pick up on everything, contributing to the film's middling-at-best reviews.

The butler exits, leaving Mustard facing a wall of books, feeling around for a doorknob. Some of the more physical comedy, including this moment, were absent from the first draft of the screenplay. The farce ramps up slowly, with small moments like this, until the movie becomes more of a slapstick comedy, with characters screaming, falling, and crashing into one another. Carved into the library wood around the room, at roughly eye level, is a face that looks suspiciously like a bust of Socrates. Intricate details like this are visible throughout the set.

The bell clangs, and there is Mrs. White, with her letter out, too briefly shown and not exactly in focus for audiences in the theater to read: "IT WILL BE TO YOUR ADVANTAGE TO BE PRESENT TONIGHT BECAUSE A MR. BODDY WILL BRING TO AN END A CERTAIN LONG-STANDING CONFIDENTIAL AND PAINFUL FINANCIAL LIABILITY. YOUR PSEUDONYM IS MRS. WHITE. A FRIEND." For blackmail victims, such a letter would be especially unsettling, little more comforting than if it had arrived with words cut out of different magazines in the style of a ransom note.

Mrs. White was, according to Lynn's script, supposed to "remind us of a woman from a Charles Adams [sic] cartoon."[18] Addams, creator of the *Addams Family* comic that would inspire a TV series, movies, a musical, and animated films, had drawn the poster for *Murder by Death*. Costume designer Kaplan and Madeline Kahn balanced Lynn's image of White as an Addams character with the demands of real life. White couldn't stand out so drastically from the other characters, but her appearance still sets her apart. John Morris's music, almost nonexistent since the opening titles, gives White an elegant twist on the main theme, with piano and strings. But lurking behind the sound is danger, or at the least mystery. We sense we cannot entirely trust this woman.

White arrived in a 1950 MG TD convertible, white with black trim, and it is the most inspired choice of all the characters' cars. It's a stunning classic two-seater, the kind of car a playboy would carelessly race around the English countryside in, running irate citizens off the road. That Mrs. White drives this car—which audiences glimpse for only a split second—is consistent with her identity as a black widow.

Photographing Kahn's entrance was tricky. Director of photography Victor Kemper said that in forty years of working on movies, it was

---

18 Lynn, "Clue," revised third draft, 5.

the most challenging contrast he had to light and shoot—Kahn's black hat with a black coat, her pale face, and then the white lining of the coat, all against a black marble background filling the frame. Kemper, who loved photographing the women of *Clue* because "they all seemed to latch onto fine characterizations," said the challenge was not to "overlight" Kahn's face but "still make her look very beautiful."[19]

It is often said that *Clue* takes place in real time, with the events unfolding in the hour-and-a-half runtime of the movie. It's not strictly accurate, since cuts were later made that trimmed a few moments here and there. Wadsworth and Mrs. White end up in the library too fast to have walked from the front entrance. But if the film doesn't play out strictly in real time in the same manner as Hitchcock's *Rope* (1948), for instance, it comes awfully close. Everything happens in one evening, with the characters even reminding one another how long they have until the police arrive. It made the choice of costumes, hairstyling, and makeup all the more important, since the actors would have only one look throughout the entire movie, giving the designers only one chance to get it right and convey all they intended.

As Wadsworth opens the library door and inadvertently shoves Colonel Mustard aside, he introduces Mrs. White to Yvette. White glares at the woman, and Yvette stares back. The script has them both looking at Wadsworth in fear, but in the film the fear is replaced with anger and irritation. Wadsworth, acting surprised, says, "I see you know each other." The key word there is "acting." Wadsworth is acting because he already knows—regardless of which ending we might see—about the women's unfortunate connection through White's deceased husband. The reasons for Wadsworth's deception—reasons we don't know yet—change depending on the ending, however, and it becomes clearer and clearer that Lynn's script is carefully constructed and densely plotted. It is much more intricate than simply having a character missing from a scene here or there because they are off murdering someone. "It was difficult as an actor," said Martin Mull, because they had to "tread that line" of acting guilty, but not too guilty, and tailoring their motivations

19 Kahan and Turner, "Clue is More Than a Game," 56.

to multiple endings.[20]

After spending the last few minutes in the mansion, we cut back to Franklin Canyon for sixty-eight seconds, the longest of the rare scenes in which we're off the Paramount lot. It's August 7, and shooting is nearing two weeks over schedule. Miss Scarlet is looking at her engine in sheer exasperation. It's the clearest look we get at a suspect's car and a chance to notice that it matches her character token. Scarlet was driving, before the engine died, a red 1946 Lincoln Continental. The bright moonlight peeking through the trees is no moon at all, but a light set up by the crew. There was a new moon for this last week of principal photography, and production teams knew better than to rely on Mother Nature to cooperate with filming schedules.

As Miss Scarlet fumes at her car, Professor Plum pulls up, the camera remaining static to capture the scene. Here, Lesley Ann Warren departs from the script. Throughout the movie, Scarlet was written more passively than she is played by Warren. She was supposed to act skittish when Plum pulls up, and then respond with uncertainty when he offers her a ride. Instead, Scarlet is aggressive, bending over the hood of her car seductively as Plum drives by. He hits the breaks, quickly backs up, and offers her a ride, which she accepts without hesitation.

The word "ad-lib" gets thrown out a lot when talking about comedic performances, and some directors do encourage spontaneity and plan for improvisation, but Lynn isn't one of them, at least when it came to *Clue*. He insisted that the actors stick to the script. Saying a different line or riffing a new joke is one thing, but it's difficult to change action on the fly. Shots are meticulously set up; lighting alone can take hours to get right. Character coverage has to be planned, especially in an ensemble movie like *Clue*. Actors have a small field to work in; they usually can't decide on inspiration to march across a room if they're supposed to be standing still. It's difficult to know, therefore, exactly what might have happened when there's a departure from the shooting script. Did Lynn have a new idea as he was filming? Or did an actor propose something? It's both, of course. The director would realize

---

20 Martin Mull, interview with *Entertainment Tonight*, aired Dec. 11, 1985.

something wasn't working and come up with a solution. But while all of the actors in *Clue* make the characters their own, none of their portrayals differs from the shooting script more than Lesley Ann Warren's.

Warren hung a sultry photo of Lauren Bacall from the 1940s in her dressing room for inspiration. In her hands, Scarlet became a no-nonsense woman, and her interactions with the pervy Professor Plum are much funnier because of it. Warren, switched from Mrs. White to Miss Scarlet at the last minute, had less than a month before shooting and less than a week before rehearsals to develop her character. All of the actors in *Clue* turn in memorable performances, but Warren stands out after repeat viewings.

Scarlet, now in Plum's 1949 Pontiac Streamliner station wagon (purple, of course), smoothly thanks him and explains she's late for a dinner date. Plum, who has transformed from a "middle aged, balding, plump" man in the first-draft screenplay into Christopher Lloyd, asks where she's going, and she replies, "Hill House, off Route 41."[21] Stunned, he grabs the letter she's reading from and realizes it's almost identical to the one he received and that they're going to the same place. Fans have tried to pinpoint the location of Hill House, and here is concrete information: Route 41. Several states have short stretches of road called Route 41 that might be candidates, but two explanations merge to potentially clear up the mystery. First, US Route 41 begins in Miami, travels the length of the state, and passes through several other states before terminating in Michigan. Its mention in *Clue* is a holdover from Landis's idea to set the movie in Florida. His original pitch included the Hialeah Race Track, northwest of Miami and not far from Route 41. *Clue* was set in Florida for so long that Lynn's shooting script left in a detail quite at odds with the New England setting: the storm outside is raging with such fury that there are "palm trees bending, nearly flattened by gale-force winds."[22] But there's another explanation. The *Clue* CD soundtrack liner notes inexplicably place the mansion

21 Lynn, "Clue," first draft, 5–6.

22 Lynn, "Clue," revised third draft, 9.

in New Jersey, a state that is not part of New England, and would therefore seem to be ruled out. But it does have a state Route 41—and it passes directly through Debra Hill's hometown of Haddonfield, New Jersey. It's not difficult to imagine that as the script shifted from Florida to the northern East Coast, Hill might have mentioned Route 41 passing through the town she thought of as home, and for that reason it was kept in the script.

Mrs. Peacock makes it inside Hill House just before the rain begins. Eileen Brennan grins broadly as a subdued Colonel Mustard and Mrs. White lazily acknowledge her. Her costume by Michael Kaplan is perhaps the most inspired of the lot. She resembles nothing less than a colorful bird, with a hat of ostrich and turkey feathers that looks like a nest above her glittering cat-eye glasses. Pinned on the left side of the jacket is a jeweled, golden peacock. Were Kaplan and Lynn trying to tell us something? Did Mrs. Peacock, so accustomed as a senator's wife to dressing for high society, go shopping for a peacock brooch after receiving a creepy, mysterious letter in the mail advising her of her alias? Regardless of how it came about, the flourish, like the fox-fur stole she is wrapped in (a detail taken directly from the script), reflects her attention to social status.

The costumes in *Clue* contribute to the overall design of the film that keep it in 1954 instead of growing dated. Getting period pieces right is notoriously difficult. Audiences subconsciously notice the anachronisms, even if they can't quite explain exactly what it is that makes the movie look less than authentic. Tiny details in costume design, hairstyles, makeup, or lighting can date a movie and give it a tinge of the uncanny—something just feels off. *Clue* avoids these traps; it might have been shot in 1985 or 2005, but it's impossible to tell from the look of the characters.

Peacock steps into the library and gladly takes a glass of champagne before she spots Yvette's bosom. Rather than glance away quickly in embarrassment, she stares, moving in and looking down as if peering off the edge of a cliff. As Yvette nonchalantly walks away, Brennan's Mrs. Peacock stands stunned, mouth agape. Throughout the movie it is Peacock who will fill the role of the prim-and-proper lady, frequently appalled and disgusted by her fellow guests' sexual proclivities, politics, and occupations. Given what we learn about her through the rest of the film, it makes her character that much funnier. Brennan manages to act like a chronically scandalized prude without making Mrs. Peacock unlikable. The first draft of the script portrays her much like Emily Brent in Agatha Christie's *And Then There Were None*, a heartless woman all too willing to condemn others for the slightest misstep while refusing to acknowledge her own shortcomings. Later drafts, and Brennan's performance, soften Peacock. The movie is such a well-balanced ensemble comedy that it's hard to elevate one performance over another. But Warren, Kahn, and Brennan make the women of *Clue* shine, both in their performances and in standing toe-to-toe with the men, refusing to let the other characters harass them, bully them, or take advantage of them. In a survey I conducted of 135 *Clue* fans, Wadsworth won out as the favorite character, followed by Scarlet, White, and Peacock.

Back in front of the mansion, Mr. Green stands huddled in the portico, out of the now-pouring rain. It feels so authentic it can be easy to forget we're still on the Paramount lot. Some forty feet above McKean, a water system simulated the rain inside Stage 18. The effects coordinators created a process that spun the water as it fell, giving it a more realistic look. The crew put the camera in a tent and donned rain gear. They fired up the wind machine and got the shot across the driveway in one take. It all worked well; many fans I've spoken to have no idea that they're watching rain fall from sprinklers indoors. The crew worked hard to get it right and to ensure the water would drain properly; there was a storage facility below the stage, and had the water managed to seep through the floor, it would have caused significant damage.

As Green waits, the audience can glimpse several of the cars and the replica of the fountain copied from the Busch mansion. Mr. Green drove a 1951 Plymouth Cranbrook—a sensible, straightforward car—to the dinner party. Wadsworth opens the door and he sternly tells the dogs to "Sit!" and Mr. Green shuffles backward onto the stone bench. This is another addition that was missing from the first draft to amp up the physical comedy. These kinds of gags are what would come to delight kids who discovered *Clue* on cable and home video after it flopped in theaters.

McKean's timing is impeccable, and only three takes were needed to get it right—the second take was the one used in the final film. Kemper said the production rarely needed more than three takes throughout the shoot, and while that was sometimes true, other scenes took more, occasionally going up to ten or eleven takes; one tricky scene had fifteen takes, then seven retakes. Years later, Jonathan Lynn would say there were no storyboards, but in 1985 Kemper said they did use storyboards, at least for some of the bigger scenes. Everything, Kemper explained, was "very well-prepared." Each scene required "extensive rehearsals" to ensure all the actors knew their lines and their places.[23] While these rehearsals may have been minimal for scenes with one or two actors, they were essential and detailed for scenes with everyone present.

With Mr. Green safely inside the mansion, Miss Scarlet and Professor Plum are approaching Hill House as Scarlet studies a map. According to the script, Scarlet was to ask Plum, with a line that was cut, "You know this part of the world?" to which he replied simply, "Nope,"[24] helping to explain the presence of the map. Professor Plum has had less chance than the other characters to reveal himself thus far. Apart from his shock at realizing Scarlet received the same letter he did, all he's done is offer her a ride. But now, upon her asking, "Why is the car stopped?" he tells her, at the sight of Hill House, "It's frightened." The moment contrasts her cool demeanor with his anxiety. It sets the tone for the rest of their interactions, which largely include him sexually harassing her and her not tolerating it.

At long last, the final two guests—apart from Mr. Boddy—have arrived, and Professor Plum and Miss Scarlet dash out of the car to the portico, covered by Plum's umbrella. It's May 21, the second day of filming. The shooting script portrays Plum as a gallant gentleman, shielding Scarlet from the rain. Lynn decided to add the brief shot of Plum groping Scarlet, and it was filmed a month later, on June 28. The

23 Kahan and Turner, "Clue is More Than a Game," 48

24 Lynn, "Clue," revised third draft, 7.

moment helps to establish Scarlet and Plum's antagonistic relationship and alerts the audience to how sleazy Plum is—and how Scarlet refuses to put up with any of it. She shakes him off just as Wadsworth opens the door, surprised to see them together, as if they might be a couple. Miss Scarlet quickly disabuses him of this notion and gives Plum a withering look. She is neither embarrassed nor cowed by him.

We lose a few seconds of real-time filming as another quick cut eliminates Scarlet and Plum being led to the library. They appear at the door, and Wadsworth introduces them to the other guests. As Yvette walks over to offer them champagne, Mustard ogles her. Scarlet stares at Yvette as the maid holds out a tray with two glasses. Is Scarlet nonplussed, even a little fearful? Or is it a look of shrewd calculation as she wonders how Yvette will perform tonight? It all depends on which ending we see. Scarlet continues to watch Yvette even after she gets her champagne, until the spell is broken by Professor Plum, who clinks her champagne glass with his own. Plum's cluelessness, coupled with his shamelessness, is what makes the character so funny. He is not so much frightening or threatening as he is pathetic.

All of the characters in this scene or in the previous library scene are shown holding a glass of champagne. The drink is specifically mentioned in the first draft, with Wadsworth asking each of the characters if they want a glass, and each accepting. These shots are setting up the fourth ending. This scene was filmed on May 22 and partly on May 23. In the first week of shooting, things have gone relatively smoothly, apart from the uncooperative dogs.

Wadsworth announces that all the guests have a pseudonym, and they look around at one another with fear, uncertainty, and suspicion. It's then that the cook bangs the gong with such ferocity that the guests are startled, and Mr. Green throws his champagne all over Mrs. Peacock. Green's clumsiness is setting up what was intended as a running gag for the first part of the movie, but a third instance of Mr. Green apologizing for his blundering in the study was later cut. For now, he grabs his handkerchief and wipes down Mrs. Peacock as best he can. It was not a random choice to have Green spill his drink on Peacock, but part of Lynn's carefully laid plans. Because she has to wait a few moments as Mr. Green wipes her off, Mrs. Peacock is delayed in crossing the hall, and she therefore just misses spotting the cook—her old cook, we later learn—whose back quickly disappears into the kitchen.

Dinner is served.

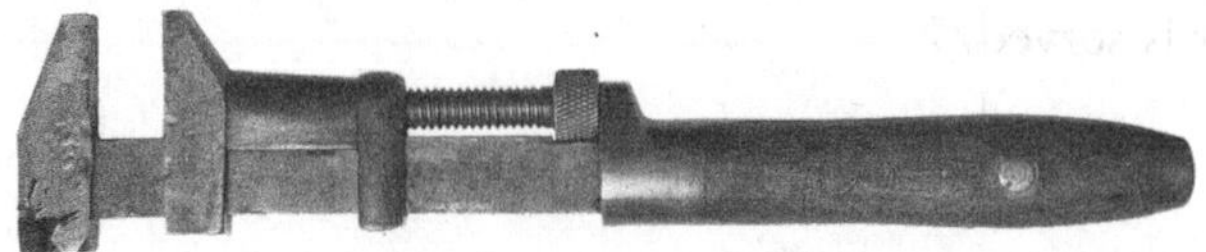

# 5. "WELL, ONE OF US MUST'VE KILLED HIM!"

"We were ecstatic and laughing and carrying on over each other's work all the time. I always say it was like herding a bunch of cats."
-Lesley Ann Warren[1]

The guests make their way across the hall and enter the sumptuous dining room, where they hope the answers they crave will be revealed. The dinner scene was filmed over four days from May 23 to May 29, 1985 (the production took holidays and weekends off, so no scenes were shot on Memorial Day), with retakes and the special-effects shots of rain and lightning outside filmed later in June. This scene highlights how challenging it is to make an ensemble movie. Jonathan Lynn used a two-camera setup in this scene instead of a single camera, to catch more action. The set walls in every room could be removed if needed to position lights and cameras, and for a handful of shots here they took out the wall separating the dining room and the lounge. Close-ups were taken of hands picking up silverware and goblets; characters were positioned to get a shot of their eyes darting or their faces trying hard to be impassive, inscrutable. Insert shots were filmed of place cards with the guests' pseudonyms, and although they were never used, the actors can be seen looking down at them, trying

1 Ivie, "Lesley Ann Warren."

to find their seats after Wadsworth announces, "You'll find your names beside your places."

The dining room, like the driveway and front facade, is a copy of another mansion, this one a private estate in the Hudson River Valley. The set designers took inspiration from East Coast mansions in decorating Hill House. Each room is different because designer John Lloyd wanted to showcase variety throughout the set, from the oak-paneled library to the green-wallpapered dining room, from the red-velvet-covered billiard room to the brightly lit kitchen. Although the dining room is seen only briefly later in the movie, this scene, with all of the main characters talking together for the first time, is pivotal, and decorating this part of the set was handled with care.

The place settings are antique Lenox china, valued at $1,700 per place setting and at $50,000 for the entire set. The chandelier is from the Victorian Era, and the table is made of cherrywood. The wallpaper is "pale green damask."[2] A fire crackles behind the guests, and candles flicker on the table. Lighting most scenes in *Clue* was tricky; nearly every room has a fireplace and ambient light from wall fixtures and chandeliers, all of which needed to be calibrated alongside the massive studio lights. Films are called films because for their first one hundred years, they were shot on . . . well, film. Movies are about story and writing and acting, but they are also about photography, and photography requires massive amounts of light. It can take hours to light a shot; *Clue* could take even longer because of the dark wood on the set and the natural light given off by the fireplaces, the lamps, and the chandeliers. Film soaks up light, but so do dark wood and fabrics. Once a scene is shot on one side of a room, turning around to shoot the other side might require two, three, or four hours to reset the lighting. As *Clue* later fell behind and the decision was made to adjust the schedule, lighting was the main reason. Lynn remembered that "it was a very slow and time-consuming process just to light everything because those rooms were so intricate."[3]

---

2 Kahan and Turner, "Clue is More Than a Game," 51.

3 Wixson, "Communism Was a Red Herring."

As the guests seat themselves, Colonel Mustard asks Wadsworth what the butler does. "I buttle, sir." Buttle as a verb is a decidedly British joke, and it was added only later, in the third-draft screenplay, as part of Lynn's effort to amp up some of the comedy. The characters, all together at last, begin to riff off of one another's lines and show off the script's crackling wordplay. So much will happen later that Lynn deliberately took his time in dialing up the action and the rapid-fire dialogue. Wadsworth quotes Tennyson's poem, "The Charge of the Light Brigade," with ours "but to do and die," and Plum responds, "Die?" The script suggested there be ominous music in response to Plum's query. John Morris, whose music has been only sporadically used thus far, thought better of this. Comedies often have sparser scores, and knowing when not to include music can be just as important as knowing when to include it.

It is at dinner where *Clue*'s genius blossoms for a lot of fans. The jokes start to come faster, and Scarlet becomes another in a long line of characters to stare at Yvette's cleavage. Lynn's wordplay is interspersed with physical and visual gags throughout the movie, and after Yvette has placed the shark's fin soup, Professor Plum and Mrs. White commence their slurping, though in different octaves. The shooting script says only that the characters eat nervously, making an effort to be as delicate as possible, since they know they are watching and listening to one another. The loud slurping was an inspired addition during filming. Even Wadsworth pauses as he pours Mr. Green's wine to watch the pair. The others begin eating, but Mrs. Peacock hesitates, then launches into her fast, nervous monologue.

Most of the dialogue in *Clue* is between more than two people, and it changed how the film was shot. While there are close-ups throughout, most of the shots are medium or wide to catch the reaction of more than one character. First-time director Lynn relied on veteran cinematographer Victor Kemper to help him block and set up these shots. He remained grateful to Kemper decades later in interviews and would say he "learned everything" about making movies from *Clue*.[4]

---

4 Lynn, interview with *Movies and Stuff*.

As Peacock speaks, there are shots of her and Plum, then a close-up of White, then a medium shot of Scarlet and Green, and then a close-up of Mustard. In the medium and wide shots, actors have to time their reactions to one another. The final shot of Mustard, Scarlet, and Green staring at Peacock, mouths open, spoons suspended in midair, is a glimpse of the ensemble work to come.

We finally begin to learn who these people are and where they come from. Peacock, eager to chat to smother the silence that's abundantly painful to her, almost reveals that she's the wife of a senator, but catches herself. In Lynn's first-draft screenplay, Peacock revealed considerably more, telling the guests that she and her husband "come to Palm Beach every winter" since "Florida has that special something that we don't have in North Dakota," to which Scarlet responds, "Alligators?"[5] From here Peacock's dialogue closely matches that in the final film, and she catches herself before she gives too much away. But Mr. Green tells her that he already knows who she is, badly unnerving the woman. The first draft has more on the Red Scare, and Peacock, upset by Green's knowledge about her, accuses him in that draft of being a Communist when he refuses to divulge more about himself by announcing that he is pleading "the Fifth." Green panics and insists he was kidding, underlining the tension. The characters are also less fleshed out in the early drafts. Mrs. White is meant to be cool and unflappable, but comes off as underwritten, something that Lynn would acknowledge was the case until his rewrites. Peacock is distinctly unlikable, but she is softened by the third draft, and she became much funnier in Eileen Brennan's capable hands.

Mrs. Peacock, both grateful for the conversation and anxious to turn it away from her, asks Mrs. White what her husband does, only to have White respond so quickly that she cuts Peacock off, then realizes how defensive she sounds. When she replies that he "just lies around on his back all day," Miss Scarlet says that "it sounds like hard work to me." The kitchen hatch suddenly slides open with a crash, and the thunder roars outside. Michael McKean nails another moment of

5 Lynn, "Clue," first-draft screenplay, 12.

physical comedy, hitting his spoon perfectly to shower Lesley Ann Warren in soup on the second take. Miss Scarlet gawks at Mr. Green, more stunned at his idiocy than angry. Once more, Warren adds to her performance and makes the moment much funnier. In the script she merely sits quietly as he begins mopping her up, but in the final film Warren tells him to "watch it!" and Mr. Green sheepishly puts his napkin aside.

Mrs. Peacock, who recognizes the sight and smell of the dish, can't help herself and immediately dives in. *Knives Out* director Rian Johnson said that viewers should have nothing but "pity" for actors they see eating on-screen; it's more than likely that they've eaten it "a thousand times" for multiple takes.[6] Mrs. Ho turns to look out of the opening for the first time at the guests, and as she does, Wadsworth steps in front of her to block her from Mrs. Peacock's view, right as Peacock turns to tell the butler that it's one of her favorite recipes. The moment is well-timed, and it's easy to miss the significance of Wadsworth's movements, designed to prevent Peacock from seeing her old cook and realizing, before he has a chance to explain everything, what is happening. In the end, it doesn't work, as Peacock later realizes that the cook must be the source of Mr. Boddy's information.

It's Professor Plum's turn to reveal a little too much. When Miss Scarlet asks if he's a "shrink" and he confirms that he knows about psychiatry, Mrs. White smiles and flutters her eyelashes at him as she asks if he's a doctor. Plum explains that he works for a branch of the United Nations Organization (UNO) called the World Health Organization (WHO); he works, in other words, for UNO WHO. This gag was originally part of the script, with Scarlet asking, "So if we ever want to find out about you know what, we could go to UNO WHO?" It was dropped for the final film, leaving viewers to work out the joke on their own. Professor Plum asks Colonel Mustard if he's a real colonel as the dialogue keeps picking up. Scarlet outs Mustard as another Washingtonian (adding that she's "certainly seen" him before—all of him, it will turn out, since she's seen photographs of Mustard

---

6 Johnson, in-theater audio commentary, *Knives Out*, 1:03:00.

having sex with Yvette), and Mr. Green asks if they all earn their living from the government one way or another. They are all starting to make sense of at least some things—but is the audience?

The movie is perhaps already moving too fast for viewers watching this in theaters for the first time to grasp the implications. It is 1954, and there's been a quick glimpse of Joseph McCarthy on the television. The McCarthy–Army Hearings were at one point in the production also playing over Professor Plum's radio as he drove, but that idea was dropped for the final film. There are no visible newspaper headlines or any other, ahem, clues that point to blackmail and the Red Scare. Detective stories require a delicate balance—reveal too much and the mystery is gone, but show too little and the audience feels cheated. *Clue* is above all a comedy, and it was written, acted, and filmed first and foremost as a comedy, with the murder mystery taking something of a secondary role. It wanted to be both, but having a real mystery embedded in a ninety-minute comedy was next to impossible. Mysteries, with misdirection and carefully placed hints, take time to unfold. Even the critics who liked *Clue* upon its initial release (and contrary to popular belief, there were some), focused almost exclusively on its comedic aspects, barely mentioning the mystery at all. Viewers watching the movie a second or third time will start to pick up on the intricate details of the mystery, but by then they already know who did it, and so it becomes an appreciation of the film's cleverness—which is exactly what Lynn intended in the first place. He would remain wary of the different endings playing in different theaters throughout the production. To paraphrase Raymond Chandler, it's the journey through the mystery, not the destination, that matters.[7]

The characters grow impatient; Colonel Mustard's frustration boils over, and he demands an explanation. Just at that moment, the bell rings. Mr. Boddy, and with him the answers the guests want, has arrived. Lynn saw Mr. Boddy as a disgusting, odious man who "picks his teeth, nose, and other orifices."[8] Lee Ving would, like all of the

7 Chandler, "The Simple Art of Murder."

8 Lynn, "Clue," shooting script.

actors, have to make the character his own, but perhaps no one was more different from the part as originally written and envisioned by Lynn. Adding to the challenge, few scenes in *Clue* underwent more revisions than Mr. Boddy's arrival, both in the script and then later during editing.

On June 18, 1985, the production set up in the driveway to film Ving's entrance. The crew fired up the rain machine and the large fans to simulate the storm still raging outside. Lynn took close shots of Ving from the waist down exiting his black Cadillac and crossing to the front door carrying his crocodile-skin bag, all meant to lend an air of gravity to his arrival. A month earlier in the production, on the second day of filming, the camera had followed in front of Wadsworth as he exited the dining room and walked to the front door, opened it, and greeted Mr. Boddy, whose face the audience would see for the first time. From there Lynn filmed the two men having a cryptic conversation, dropping nuggets without revealing too much. Shots were also filmed of the guests at the table listening and of Yvette and the cook eavesdropping.

The conversation between Wadsworth and Mr. Boddy changed across the script drafts, and most of it was cut by the time the film was released. In the first draft of the script, Boddy asks whose mansion he is in, and Wadsworth responds that "it belongs to an acquaintance."[9] Boddy looks around impressed and says it must be a "rich acquaintance, noblesse oblige, eh?" and Wadsworth quotes the writing above the fireplace in the library: "Nouveau riche oblige." The joke, had it been kept, would likely have sailed over most viewers' heads, especially American audiences. "Noblesse oblige" means nobility obliges or obligates—that is, the rich have a responsibility to both the poor and to their high station. They are expected to behave a certain way. Boddy is insulting Wadsworth, in other words, telling him that he relies on rich friends for help. Wadsworth is responding that his acquaintance is new money, often an insult in itself, meant to imply that the newly wealthy do not know how to behave as nobility is expected to. By

9 All of the dialogue quoted here is from Lynn, "Clue," first-draft screenplay, 18–20, and Lynn, "Clue," second-draft screenplay, 18–19A.

the third draft, all of this is eliminated, replaced by a single line from Wadsworth that the house "is on loan." Boddy then looks Wadsworth up and down and asks who he is "supposed to be." Wadsworth answers that he's supposed to be polite, "though when talking to you, I find that the task is almost beyond me." In the script, when Boddy uses the name "Wadsworth," it is framed in scare quotes to suggest that the guests are not the only ones using an alias tonight.

Boddy warns Wadsworth that he "knows who you really are," and Wadsworth retorts that he also knows who Boddy is and that's "why you are here." Lynn added another hint in the second draft as Wadsworth asks Boddy if he's "just arrived from Washington." In a silly bit of wordplay, Boddy says, "Yes, it's a long haul," while Wadsworth looks around the cavernous hall and answers, "Indeed, it is a long hall." Finally, in the first draft, when Boddy asks for the key to the front door, which Wadsworth has just locked, Wadsworth tells him he'll get it over his dead body, and Boddy replies that "I'm sure that can be arranged." Wadsworth warns him not "to make that kind of suggestion this evening, sir." Some of this dialogue was included in the shooting script and was filmed, then later cut as changes were made.

The shots of Boddy's arrival in the driveway, Wadsworth leaving to answer the door, and their conversation in the hall were all scrapped in favor of voice-overs as everyone else listens in. Getting the conversation at the front door took longer than most scenes. They shot seven takes of Wadsworth leaving the dining room, crossing the hall, and opening the front door to admit Mr. Boddy. But Kemper still wasn't happy, and he "begged" Lynn and Debra Hill for more time to reshoot.[10] He wanted to be able to zoom in on Ving's face to give Boddy's first reveal more impact. Near the end of filming on July 30, they did five retakes. Twelve takes for a shot isn't uncommon in many productions, but it wasn't the norm in *Clue*, as the production team struggled to stay on schedule. Some of the takes in the shot log include the note that a boom mic was visible, and ADR—automated dialogue replacement—was used over some of the lines that didn't work—including all of

10 Kahan and Turner, "Clue Is More than a Game," 54.

Ving's lines.

Wadsworth escorts Boddy to the dining room, and in the final cut of the film, this is where the suspects and the audience get their first look at him. His black costume helps with his malevolence, but there's a hipness to it. Ving is unshaven, to suggest Boddy's slovenliness, but it only adds to the rock star's good looks. Paramount, hoping to make Ving into a bankable actor, had no interest in making him appear unattractive. But Ving does his best to lean into the role, and he immediately establishes himself as an aggressive, rude pig. He's helped by Morris's music, now at its most ominous. As everyone takes Boddy in, surprised that he knows Yvette and appalled as he gropes her, Morris's music continues in undertones until it swells later in the study. The shot of Boddy grabbing at Yvette, originally part of a longer shot, was a retake filmed in July to emphasize her discomfort as she jumps away from him.

A shot taken from above looking directly down on the guests as they finally leave the dining room, following them across the hall to the study while Colonel Mustard and Miss Scarlet wonder aloud who is waiting for them, was cut in editing, and instead there's a brief time jump as everyone makes their way into the room. More action takes place in the study than in any other room, totaling almost exactly twenty-four minutes of screen time. It's also where most of the ensemble work takes place, as the characters interact with each other before splitting up to search the house. Thus, special care was given to decorating this room.

The large paintings covering the walls are all of US presidents. Near the door is George Washington, and then on the same wall is James A. Garfield. On the other side of the room, doubling as the entrance to the secret passage, is a portrait of William McKinley. Garfield and McKinley were both assassinated while in office, adding to the theme of murder. These paintings are based on existing portraits, but they were created by the production team to be the right size and were therefore not exact copies. McKinley's portrait is based on August Benziger's painting of the president in 1897, shortly after he had taken office. Garfield's is titled "James A. Garfield, 20th President of the United States," painted in 1882 by Eliphalet Frazer Andrews a year after Garfield's death. Washington's portrait is the most curious, an amalgamation of popular paintings of the first president by Charles Willson Peale and John Trumbull, with a dash of Gilbert Stuart thrown in. Other paintings in the room are from the Victorian era or Edwardian era, including one of a sailor and a woman from 1906, called "Off Duty," by Julius Mendes Price. The framed painting of the lion and lioness on the seashore was done in 1913, meant to symbolize Britain's defense of the home country.

The busts around the room are of Greek figures. The furniture is again a mix of antiques obtained with the help of the Antiquarian Guild, a rental company specializing in locating furnishings for films, and props from Paramount. The cobra floor lamps fit perfectly with set decorator Tommy Roysden's animal motif throughout the mansion. Eagle-eyed viewers can spot them in the background—the gold body of the snake acts as the stand for the lamp, starting with the tail at the bottom and getting thicker as it rises to an inverted lamp shade with a distinctive cobra head against it, and the tongue wrapped around the shade.

In the *Handbook of Production Information* sent by the Paramount marketing department to reporters and news organizations, the studio went to great pains to emphasize the antiques used and the lavish decor of the mansion. They touted that the study features a "desk with a bookstand" that comes "from the Teddy Roosevelt estate."[11] Throughout the summer and fall of 1985, smaller newspapers across the US, unable to visit the set or secure interviews with the cast and crew, would sometimes pull directly from this production handbook to write articles about *Clue*, using the quotes provided by the studio from Lynn, Hill, and the cast.

The scenes in the study, filmed before the cast leaves to check on Yvette in the billiard room, were shot over seven days. Retakes were done at the end of July. But most shots took only two to four takes. The guests settle in with great trepidation over what Wadsworth will do next, and Morris's music quiets—but only for a moment, and it picks up again as Boddy tries to flee. There are more differences between

---

11 Paramount Pictures, *Handbook of Production Information*, 9.

the finished film and the early script drafts during the escape attempt. Initially, Mr. Boddy was to run into the billiard room, described in the first draft as a "bleak empty room," before acting as if he is going to return to the study.[12] He pretends he has to use the bathroom, then races down the hall to the conservatory. Instead, these scenes were simplified for the movie. The shots of Boddy running in the hall were filmed on May 21, the second day of shooting. Two weeks later, the brief scene in the conservatory was filmed with Curry and Ving.

In the board game, the conservatory is a music room, complete with a grand piano. For the movie, it becomes a decrepit greenhouse. Lynn knew he needed a way to keep the guests trapped in the house or at least make them believe they were trapped. His first idea was to fake out the guests with an armed guard that would later be revealed to be a mannequin holding a rifle. As Boddy picks up a pot to break the glass, Wadsworth tells him in the first and second drafts that if he looks carefully, he'll see the guard. At that moment, another flash of lightning reveals the mannequin, waiting still and patient in the rain. Wadsworth warns Boddy that the guard "has orders to shoot anyone breaking out." Boddy drops the pot as the other guests huddle around the conservatory door, looking horrified at the news of the guard. Only later, when the Singing Telegram Girl arrives, is it discovered that the guard is a mannequin. But by the third draft, Lynn had settled on the dogs as the motivation for keeping the guests inside. Wadsworth adjusts the chains when he first arrives, and guests could come and go from the front door, which is why he kept it locked. But the dogs were able to prowl around the side of the house. They would also play a crucial role in the fourth ending.

Boddy's escape is thwarted, and the guests return to the study, where they will learn why they have been ordered to Hill House. Wadsworth reveals that they are all being blackmailed, and he has the evidence to prove it. He walks around the room, confronting each character as the other guests move in and out of frame. This was one of *Clue*'s more complex scenes to shoot. First, the crew filmed a master shot of

---

12 Lynn, "Clue," first-draft screenplay, 24.

Curry as he moved from person to person. Then, everything was reset to get close reactions from individual actors and shots of two and three characters together. Most setups needed only a few takes, but some took as many as nine. The master shot of everyone confronting Boddy when he's revealed as the blackmailer took twelve. Filming Wadsworth revealing everyone's secrets until Mr. Boddy turns out the lights took three full days.

Everyone knew their lines and their marks, and rehearsals helped things run smoothly. Only one spot was improvised. Martin Mull was supposed to tell everyone that he got his money after he "lost my parents," but he used the line "lost my mommy and daddy." They filmed it with both lines, but Lynn liked Mull's idea and kept it. Dialogue was cut from the first draft that added more references to communism and the Red Scare. The shooting script calls out that the dialogue should be "going very fast." Lynn's wordplay is at its peak, full of double meaning and misunderstanding. Scarlet asks Mrs. White about the latter's husband. Warren continued to make Scarlet more aggressive, especially when dealing with Plum. While the other guests seem miserable and defiant, Miss Scarlet is thoroughly enjoying herself in this scene as everyone's secrets come out.

Mr. Green gives his speech announcing his homosexuality, awkwardly concluding with "Thank you," which was not part of the shooting script, but it makes the moment funnier. He has told everyone that he needs to keep his sexuality a secret or he would "lose his job on security grounds." In reality it would have been much worse. The United States acted aggressively in the 1940s and 1950s against LGBTQ+ people. Mr. Green would have been barred from service in the United States military during World War II, something alone that might have raised suspicion among his family, friends, and neighbors. President Harry S. Truman and his successor, Dwight D. Eisenhower, signed executive orders that would have made it easy to fire Green for "sexual perversion"—there was no need for the government to cite "security grounds." The District of Columbia had criminalized sodomy in 1948, a label frequently used to target gays and lesbians. Beyond losing his job, Mr. Green may well have gone to jail as a gay man in 1954.

The revelations culminate in Mr. Boddy being unmasked as the blackmailer, and everyone jumps up to confront him. Colonel Mustard raises his dukes, ready to fight, and Morris's music begins with the same ominous undertone as when Boddy was revealed before switching to a comedic melody. Lynn later said he enjoys the moment when Boddy pokes Mustard in the eyes because it's an "old move from the Three Stooges."[13] As Mustard writhes on the floor and they drag Boddy off of him, Mrs. White calmly approaches and knees Boddy in the groin. As filming wound down at the end of July, they did another take of White attacking Boddy, but this time she punches him in the stomach so that the shot could be used for the television and airline versions if censors nixed the knee-in-the-groin shot. Such alternate takes were becoming more common in the 1980s; filmmakers knew their movies would likely be broadcast on basic cable. *Ghostbusters*, released a year earlier, had filmed a handful of alternate takes to eliminate profanity that would have to be bleeped or redubbed for broadcast television and basic cable.

After the chaos of Boddy's reveal as the blackmailer, Wadsworth announces that the police are coming. It is a clever way to keep the action moving against a ticking clock, and it reinforces the sense that the events of the movie are happening in real time. But Boddy, rising after being flattened by Mrs. White, has other plans, and so he steps out into the hall to get his suitcase. He opens the crocodile-skin bag and passes out gifts in black boxes. Miss Scarlet, at Boddy's urging, opens hers first. A bit of suggestive dialogue about what Scarlet might imagine doing with a candle was cut from the first draft. Each of the characters opens their gifts in turn, with Morris's music ratcheting up the tension. Instead of designing elaborate weapons specifically for the movie, the production team looked for existing items. Because the weapons, apart from the lead pipe and the rope, were real products, a handful of *Clue* fans have gone to truly herculean efforts to identify and collect them.

Colonel Mustard's gift is a twelve-inch Billings & Spencer monkey

13 Brandon and Lynn, "*Clue*: The Director's Commentary," 1:00:48.

wrench. It was originally made by Coes, but purchased by Billings in 1939. Of all the *Clue* weapons, it is the easiest to find, regularly offered for purchase by online sellers and auction sites. Professor Plum's revolver, a Harrington & Richardson 733 .32 caliber, is rare because of its four-inch barrel—only a small number were made, while most of the 733s had a 2 ½ inch barrel. It is nickel plated and was first manufactured in 1956—two years after the movie takes place. *Clue* collectors eager to find the model often resort to plastic replicas because hunting it down is especially difficult and, in the off chance they find one, expensive. The dagger is a World War II Fairbairn-Sykes British commando fighting knife, named after its two inventors. The one Mrs. Peacock unwraps is the third iteration, a simplified design developed near the end of the war and mass-produced. Although as many as two million of these knives may have been manufactured, today they are difficult to find, and the many variations introduced by different companies means that hunting down the same model used in the movie is challenging at best. Another Fairbairn-Sykes knife, identical to Mrs. Peacock's, can be spotted protruding from the body of a murder victim in the Italian *giallo* film *Deep Red* (1975). The candlestick was made in 1897 and sold in Britain to celebrate the diamond jubilee of Queen Victoria's reign. It is part of a series of four nearly identical candlesticks—the King of Diamonds, the Queen of Diamonds, the Diamond Prince, and the Diamond Princess. The candlestick gifted to Miss Scarlet is the Diamond Prince. The designs proved so popular that they were made well into the twentieth century, and by the 1940s they were being shipped to the United States for sale in retail stores. Replicas of each weapon were also made by the production team so that they could be safely used later to protrude from Kellye Nakahara's back or topple onto Curry's head.

Mr. Boddy doesn't intend to go along with Wadsworth's plans to notify the police. He tells the guests he's blackmailing that if the cops find out, they'll all be publicly exposed, but if they kill Wadsworth, everything will remain under wraps. As Boddy stalks the room, Morris's music slowly builds, until Boddy hits the lights. There's a scream and a gunshot, and when the lights come on, Boddy is lying on the floor, "apparently dead" but with no apparent serious wounds. There's a cut to Wadsworth, who reacts in shock—then he's nowhere to be found for the next ninety seconds. Wadsworth, unnoticed by the other guests, has taken the secret passage through William McKinley's portrait to the kitchen as part of a key plot point for the scrapped fourth ending. While he is absent, the guests examine Mr. Boddy. A small trickle of blood can be glimpsed on his left ear, another important detail that plays into all possible solutions.

As the guests begin to panic and Mrs. Peacock takes a large gulp of Boddy's brandy, Plum suggests that perhaps Boddy was poisoned by the drink. Peacock begins frantically screaming until Mr. Green slaps her across the face. The next shots were cut, but a brief clip can be seen in the film's trailer. In the final movie, after everyone stares at Peacock wondering if she's going to die, they rush to the billiard room, where Yvette is screaming. As the scene was originally written and filmed, Mr. Green begins screaming in response to Yvette's screaming, and Colonel Mustard slaps him across the face. Mustard asks him why he's screaming, and Green responds that he's frightened. At one point or another, every character in *Clue* will be smacked, knocked to the ground, pushed, hit over the head, or otherwise physically harmed. It is all played for laughs in the way that only movies can make funny. Ten takes were shot of Green being slapped in June; then the scene was reshot at the end of July. Lynn also shot an alternate version of the scene without Green screaming, and that was the one used in the final film.

Everyone rushes out of the study to see who is screaming in the billiard room. The last two people to leave the room are Wadsworth and Mrs. Peacock. Wadsworth is one of the last because he has just reemerged from the secret passage, and Mrs. Peacock will sneak by everyone huddled in the billiard-room doorway because she now has business in the kitchen. The rest of the group pounds on the billiard room door, and Yvette finally lets them in.

The billiard room became a popular place for some of the cast to hang out while *Clue* was being shot. Michael McKean has said that he and others would retire to this room to shoot pool while scenes were being reset. The table wasn't a prop, it was an antique Brunswick with pearl inlays. Cost: $14,500, as trumpeted by Paramount in its press materials. Warren has reminded interviewers a few times that she wasn't able to play pool because of her restrictive costume. Designer Michael Kaplan included a corset for Warren, since he wanted "Scarlet to have a very hourglass shape."[14] Bending or sitting down became next to impossible for her. Sometime after shooting began, Kaplan created another dress for Warren, which included a hidden zipper so that she could run and be more active. Kahn often retired to her dressing room in between shots, and Nakahara felt more comfortable spending time with the crew, chatting with them and playing cards. But at one time or another, most of the cast picked up a pool cue and relaxed in this room.

In a 1985 article about *Clue*, a reporter wrote that Michael McKean "reluctantly relinquishes the pool table to a couple of children and perches at the library's bar."[15] The kids were on set as part of the press day on May 17, the Friday before filming began. Debra Hill had also suggested that Lynn's son Teddy help out with the production. Filming days were filled with long hours of work, and children playing pool were nowhere to be seen. But on occasion, the families of the cast and crew could be found on Stage 18, reveling in the luxurious mansion. Nakahara's husband and daughter remember visiting and being mesmerized by the "grandness" of the set: "You walked in and it felt like you were in a real house."[16]

The billiard room, in addition to its expensive bar and Brunswick pool table, had real red velvet–covered walls and more of Roysden's animal vibe. While most of the other rooms had multiple sources of light, the billiard room was supposed to have only one. Kemper and his crew wanted the lamp above the pool table to seem as if it were the only source of light in the room, which could make it difficult to shoot. The scene with Yvette, including the cast running down the hall to the billiard room doorway, was finished in one day. The cast and crew had one more shot to get in the hall, this time from a slightly

---

14 Ivie, "Lesley Ann Warren."

15 Rabkin, "Whodunnit?" 37.

16 Coleman and Wallett, interview with the author.

different angle. It would show Mrs. Peacock making her way past the oblivious group into the kitchen as she raises the dagger. This shot was cut, but other flashback scenes would be filmed to be used in the four different endings to show whodunit.

After Colonel Mustard and Miss Scarlet calm Yvette, the group moves to return to the study. In this scene, as Mustard rattles the wrench, a wedding ring can be glimpsed on his finger, making the stakes that much higher for him if his secret affair with the fake French maid gets out. Wadsworth moves to the tape recorder, shuts it off, and gathers the reels. Lynn left the tape recorder running in the first draft so that it could later capture the murderer's confession in the fourth ending. But in the second draft, Lynn rewrote the ending, and the tape recorder is turned off by Wadsworth.

The guests return to the study, where the butler gives a long confession—not of murder, but of his wife's involvement in socialism and of Mr. Boddy's domination of the couple. The presence of the Red Scare makes the movie something of a political satire. Lynn wrote *Clue* shortly after he had written *Yes Minister*, a satire of British politics. Throughout his audio commentary, recorded in 2017 with Josh Brandon, Lynn points out the politics of *Clue*. He says it's amazing how little has changed over thirty years. Sex scandals, war profiteering, and corrupt politicians—all of it continues in Washington, DC. Lynn adds that bribery, the crime of which Mrs. Peacock is accused, is essentially legal thanks to donations from corporations and PACs, which are repaid when public officials act in the best interest of their donors rather than their constituents or the country at large. He also expresses his belief that the gasps and shock from the guests when Wadsworth admits that his wife had "friends who were socialists" wouldn't have been out of place in 2017.

Lynn's earliest ideas for this scene, later abandoned, included a harsh critique of what he saw as American hypocrisy. Wadsworth explains that his wife tried to stop befriending socialists, "but she couldn't kick the habit. She had become addicted to notions of equality and freedom. She even argued that Thomas Jefferson was a form of early socialist and that life, liberty, and the pursuit of happiness were not incompatible with the American way of life."[17] But Mr. Boddy, the consummate capitalist, has his own retort to that. Wadsworth tells the group that "we were slaves—but Mr. Boddy reminded us that Thomas Jefferson had slaves and that this was the American way." Americans, Lynn seems to be saying, are terrified of socialism but are more than willing to turn a blind eye to slavery and racism in order to whitewash their inflated notions of their nation's founding and democratic ideals. These lines, which appear only in a preliminary draft, are struck through with black ink in Lynn's own hand.

His next draft revised this idea to more closely match the experience of Donald Ogden Stewart, Lynn's expat friend who had inspired him to set *Clue* during the McCarthy era. Wadsworth's wife joined an anti-Nazi league (just as Stewart had done in the 1930s), but it was there that she met socialists and Communists. All of this was eventually dropped for the simpler version in the final film. Wadsworth's wife is refashioned as a naive woman who made friends with the wrong people instead of as an idealistic crusader.

After Wadsworth's tearful admission, Mrs. White approaches and gives him a handkerchief. Kahn told reporters in 1985 that normally working with "a first time director is never a plus, " but she felt that, with Lynn, it was different because of his experience in theater and farce. If another director had "ten hit films but had never directed classic farce in the theater, it would be a terrible experience," she concluded.[18] That feeling of respect was reciprocated by Lynn, who felt that Kahn was a comedic genius, and some of his rewrites throughout 1985 added more to Mrs. White's character once Kahn was cast.

The guests are baffled by Boddy's death, unsure what to think, and terrified that the police will soon learn all of their secrets. It's then that they realize there is only one other person in the mansion: the cook. They race down the hall as Morris's music is at its most recognizable. The kitchen is brightly lit and decorated in such a way as to provide a stark contrast to the other rooms, especially the hall, with its dark

17 Lynn, "Clue," preliminary draft, 45

18 Farber, "Off the Board."

wood paneling. Scattered throughout the room are products from the 1950s—or at least close enough. A six-pack of bottled Coca-Cola is from the 1960s, though it sits far enough back that it's hard to make out. A can of Bon Ami cleanser is from the mid-1950s. Once again, there is the attention to detail common in Hollywood productions, but easy to miss. There's tile, dingy walls, dish towels from the era, and a rusty pipe that looks like it's corroding. The paint around the knobs on the drawers and cupboards is worn from years of use. All of this was done on the Paramount set to give the mansion a lived-in feel. The chocolate cake on the table was originally meant to be shown in the opening credits as the cook prepared dinner.

Mr. Green stalks carefully around the room, looking for the cook. When the freezer door opens and she falls into his arms, it sets up another repeating gag, first envisioned by John Landis: Mr. Green insisting he is innocent. "I didn't do it!" he yells as he struggles to hold the large Mrs. Ho. "I didn't do it" would become Green's rallying cry. Nakahara's family noted the irony behind the offensive fat jokes made at the cook's expense. The actress, who had starred in an episode of *M*A*S*H* three years earlier about how the nurse-chasing Hawkeye Pierce ignored her because of her physical appearance, had recently lost a significant amount of weight. Nakahara's daughter recalls that her mother had to wear a fat suit or additional padding to make her look bigger than she was. Occasional notes in the shot log confirm her memory and indicate in one case that because some of the cook's padding is visible, a take is no good.

As the guests tangle over who killed the cook, there is a brief shot of Wadsworth on the kitchen landing. Professor Plum and Mrs. Peacock are nowhere to be seen. Most of the action for the next minute will center on Mustard, White, Green, and Scarlet, since either Professor Plum, Wadsworth, or Mrs. Peacock, depending on the ending, cannot be present. Lynn wrote this carefully, so that when we cut back to the landing, it's because Colonel Mustard has addressed Mrs. Peacock, giving the audience the impression that the three have been there all along. It can take several viewings to realize what is happening. This scene, shot on June 12 and June 13, 1985, was carefully rehearsed to get the timing just right. At one point both McKean and Kahn needed to rise into a shot and glare suspiciously at Mull. What looks effortless on camera took a lot of practice to get right. Of the seven takes, only one was usable. As Mustard confronts White, Lynn's wordplay is at its finest—"Flies are where men are most vulnerable." She somehow wins the argument with a non sequitur.

The guests scoop up the cook on Wadsworth's instruction and carry her body to the study. The cut from the kitchen to the study doorway allowed the production to swap out Nakahara for a dummy dressed as the cook that could be dropped painlessly on its face. The thud of the cook's head hitting the floor was added later, in postproduction. Most of the time, however, the corpses in *Clue* were played by the actors. They were dropped, pushed, shoved, and thrown around, all while trying hard not to breathe, move, or so much as twitch an eye. Nakahara came home from work on *Clue* one day to show her family some bruises she had from being dropped, then flung herself over her couch to recreate, for her delighted children, the shots she had filmed that day.

After the guests realize that Mr. Boddy is gone and they search for him, Mrs. Peacock excuses herself to the bathroom. Miss Scarlet finds the negatives of Colonel Mustard at her brothel, and turns to Yvette to ask her if she'd like to see them. "They might shock you," she says. Scarlet knows what the audience doesn't yet—Yvette is in the pictures with Mustard. She also mocks Yvette's fake accent, asking her how she knows what's in the pictures if she's "such a lay-dee." As the other guests gather around, anxious to glimpse the pictures, Professor Plum grabs Mrs. White and begins to climb on top of her before they are interrupted by a screaming Mrs. Peacock in the hall.

The guests sprint out of the room to find Mr. Boddy "attacking" Mrs. Peacock. Except now he is really dead, with blood on his face. The production team shot three takes and used the third, which had "less blood" and would therefore not jeopardize the intended family nature of the film.[19] The other guests lower Boddy to the ground as Mrs. Peacock fans herself, about to pass out. This was another difficult

19 Paramount Pictures, Script Department, *Clue*, shot list, scene 46.

shot that took careful planning. First, the cameraman needed to pan down to match Eileen Brennan's timing as she collapsed through Tim Curry's outstretched arms. Second, Brennan was still in pain from her terrible car accident three years earlier. The actors and crew rehearsed it and got the shot in just a few takes. They used the first because takes two and three had Wadsworth saying, "Oops, butterfingers," as he dropped Mrs. Peacock; instead, Lynn wanted to use the simple apology "Sorry." As Wadsworth rants, we see the candlestick perched precariously above him on the bathroom door molding. Two insert shots of the candlestick wobbling were taken, one with blood smeared on it, one of it clean; neither was used. Instead, Lynn stuck with the wide shot of Wadsworth, Green, and White as the candlestick topples over after a small peg pushes it off the ledge through a hole in the wall. This replicant candlestick—made by the production team—hits Curry and then falls to the floor; the clanging sound effects were added later.

The characters assemble back in the study, now with two bodies to stash. The dummy dressed as the cook that was dropped on its face has been swapped back out for Nakahara. For Yvette, Miss Scarlet, and Mrs. White to drag the cook across the carpet, Nakahara was put on a dolly and pulled, with her costume strategically hiding the wheels. When they stop, she rolls off to one side to continue hiding the dolly; then, when the camera cuts, she is lying flat again with the dolly gone. There's another brief moment shown in the trailer that was cut from the final film: as Wadsworth instructs the guests not to get blood on the sofa, he says, "Look, Professor!" to Plum, telling him to watch what he was doing. Plum, staring at Yvette's cleavage, responds, "I'm looking, I'm looking!"

The production made excellent time with these scenes. Most shots outside of the bathroom and in the study were filmed in one day, on June 17, 1985. A few quick shots were taken on June 18, and a handful of shots were taken later in July. The shot of Wadsworth stalking around the room to collect the weapons ends with everyone racing to the front door to throw away the key. But when Wadsworth pulls open the door and raises his arm, there's a surprise waiting for everyone. The Motorist has arrived.

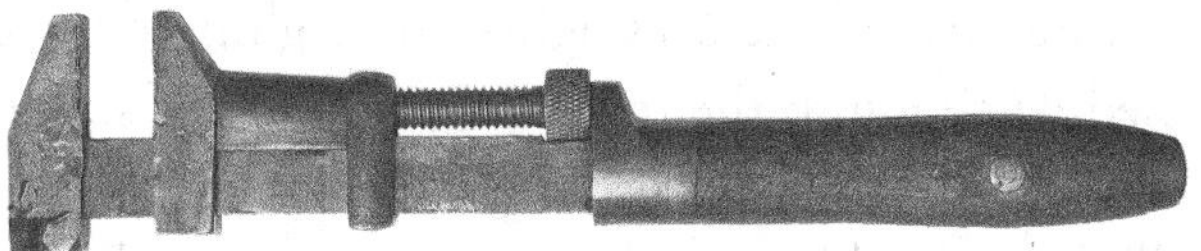

# 6. "THIS IS WAR, PEACOCK!"

"I can't think back to the last balls-out mystery comedy that worked."
-Michael McKean[1]

The rain is pounding on the windshield. The Motorist squints through the drops of water with his wipers at full speed, trying to keep the storm at bay. The car radio is on, pumping the Army–McCarthy hearings through the staticky speaker. The man is nervous, unsure of where he is going and why he was invited there. The bright headlights shimmer off the wet pavement, throwing out reflections and making it even more difficult to see. He takes a tight curve that seems to catch him off guard. He manages the turn and begins to relax. Just then, a cat darts across the street. The Motorist swerves to miss the cat and his car runs off the road and stops, the front wheels dangling over an embankment. Shaken, he decides to walk to Hill House.

So it went in a scene that was written and filmed but never seen by audiences.

On July 12, 1985, these shots of actor Jeffrey Kramer in the car were filmed. There were close-ups on his face as he tried to squint through the rain on his windshield. A reaction shot was filmed as he looks off-screen at the cat. Inserts of his foot slamming on the brake pedal and of the car radio were shot on July 15. A month later, on August 9, the second-to-last day of principal photography, two cameras were set up on Franklin

1 Rabkin, "Whodunnit?"

Canyon Drive to film as the Motorist's mint-green car, a Chevrolet Bel Air driven by a stunt crew member, swerved around the curve and crashed onto the embankment. A stuffed cat was filmed crouching in the middle of the road as the car's lights hit its glimmering eyes. A real cat was filmed darting into the road and jumping off-screen as the car approached. Finally, footage was taken from the cat's point of view as the headlights grew larger and the oncoming car drew nearer and nearer.

All of these moments were to be intercut with the action over at Hill House. We would see the Motorist in his car, hear his radio, and watch as he made his way down the road. Then we would jump back to the Motorist, this time crashing as he swerves to avoid the cat. Instead, all of this was deleted, and we first see the Motorist at the front door as Wadsworth is about to throw away the key to the weapons cupboard.

Deleting the car crash was not an inexpensive choice. There's no indication of any issues with the scene. During editing, the decision to lose this scene, brief as it was, was made to keep the focus on the action at Hill House. Intercutting the Motorist's approach slowed the pace of action at the mansion. This sort of intercutting works well later on, when the film cuts back and forth between the Cop discovering the Motorist's car and the search at the mansion, but it wasn't working here. Also, keeping the runtime at around ninety minutes was important to Lynn and the producers. Comedies, especially parodies, can wear out their welcome. Mel Brooks's longest parodies run an hour and forty-five minutes; most are around ninety minutes. Throughout the editing process, Lynn and editors David Bretherton and Richard Haines trimmed shots to tighten the film. Lynn would later lament the loss of some of the sweeping shots of the hall and other moments that he felt added to the film but were cut to accommodate the preferred runtime.

Behind the Motorist, as he stands huddled at the front door, is Mr. Boddy's black Cadillac sitting in the driveway. Kramer redubbed some of his lines later; the artificial rain drowned out his dialogue. This scene was shot on June 18, the same day as Mr. Boddy's arrival, since the rain machines were required for both. Later in the day, the shot of Wadsworth tossing the key into the bushes was filmed. After the group ushers the Motorist in and Wadsworth shows him to the lounge, the hapless driver's demeanor changes. He is now alone with Wadsworth, and he knows he's been invited to the house. He is nervous, unsure of what to expect or what is happening. He watches the key turn and the door lock.

The lounge has more of set decorator Tommy Roysden's animals, including a stuffed bird in a glass case on a table. The room also has a $30,000 rug and a Tiffany lamp. The couch that Miss Scarlet and Professor Plum will later throw themselves on is an expensive antique with needlepoint upholstery. But this room is glimpsed less often than some of the others, and much of what is here fades into the background. Apart from one portrait over the fireplace and a photograph of an unidentified couple on the mantle, the paintings and pictures in the lounge are simple landscapes. Unlike the production-created paintings of US presidents, these were snagged from the Paramount prop department and antique stores. There is also a mirror, which will be used later.

After Wadsworth locks the Motorist in and returns to the hall, the guests continue to insist that he throw away the key to the weapons cupboard, and this time he does. The split-second footage of the key hitting the concrete ledge and flying into the bushes was filmed four weeks later, on July 15—and it was tough to get right. Lynn and Victor Kemper shot it at thirty-four frames per second and played back at twenty-four frames a second, to make the key more visible. When we cut back across the driveway to Wadsworth standing in the doorway, there is Mrs. White, trying to sneak around him to escape. The whole moment is easy to miss as he grabs her and pulls her back inside. It's then that she confronts him, telling him to let her out. The others object, and Mustard announces that he could use a drink. The guests head for the library.

All of these scenes were filmed on June 18 and June 19. At one month into principal photography, the production was only about two days behind schedule. Debra Hill would tell reporters that "it's the easiest film she's ever done."[2] While there is always motivation to put

---

2 Bygrave, "The Man Whodunnit."

the best possible face on things for the press, after a rocky start during casting, things were running smoothly at this point. Of course, smooth should not be confused with easy. Lynn was working tirelessly, and Tim Curry, who had the most lines, was still learning them.

The days could be long and tedious. Each morning, the actors would arrive for makeup and wardrobe. Depending on the schedule, Colleen Camp and Lesley Ann Warren got there earliest, as their hair, makeup, and costumes took the longest. Eileen Brennan and Madeline Kahn averaged about an hour to get into their clothes and get their hair and makeup done. The men had it easier: Curry took a few extra minutes to get into his butler's outfit, but Christopher Lloyd, Michael McKean, and Martin Mull each usually needed no more than thirty minutes in wardrobe and makeup before they were on set. The actors got along and, years later, would remember having an awful lot of fun. McKean said the group would be "just digging life and laughing," and when Lynn was ready for them and they needed to get serious, they "would say to each other, 'Something terrible has happened,' and that became the mantra."[3] Warren captured the essence of working on *Clue* when she remembered, "It was such a riot . . . but it's exhausting. You're not just having fun, you're working hard."[4] Kahn, during an appearance on *The Tonight Show Starring Johnny Carson* to promote the movie, had a different take. She compared filmmaking to a Twinkie. Consuming it might be fun, but "it doesn't mean the people in the kitchen making it are having a party."

Lynn would get to Stage 18 early each morning to review the schedule. The production was behind by only a couple of days, but even so, that meant that the entire timetable moving forward needed to be revised. Filming was supposed to be completed at the end of July, but now it was pushing into August. He would also have to review dailies—the previous day's footage—with other members of the crew to ensure there were no issues. In July, he would have to rewrite an important scene to clarify some details. He also had to answer to several

3 McKean, interview with Andy Richter, 30:20.

4 Ivie, "Lesley Ann Warren."

producers. At any time Hill, Jon Peters, or Peter Gruber could pop onto the set and demand to know how things were going. The first-time director was aided by crew members, including Jeffrey Chernov, the production manager, and cinematographer Kemper. But if something wasn't working—if an actor wasn't happy, if a shot was out of focus, if a boom mic appeared in frame, if an antique rented for the set was damaged, if crew members were grumbling—the buck stopped at the director. Lynn was *Clue*'s Atlas, carrying the weight of the picture on his shoulders.

He was managing the heavy burden well. Lynn's stage experience gave him a good rapport with performers, and he understood that this was, at least in part, why he was hired. "There's a particular skill in keeping eight leading actors happily working together as a team for eleven weeks," he told one reporter during filming. Lynn continued to make good time for the scenes in the library and in the kitchen following the Motorist's arrival, finishing those shots by June 21. While *Clue* proceeded to be filmed in largely chronological order, there were some deviations. On June 19 the crew took footage of the Motorist and filmed everyone in the library. They also shot each guest sniffing around after they get a whiff of the dog excrement on Wadsworth's feet. Also filmed was Wadsworth's arrival in the hall as he scrapes his shoes off, the front door opens, and he hangs his coat and hat in the closet. Finally, the crew shot Colonel Mustard surreptitiously reaching into Wadsworth's pocket to take the key to the cupboard and replace it with another. This was later used in a flashback scene for what was then being called ending B.

Once the guests are assembled in the library, Colonel Mustard wants to clear up some things and make a pitch to split up and search the house. It was Mull who came up with the idea of pouring the whiskey across three glasses at once, spilling it over the sides. Lynn agreed, and a quick shot, done in one take, was filmed of Mustard making the mess. Mr. Green side-eyes him as he shakes the dripping whiskey off of his hand. It's an example of how improvising isn't as simple as it looks—these things take planning. A close-up needed to be taken of Mull pouring the whiskey, with the glasses arranged correctly; otherwise the gag would be missed. Also filmed, but unused: a reaction shot of Wadsworth wincing at the spilled booze.

Mull thought of Mustard as the embodiment of the guy who's "supposed to come up with more information than he actually has and he tries to fake his way through things."[5] The wordplay in this scene is vintage Lynn. Any fans of *Yes Minister* will recognize the back-and-forth between Wadsworth and Mustard kindred in spirit to conversations between Minister Hacker and Sir Humphrey. There is the rapid-fire dialogue, the confusion, the misunderstanding, and the detour as other characters jump in. It builds, moving too fast at times for viewers to pick up on the layered jokes and subtleties, and then resolves itself as one character finally acquiesces—in this case, only after everyone else has yelled "No!" at Mustard.

Inscribed on the fireplace is "nouveau riche oblige," relegating Lynn's earlier obscure joke between Wadsworth and Mr. Boddy (cut in editing) to the background. Kahn nailed breaking the champagne flute, her lines, and then throwing the glass, all in one take. Brennan begins yelling that the Motorist can stay "locked up for another half an hour" as she grows more and more animated, flapping her arms and stamping her foot. She was at times in pain after her car accident and rehabilitation. Christopher Lloyd would remember that during filming, "she was still struggling. . . . I could see the effort it took for her to get up and do what she was doing."[6]

Mustard storms around the room, trying to convince everyone they need to split up, and the library comes more fully into view. On a bookstand is The White House Gallery of Officials Portraits of Presidents, open to a portrait of Abraham Lincoln. This painting of Lincoln was originally created in 1869, four years after his assassination, by William F. Cogswell. Outside of the room, on the landing of the main staircase, there's a painting of someone who looks to be William Howard Taft. The extensive use of US presidents served a few purposes. These images were easy to find and duplicate for the production; they seemed to fit neatly with the atmosphere of the setting, a gothic

---

5 Rabkin, "Whodunnit?," 38.

6 Vary, "Something Terrible Has Happened Here."

mansion in the American Northeast; and they hint at the political themes of the film.

After Mustard and Wadsworth's spat, the guests reluctantly agree that they need to split up and search the house. In Lynn's preliminary draft, all of the men, including Mr. Green, want to pair off with Yvette, admitting that they too are afraid of the dark. Scarlet replies, "They don't even care that you might be a killer so long as you got big tits."[7] Through each draft, Lynn toned down the profanity and some of the more aggressive sexual innuendo. Camp played Yvette as shrewd, although it takes repeat viewings to pick up on it. In an interview with me, she explains that everything Yvette does is "calculated," then slips easily back into Yvette's French accent and offers an example: "But I am frightened of zee dark. Will anyone go wis me?"[8] Yvette was not frightened of the dark, but she did have a reason, depending on the ending, to lure one of the men anxious to be alone with her into the attic.

With the search plan settled, Wadsworth grabs a handful of matchsticks and gestures toward the kitchen, signaling for everyone to follow. Lynn and Kemper took footage of the actors crossing from the library to the kitchen here but didn't use it, and there is another brief time jump. Takes of the guests gasping when Wadsworth grabs the large kitchen knife to cut the matches also were left out. Lynn later remembered that the long shot of everyone coming forward to get a match required just one take. However, the shot list says it took two—still impressive for a complicated scene with seven actors and a pan in which everyone is shown picking the right match at the right time, followed by a slow pan back to Brennan. Everyone needed to be flawless, hit their marks, and react accordingly. Warren is especially expressive, with her disgust at being paired with Mull's Colonel Mustard. Why then did they need two takes? At the end of the shot, Lloyd approaches Brennan, puts his match against hers, and purrs, "It's you and me, honey bunch"—and Brennan busted up with laughter.

---

7 Lynn, "Clue," undated preliminary draft, 66.

8 Camp, interview with author.

The second take was used, and in the split second before the scene cuts, it looks as if she's still fighting back laughter. This brief moment between the two actors replaced a longer exchange in Lynn's first draft: Peacock exclaims to the other guests, "I can't do it. Me, alone, in the pitch darkness with this sex maniac?" "I assure you, Mrs. Peacock, that there is absolutely no chance of my so much as laying a finger on you, even though your appearance would undoubtedly be improved by pitch darkness," Plum replies.[9]

Everyone emerges from the kitchen, and John Morris's music playfully returns. Yvette still holds her matchstick upright as if it's a talisman protecting her. She won't drop it until she and Mr. Green struggle to climb the attic stairs side by side. It's easy to miss, but funnier once it's spotted. Professor Plum and Mrs. Peacock head to the cellar, and Colonel Mustard and Miss Scarlet make for the billiard room. When Green, Yvette, Wadsworth, and Mrs. White ascend the stairs to the upper landing, we notice dust on the floor and molding. The window is dirty and the walls stained by water damage throughout the years. In some spots, the wallpaper is peeling, exposing mold underneath. The ramshackle upstairs adds to the tension as lightning flashes and thunder roars outside. The camera stays on Green and Yvette as White and Wadsworth walk out of frame, headed for the bedroom and nursery.

While Syd Dutton and Bill Taylor of Illusion Arts handled the lightning effects on the matte painting, the production crew working at Paramount were responsible for the rain that beat against the windows, the wind that howled outside, the thunder that roared through the house, and the lightning that flashed against the windows. Lighting tech Earl Gilbert and his team used two machines made out of a welding transformer that could produce a lightning arc. The wind blew from large fans, and the rain was coordinated by the effects team. McKean and Camp coordinated their timing with the effects as they passed by the window.

At the cut, as Morris's shivering strings fill the soundtrack, Mr.

9 Lynn, "Clue," first-draft screenplay, 67.

Green gropes for a light switch. McKean and Camp have moved to Paramount Stage 17. Here the production recreated the attic (including the stairs), the hallway in front of the bedrooms, the master bedroom, the nursery, the dressing room, the bathroom, the cellar (and the stairs leading down to it), and the secret passages. Filming all of the upstairs, downstairs, and secret passage scenes was done over three days in early August 1985. These rooms were, like the upper landing, weathered and dingy. Although only briefly visible, the master bedroom and nursery have holes in their walls. The floor of the bedroom is covered in crumbling chunks of plaster. Had Lynn been able to keep everything he shot, audiences would have seen a lot more.

No sequence had more deleted shots than the upstairs search. Many more shots were taken of Curry and Kahn timidly prowling around the upstairs bedroom and child's room and of McKean bumbling his way through the attic as Camp searches alongside him. Most of this footage was discarded in editing. One unused shot established that Mrs. White was in a child's nursery by panning across the room, showing toys and dolls. Kemper and Lynn shot two versions, one panning slowly and one quickly. But deleting the shot makes it unclear where White is; plus, a later scene, during the second search of the house, when a giant jack-in-the-box pops out, seems rather bizarre as a result. Also deleted from the first search of the house: Wadsworth and Mrs. White searching through a hallway hidden behind curtains and looking under a couch, then startling each other through another set of curtains; Wadsworth more thoroughly searching the bedroom, knocking over a lamp; and Mrs. White becoming startled by the shadow of a doll on the wall after switching on a lamp in the nursery. Attic shots of Mr. Green tripping over golf clubs and jumping at a flash of lightning also got tossed, as did Green reacting to a head in a glass case; Yvette being frightened by Green's crashing and falling; and Yvette discovering a stuffed reindeer. While many of these shots were discarded to keep the runtime down, Lynn later lamented losing them, opining that the film is "less visually interesting" without them.[10] Without these scenes, the upstairs search

10 Brandon and Lynn, "*Clue*: The Director's Commentary," 1:24:45.

is left with only one brief shot each of Wadsworth and Mrs. White, in separate rooms, and one shot each of Yvette and Mr. Green after ascending the attic stairs.

Although it can feel as if the characters are upstairs and in the cellar for quite some time, they are on-screen for only about two and a half minutes during this first search. Mrs. Peacock and Professor Plum don't get much screen time in the cellar either. All of their scenes on Stage 17, including both the first and second search of the house, were filmed in one day, on August 2. One of the production's light stands is visible for a brief moment as the camera pans to follow Brennan running away from Plum. The shot of the rat turning and crawling into the wall is stock footage. The sets on Stage 17, particularly the attic and the cellar, were small, especially compared with the massive set on Stage 18. The camera filmed most everything from one angle, and each room was stuffed with props and furniture to make it appear crowded and messy.

The scenes of Colonel Mustard and Miss Scarlet on the ground floor, of the Cop finding the Motorist's car, and of the Motorist in the lounge are twice as long as those filmed on Stage 17. On Monday, June 24, while the rest of the cast got a rare weekday off, Warren, Mull, and Kramer got to work. All of the scenes of Mustard and Scarlet searching the ground floor for the first time were filmed on this day except for the shots of them in the ballroom. Warren and Mull worked well together and became friends on the *Clue* set. As they search the billiard room and have to squeeze through the bar, Warren struggles not to laugh, and it required nine takes to get it right. As written in the first draft, where the tape recorder plays an important role in the fourth ending, the pair notes that it is still running, and Mustard and Scarlet leave the recorder alone. Filming the rest of their search went smoothly, as the two are shown opening closet doors and looking in on the ballroom.

The ballroom is never glimpsed from the hall and vice-versa, because each is about twelve miles apart from the other. The shot of Mustard and Scarlet framed in the ballroom door when he searches her and she tells him to take his mitts off of her was taken on Stage 18. The camera was set up outside of the mansion, on the soundstage. When the shot cuts to Colonel Mustard and Miss Scarlet feeling their way into the room and looking for a light, it is six weeks later and production has moved to the Busch mansion in Pasadena. The actors spent one day there, August 6, and both the interior shots of the ballroom and the exteriors of the house were captured on this day.

The footage of the Cop discovering the Motorist's car was filmed on the same day as the Motorist's crash, August 9, the second-to-last day of principal photography. Bill Henderson was the only actor needed, and it was his one day away from Stage 18, as production returned to Franklin Canyon Drive. Rain machines were set up by the crew for the scenes in which the Motorist's car veers off the road and the Cop later finds the car. As the police car makes its way down the road, the driver's-side window is rolled down to allow the stunt driver to see better and hit the mark to turn the car around. Despite the fake rain and shooting at night, everything went quickly and was captured in a handful of takes.

Mustard leaves Scarlet in the ballroom to go search the kitchen. It was essential to split the duo up for two of the four endings to work, since one of them had to be murdering the Motorist. A brief scene was filmed of the two reuniting on the hallway landing as Mustard leaves the kitchen, after Scarlet has crossed the ballroom. However, this moment went discarded because it implied too strongly that neither could have been the killer. As we shall see, this wasn't the only sequence deleted for suggesting that one of the murderers was somewhere they couldn't have been.

With Scarlet and Mustard separated, the killer is wearing gloves in the study, collecting Mr. Boddy's blackmail evidence, destroying it in the fire, and getting to the weapons. This gloved hand could belong to any of four characters, depending on who kills the Motorist in each of the film's four endings. In reality, it belonged to a crew member, possibly Lynn, who occasionally stood in on shots of hands gripping weapons. The footage of the evidence being gathered and destroyed was taken on July 3, while the brief shot of the gloved hand opening the cupboard was filmed a week later, on July 10.

The production team created the evidence photographs, glimpsed for only a split second on the desk in the study before they're tossed into the fire. They are black-and-white images of Mrs. White on a porch,

Colonel Mustard in front of a jeep driven by the Motorist, Mr. Boddy in his car, and Mr. Green at US State Department headquarters. The photographs of Green and White are difficult to make out but appear not to be of McKean or Kahn. The image of Lee Ving shows him in the same costume he wears in the movie. In the picture of Mustard and the Motorist, Kramer and Mull are in Army uniforms in front of a set designed to look like an Army hospital. All of these moments were photographed nearby on the Paramount backlot.

Back in the locked lounge, the scene of Kramer on the telephone was filmed on the same day that Mull and Warren searched the ground floor, June 24. The Motorist doesn't realize it, but he's in trouble; the murderer begins to emerge from the secret passage. The viewer sees this, but the motorist does not. Alfred Hitchcock famously said that if a bomb goes off under a table, the audience is surprised, but just for a brief moment. However, if the camera pans down below the table to show a bomb about to go off, with a timer counting backward, the suspense is prolonged. In other words, anticipation is more suspenseful than surprise. So it is here. As the secret passage opens, the murderer, with a wrench clutched in his or her gloved hand, moves slowly across the room, tension building before the wrench at last comes crashing down onto the Motorist's skull.

The production ran out of time to film the final moments of the Motorist's murder on June 24, and June 25 and 26 were scheduled for stunt doubles and the dropping of the chandelier, so the scene was finished on June 27. There were several takes of the fireplace opening, the wrench moving across the room, and the Motorist falling. Retakes were shot in July of the fireplace opening even more slowly. Lynn remembered that the murder was initially more gruesome, with shots of Kramer's face doused in fake blood, but to accommodate the PG rating, he wound up cutting the more graphic closeup of his head. The brief shot of the gloved hand replacing the receiver onto the phone cradle was filmed a week later, in July.

Hill House's phone number, YL-7091, uses the typical two-letter, four-number system of the time, though some metropolitan areas were converting to a seven-digit system by 1954. Anyone who has seen a movie made before 1950 has likely heard a character pick up a phone and say something like, "Operator, give me Belmont 4542." It has an old-timey vibe to it, separating our world of cellphones from what feels like a distant past. The word prefix represented a city or town where the telephone exchange, or central office, was located. That exchange would host up to 10,000 numbers, from 0000 to 9999. An operator would use the first two letters of the name to identify the right exchange and then the last four numbers to pinpoint the right home or business. Belmont 4542 would be BE-4542, or 23-4542. By 1954 some areas had instituted direct dialing, meaning that a caller would hear a dial tone instead of an operator picking up, so they could dial the number on their own. Depending on where Hill House was, the Motorist may have still needed to ask an operator to connect his call or he may have been able to call without help.

Does the YL on the phone at Hill House identify its exchange and therefore give away its location? No, since there are no cities, and therefore no exchanges, that begin with YL. Instead, American Telephone and Telegraph reserved YL for mobile phones. In 1954, these car phones were large and expensive. They used VHF radio frequencies to connect to telephone exchanges. Using the YL exchange allowed the production to use an authentic number while not identifying the location of Hill House.

The script, through all drafts, called for Colonel Mustard and Miss Scarlet to fumble around in the dark in the lounge until they tripped over the Motorist's body. Scarlet was to feel around and find his head. Then Mustard would switch on the flashlight, but a gloved hand (belonging to the murderer) knocks the flashlight away. Both Mustard and Scarlet would begin screaming that they were trapped with a murderer. This was scrapped during filming when Lynn realized that it didn't work for two of the endings. As originally planned, there were four people, depending on the solution, who killed the Motorist: Mrs. Peacock, Wadsworth (in the cut ending), Colonel Mustard, or Miss Scarlet. There couldn't have been a third person in the room in the endings where Mustard and Scarlet were the guilty party. Lynn changed the scene and filmed the fireplace slamming shut and the pair panicking and pounding on the lounge doors.

All of the characters respond to the screams and emerge running from the rooms they were searching. There is a peculiar blink-and-you-miss-it shot of Mr. Green looking at a sculpture of the head of Vladimir Lenin in a glass case, and Yvette is staring at a stuffed reindeer head. Both of these moments originally ran longer. Viewers could be forgiven for wondering: What on earth is going on in the attic of Hill House? The answer: a production team was determined to make the mansion as spooky and weird as possible, especially upstairs. Set designer Lloyd echoed Lynn when he said they wanted it to feel like "sort of a Charles Addams place."[11] Before audiences can process what they just saw, the action cuts to Curry and Kahn running through a curtain, then Camp and McKean bursting down the stairs from the attic. With another cut, the actors are replaced with stunt doubles. The doubles were required for just two days, on June 25 and June 26. The shot of Mr. Green, Yvette, Mrs. White, and Wadsworth crashing into each other at the top of the stairs was filmed on June 25 and needed two takes. Lynn and Kemper used a two-camera setup, with one camera facing the doubles on the second floor and the other on a crane. The stunt doubles, practically sprinting, crash into one other. Chére Bryson was Yvette's double, Robert Fisher was Mr. Green's, Dan Costa stood in for Wadsworth, and Jean Malahni became Mrs. White. Fisher and Costa slam into each other hard, sending Fisher flying into the air.

With one more cut, the doubles are gone and the actors are back, picking themselves off the floor and racing down the main stairs as the camera, mounted on a crane, tracks them. In another shot that was removed from the final film, Mr. Green, Mrs. White, Professor Plum, and Mrs. Peacock crash into one another again, this time just outside the door to the cellar. Doubles were used here as well with one exception. John Scott was Professor Plum, Malahni was once again Mrs. White, and Jeannie Epper stood in for Mrs. Peacock. But McKean remained as Mr. Green. It's not clear why no double was used for Green—his face wasn't so visible that a double couldn't have taken his place. The shot, cut from the final film, is immortalized in the

---

11 Kahan and Turner, "Clue Is More than a Game," 51.

trailer for fans to see.

As everyone's panic mounts and Morris's music is at its most frenzied, the action gathers at the front of the hall. This scene was more or less consistent across all drafts of the script, with very few changes made. No stunt double was used for Wadsworth to crash into the lounge door, and Curry gives it his all. The door doesn't give, and he clutches his arm in agony, writhing around on the floor. Yvette runs out of the study and trips over Wadsworth; Camp once again has been replaced by Chére Bryson. This required seven takes, the most of any scene with a stunt double. Bryson has a fake gun, and the gunshot effect was added later. No stunt doubles were used for Lloyd or McKean as they hit the deck after the gun is accidentally fired. The footage of the chandelier being hit and spinning as the rope begins to unravel was taken on August 1, with the chandelier hanging from a false ceiling.

Once more, Bryson is gone, and it is Camp rising, aiming, and shooting through the door lock. The production team rigged the door with a small explosive to blow out part of the lock; it took three tries to get it right. When Colonel Mustard and Miss Scarlet finally emerge from the lounge, there is white fabric exposed on Mustard's left shoulder, where the bullet Yvette fired ripped through his clothing. He isn't just being dramatic when he yells, "I've been shot!" This was, of course, planned by the production team, and his costume is altered appropriately. Mustard begins pushing Yvette, yelling at her and the pair stop underneath the chandelier.

Dropping the chandelier took time and careful planning. One of the more memorable stories to come out of Adam Vary's oral history of *Clue* was of Lynn admitting that he was especially cautious with this scene because of Landis's *Twilight Zone* accident. Lynn felt like the chandelier "should have only just missed them."[12] As it was, it came reasonably close to Mull.

The chandelier was dropped twice, first on June 26 with stunt doubles, then on June 27 with the actors. The chandelier was attached to rigging above the mansion on Stage 18. None of the rooms, including

12 Vary, "Something Terrible Has Happened Here."

the hall, had ceilings allowing lighting and cameras to peer down onto the set. By cutting from different angles, Lynn was able to obscure the use of the doubles. There is the down-angle shot of Colonel Mustard pushing Yvette underneath the chandelier for which all of the actors are present and then a cut to the actors on the floor. But when Lynn cuts to the high angle overlooking the action, the stunt doubles have replaced the actors. The doubles are looking down slightly so that the camera doesn't catch their faces. Two cameras were set up, one pointing down and another panning with the chandelier as it falls. This version, with the doubles, was filmed at thirty-four frames per second, to slow down the fall when it was played back.

After another cut, Mull says, "I can't take anymore scares." Then the shot cuts back one last time to the down angle and the stunt doubles. When the rope snaps, the doubles are ready as the chandelier falls and shatters. For this shot, the chandelier was dropped free from any support. The next day, it was done again, with two cameras, both on the ground floor. Curry, waiting for it to fall so that he can turn away at the right moment, can be seen glancing upward for a split second. With the actors there and the doubles gone, the chandelier was kept on a pulley so that the production team retained more control. A split second after the chandelier crashes and glass shatters, there's a cut to the footage captured by the second camera to hide the rope attached to the pulley and rigging far above the hall.

This was *Clue*'s toughest practical effect, and it went off well. Stunt coordinator Terry Leonard toyed with Mull by pretending to be drunk before the chandelier was dropped and, slurring his words, said he hoped everything worked out. It did. After the second drop on June 27, the cast was able to film several more scenes, including the Motorist's murder, Scarlet and Mustard's discovery of the dead man, and the rest of the guests' congregation in the lounge as they stared at the body. They also filmed Yvette tossing the gun on the ground and everyone running into the study when she reveals that the cupboard was open. However, the shot of Green, Plum, Yvette, and Wadsworth in the lounge doorway as Plum asks if it's the same gun was not filmed until a month later, on July 26. The crew originally shot the conversation at a wider angle as everyone stood crowded in the doorway. But at some point Lynn decided it wasn't working and added the separate shot of Green, Plum, Wadsworth, and Yvette.

Back in the study, the guests gather around the now-open weapons cupboard, stunned and a little suspicious of Yvette's story. But before she can explain beyond saying it was already open, the doorbell rings again. On May 23, two and a half minutes of footage was taken of the bell ringing from two different angles, one tighter on the bell, one a little wider. This was cut in throughout the film anytime the bell was rung. Now, another guest has arrived: the Cop.

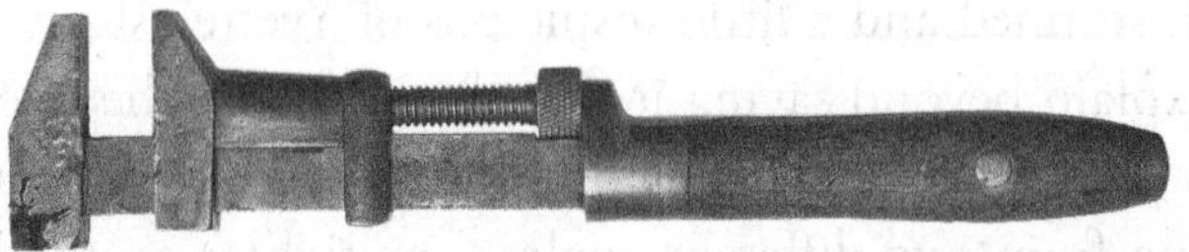

# 7. "IT'S ALL TOO SHOCKING!"

"The best thing about our movie is that I don't see how there could possibly be a *Clue II*."
-Martin Mull[1]

The ink on Bill Henderson's contract was barely dry when he walked onto Paramount Stage 18 on Friday, June 28, 1985, dressed in a police rain slicker that covered his neat uniform from head to ankles. Henderson was recommended by Debra Hill after Tim Reid withdrew from the cast, and he had signed on only a week before. The production team filmed his arrival and awkward entrance into Hill House as everyone quietly stares at him when he asks Yvette, "Don't I know you from someplace?" She feigns ignorance as Wadsworth offers the shattered chandelier as the excuse for everyone's odd behavior.

The production would spend the rest of the twenty-eighth and the first three days of July filming the next few scenes with Henderson before the guests split up to search the house again. The cast and crew had more than half the film in the can. They were approaching the home stretch, but still had a lot left to shoot, including Wadsworth's hyperactive retelling of the evening as well as all four endings. Also left on the shooting schedule were several flashbacks showing who had committed the murders and how it was done.

Wadsworth ushers the Cop toward the library, desperately trying to

1 Farber, "Off the Board."

keep him away from the study and lounge. Lynn later remembered that getting the timing right as Miss Scarlet and Professor Plum slam the doors to the incriminating rooms was difficult. It's "easier to do on stage," he recalled, "where everybody can see all the action." The difficulty in cutting it for film was making it appear as if all the action is happening at once.[2] Almost nothing is as easy as it looks to the audience at a movie. Case in point: after Wadsworth escorts the confused Cop to the library and shuts him in, the fake cardboard books rattle on the library doors, exposing a bit of movie trickery.

This segment of the film, from the Cop's arrival to the time the power is shut off, remains virtually unchanged across all of Lynn's drafts. One exception: additional dialogue when the Cop answers the phone and learns it's J. Edgar Hoover calling. In the first draft, he replies sneeringly at the stunning identity of the caller, "And I'm the Pope," only to quickly realize his mistake. In a later draft, the Cop says, "And I'm Harry Truman," before his sarcasm is abandoned altogether in the final film. Henderson nailed in two takes crossing from the door through the library to the phone, answering the phone, and crossing back to bang on the door. The shot of the group laughing uncomfortably at the Cop's phony threat to book them for murder was done in seven takes, but most scenes with Henderson needed only three or four.

The group is gathered in front of the library when Mr. Green asks Wadsworth why on earth J. Edgar Hoover is on his phone. The butler's reply, that Hoover is on everyone's phone, is a joke about wiretapping subtle enough that it can be missed. Hoover did order the phone lines of many Americans tapped, including Martin Luther King Jr. and other civil rights leaders. The butler steps into the library and shuts the doors to take the call. In two of the endings, it is explained that Hoover is calling to talk to someone who works for him; in the other two, the reason for the call is left unsaid.

When Miss Scarlet approaches the Cop, grabs his lapel, and draws him in close to tell him that the group is "having a party," it seems

---

2 Brandon and Lynn, "*Clue*: The Director's Commentary Track," 1:34:35.

impossible that he wouldn't realize who she is. She certainly recognizes him, as she later admits, as the Cop she bribes once a week to turn a blind eye as she runs her house of ill repute. But what Mr. Boddy's informers were told about why they were being invited to this house is left unexplained. As is why they agreed to behave as if they were (in the case of Yvette and Mrs. Ho) employees or (in the case of the Motorist, the Cop, and the Singing Telegram Girl) people who had innocent reasons to be at the mansion. Early in the film, Lynn crafts elaborate staging to ensure that Mrs. Peacock never sees the cook; the need to hide Mrs. Ho's presence from her former employer is part of the script from the earliest drafts. But no attempt is made to keep Mr. Boddy's other informers—the Motorist, the Cop, or the Singing Telegram Girl—hidden from the guests who will recognize them.

The Cop is not to be dissuaded from wanting to check the house, and Mr. Green is volunteered by Scarlet to show him around. With Wadsworth still stuck in the library on the phone with Hoover, the others race to hide the crimes awaiting the Cop in the study and lounge. Miss Scarlet tells Mrs. White, Miss Peacock, and Colonel Mustard to make their cover up of the murders "look convincing." In the first draft of the screenplay, Mrs. White asks, "What are you going to do?" and Scarlet answers that she will "deal with the Motorist," but this was cut. The Cop quickly loses patience with Mr. Green's lackluster tour of the house and demands to know what's going on in the rooms teeming with dead bodies. Green can't deter him, and the Cop throws him aside (McKean and Henderson got this bit of physical comedy in six takes) and steps into the study and into *Clue*'s most infamous scene.

The Cop's line upon seeing what is going on—"It's not all that shocking; these folks are just having a good time"—contrasts with what's actually happening. It is in fact shocking, and Mrs. White, Colonel Mustard, and Mrs. Peacock are decidedly not having a good time. The guests have positioned the corpses to make it appear as if they are alive. To sell it, Mrs. White kisses the very dead Mr. Boddy, while Colonel Mustard canoodles with the cook in front of the window. Dark comedy indeed, in a PG-rated movie that a toy company was hoping would help sell its family board game. Mrs. White kneels on the couch over Boddy, wriggling her body as she kisses him. Colonel Mustard clutches the dead cook, the knife still protruding from her back, as Mrs. Peacock doubles as her arms. An unreleased publicity still shows Mrs. White leaning up after kissing Mr. Boddy, her hair askew, staring off in the distance looking as if she is wondering how her life got to this point. The scene is helped along by the cheery music; it's such a stark contrast to what is happening that it's a bit like stepping into a somber funeral service only to hear the Benny Hill theme.

The song playing is "Sh-Boom" by the Canadian doo-wop group the Crew Cuts. Lynn would recall that he used it because it cost next to nothing to license. It was originally written and performed by a Black group, the Chords. But in the 1950s, white groups often covered—stole might be a better word—music by Black groups, covers that sometimes rocketed those white performers to fame. Toothless copyright laws and a music industry that encouraged the appropriation of the music of Black artists made it impossible for those artists to get fair compensation for their work. White cover versions were often reworked to remove anything that sounded too "Black." "Shake, Rattle, and Roll," heard at the beginning of the movie as Yvette dances in the library, was first performed by the Black artist Big Joe Turner. Two months later, Bill Haley and His Comets released their version (the one heard in *Clue*), which got much wider play than Turner's. While the Chords' version of "Sh-Boom" got some attention, it was the Crew Cuts release that climbed to the top of the *Billboard* charts. It was the Crew Cuts who performed on *Toast of the Town* (later renamed *The Ed Sullivan Show*). And it was the Crew Cuts who toured the world, appearing in Liverpool, England, where twelve-year-old George Harrison saw them at his first concert and thirteen-year-old Paul McCartney got their autographs, asking them, "What's it like in America?"[3] When newspapers across the United States profiled the Crew Cuts and their newfound success thanks to their number one hit, they almost never bothered to mention the existence of the Chords. The version of the song spinning on the turntable in *Clue* belongs to neither band, since the label says Decca. The Chords released "Sh-Boom" on Cat Records;

3 Lewisohn, *The Beatles*, 227.

the Crew Cuts recorded for Mercury.

The scene in the study, including insert shots of the record player, was filmed on July 2, while most of the action in the next scene, with the Cop in the lounge, was shot the following day, along with other pickups and inserts. Shooting everything in the lounge, including the drunken Motorist and Scarlet and Plum on the couch, went quickly. Christopher Lloyd is at his most expressive, giving viewers a glimpse of his Doc Brown persona. Lesley Ann Warren would laugh about Lloyd's performance later, saying that she was never sure "whether he was acting or this was really who he was, because he's an odd guy."[4] Jeffrey Kramer, contracted for five weeks of guaranteed work, was often not needed on set unless his corpse was in a shot, such as when the Cop visits the lounge. He later said, "I wished I'd lived another reel or two" longer so that he could be a part of the fun the cast were having on set.[5]

The Cop has seen the house, and he is finally satisfied. The shots of Tim Curry speaking to Henderson after he has "seen it all" were filmed two days earlier, on July 1. When Wadsworth locks the man back in the library, he leaves the key in the lock, foreshadowing how the murderer will get in. The guests agree they need to split up again to finish searching the house. The production team shot everyone in the hall as they separate, then the crew reset in the kitchen to follow Colonel Mustard and Miss Scarlet as they prowl around. Martin Mull needed three takes to get hit in the head with the ironing board. After Mustard and Scarlet discover the secret passage, they were supposed to run down it. A scene was filmed on Stage 17 of the pair racing through the passage, but that shot was cut, and instead we jump to the two emerging from the painting of William McKinley in the study.

These scenes of Mull and Warren on the main mansion set were filmed in early July, and the rest of the cast shot the remainder of their upstairs and downstairs scenes on Stage 17 at the end of the shoot in early August. The schedule was getting more jumbled, and ensuring script continuity was growing more complicated by the day.

---

4 Smith, *Who Done It?*, 33:30.

5 Smith, 53:00.

Fortunately, an old pro was on hand—Doris Grau, who'd been working as a script supervisor since the late 1950s. Her job was primarily to ensure consistency throughout the film. She confirmed that costumes matched from scene to scene or that a performer's line of sight hadn't changed between takes. If filming was set to begin and Grau spotted something amiss, she would leap to her feet and yell, "Stop the presses!"[6] Shortly after working on *Clue*, she landed her first acting role, and she would go on to appear in a handful of *Cheers* episodes. She became best known as the voice of Lunch Lady Doris on *The Simpsons*.

Grau's copy of the *Clue* script is filled with her notes. Unused scenes are struck through, and new lines are penciled in. Grau would write the shot number on the script, then draw a line to the shot list detailing how many takes were made, what type of lens was used, how long the take lasted, what kind of shot was filmed (wide, medium, close, low, or high angle), and whether a take was printed or discarded. Shots could be labeled unusable for any number of reasons—an actor flubbing a line, a boom mic shadow in frame, the camera out of focus, someone missing their mark. All of it happened on *Clue*, though infrequently. First assistant camera (focus puller) Bill Roe was responsible for keeping the camera focused on the action no matter how complicated the shot. He had begun working in Hollywood a few years earlier as a second assistant and would go on to become a prominent television director, working on *The Rookie*, *Castle*, and *The Blacklist*, among other shows. Practiced expertise was vital. Everything was tactile in this analog world; if a take went awry, there was no deleting it off a hard drive or Photoshopping something out of the frame. If second assistant cameraman Mario Zavala dropped the camera magazine and the reel unspooled out onto the soundstage floor, a day's work, and with it tens of thousands of dollars, would be lost. Everyone who worked on the film knew the stakes and knew how to do their jobs, whether they had been in movies for five years or thirty-five years. Mistakes are inevitable, but none on *Clue* were catastrophic, and the movie continued its march toward the end of principal photography.

---

6 Brandon and Lynn, "*Clue*: The Director's Commentary Track," 1:27:30.

The scenes of the Cop's arrival, his search of the house, and the guests splitting up again to conduct their own search wrapped on July 3. Production took the Fourth of July holiday off, then resumed on July 5 to film two murders. A gloved hand, belonging to one of four people, depending on the ending, throws the main electricity switch. There is another brief shot of Syd Dutton and Bill Taylor's matte painting of the house. The painting still exists, now in the safe hands of Jeff Smith, director of *Who Done It? The Clue Documentary*. The shots of the matte were done with older, VistaVision cameras because veteran artist Albert Whitlock wasn't comfortable with the newer, Panaflex cameras the production was using.

The guests fumble around in the dark, all of them seemingly caught off guard by the sudden loss of power. It took ten takes on August 2 for Lloyd to burn himself with the match. A few of those included him lighting his pipe and putting it in his mouth. That same day, Brennan was filmed backing into the ductwork of the furnace and then turning to beat it with her purse. Wadsworth is upstairs in a dressing room when the wind blows the door shut, and Mrs. White is back in the nursery where a window is thrown open, and she begins screaming.

But some of the footage of Tim Curry and Madeline Kahn was cut when Lynn realized later that their presence upstairs wouldn't work for two of the endings. Both killed at least one of the victims in different endings, and therefore couldn't be bumbling around in the dark in one room at the same time they were killing Yvette, the Cop, and the Singing Telegram Girl downstairs. The same problem arose with Martin Mull and Lesley Ann Warren. Both were filmed in the ballroom at the Busch house in Pasadena, this time trying to find their way forward in the moonlight peeking through the window. But since both Mull's and Warren's character were off murdering people in two of the endings, this shot was cut.

Yvette makes her way downstairs in the dark and crosses to the billiard room. A shot of the Cop reacting to Mrs. White's screaming went unused, and instead he repeats "Hello?" into the library phone. The first murder filmed on July 5 was Yvette's. Lynn later told Josh Brandon that it might be his voice in the billiard room calling out to Yvette. It might take audiences a few viewings to pick up on a crucial detail: Yvette's French accent is gone. She's dropped the charade of being Hill House's maid. The dialogue was also changed to give away fewer clues. In the shooting script, the disembodied voice asks Yvette if the Cop recognized her. This was changed after filming began, so that Yvette is asked if "anyone" recognized her. It took a few tries to land the rope around Camp's neck exactly right

Throughout these scenes, John Morris's music enhances the mood. He switches with ease between frantic farce and genuine terror, punctuating the effect with silence or soft notes. Music journalist Thomas Hobbs calls Morris's score "the glue holding the film together" and "the fuel that powers Curry" throughout the butler's explanation of the ending.[7] The spooky music leads perfectly into the next murder: the Cop's. He's locked in the library, but Wadsworth has left the key in the lock, allowing the murderer to make their way inside. It required seven takes on July 5 and four retakes a week later to assemble enough usable footage of the pipe being raised behind the Cop and then swung down. One more down, one more to go.

In the first draft of Lynn's screenplay, the Singing Telegram Girl's beat-up car makes its way up the long drive, headlights shining through the front door and illuminating the ornate hallway. She stops, stares in bewilderment at the dark house, looks around at the other cars, spots a man standing outside the conservatory window. As she approaches him, she explains that she is "from Western Union" and has "a telegram to deliver." But as she draws nearer and taps the man on the shoulder, he falls over onto his back. She stares down in shock and realizes that it's a mannequin. After Lynn replaced the mannequin with the dogs in the third draft, he deleted the sequence in which she approaches the dummy but kept the drive up to the house. However, by the time principal photography got underway, that too was dropped. Instead, an insert shot was taken of the bell ringing while the power is out. The close-up reactions to the bell were all taken on different days. Warren's was filmed in the ballroom at the Busch mansion on August 6; Mull's was filmed on Stage 18 in July. The others were taken on Stage 17

---

7 Hobbs, "Know the Score."

at the same time each of the actors was filmed searching the upstairs rooms or, in the case of Lloyd and Brennan, the cellar.

Jane Wiedlin has the fewest spoken words in *Clue* (just edging out Kellye Nakahara), but they are some of the most memorable. Many a kid has belted out, "Da da da da da da! I am your singing telegram—bang!" It's one of the better examples of the tightrope *Clue* walks throughout the film, balancing between scary and funny. The film is like a balloon being blown up with tension until it's just about ready to pop, at which point something funny happens, letting all of the tension out. Wiedlin was guaranteed seventeen days of work for just under $5,000, from July 1 to July 17, but with shooting behind schedule and her drive up to the house eliminated, she was on set for just two days, Friday, July 19, and Monday the twenty-second. Her murder was filmed first as a wide shot; then the camera was moved closer, to medium range.

At the sound of the gunshot and the slamming of the door, Mr. Green jumps into a closet for safety and Colonel Mustard dives under the dining room table in fear, smashing his head. In the final film, it's not clear that the gunshot is what they're reacting to, especially since none of the other characters seem startled. Mrs. White begins screaming again only when the jack-in-the-box pops out. Wadsworth is still stuck in the dressing room, until he finds his way into the bathroom, where he walks into the shower. Lynn's preliminary draft has Wadsworth yelling, "I'm in the fucking shower!" when he ends up soaking wet, but the profanity is dropped in later drafts. All of these upstairs scenes were filmed on August 5; Curry running down the stairs to turn the power back on was filmed a month earlier, on July 5.

As the music playing in the study slowly cranks back to life, the guests emerge. Warren comes out of the ballroom, and she is careful not to open the door too wide, lest she expose the bare soundstage behind it. Colonel Mustard walks out of the dining room, Mrs. White and Mr. Green trudge down the stairs, and Mrs. Peacock and Professor Plum emerge from the cellar. They gather together and peer into the billiard room. Yvette is lying on top of the pool table, strangled to death, the noose still around her neck. The guests walk in, look for a moment, then walk out. They make their way into the library, and only Mr. Green seems shocked to find the dead Cop. They filmed two versions of this scene: one with the lead pipe on the floor, so that Lloyd has to bend down to pick it up, and one in which the pipe is on the table next to the bloodied policeman (they used the first).

Wadsworth's line upon realizing the body count has reached six begins, in early drafts, as a British idiom: "This is beyond a joke." Lynn realized, however, that Americans weren't getting it, so it became "This is not funny anymore" before finally landing on the version that appears in the movie: "This is getting serious." After the guests gawk at the dead Singing Telegram Girl, they shut the door again, and Wadsworth leads everyone to the shattered remnants of the chandelier in the hall. Yvette had thrown the revolver in the mess after she shot open the door to the lounge to free Mustard and Scarlet, and Wadsworth had swept it up with the shards of glass. Now the butler points out that the gun is missing. He is still dripping with water from the shower; over the next three weeks, Curry would don his character's costume and then be doused with water. The butler stuns the guests when he announces that he knows who did it, and he's going to show them how it was all done. What comes next is many fans' favorite part of the movie.

Wadsworth is ready to reenact everything that has happened thus far. Landis had envisioned this part of the film since at least 1982, and he saw it as a chance for an actor to deliver a "tour de force" performance at top speed.[8] Curry's manic recreation is a riff on a longstanding tradition in detective fiction: now that all of the clues have been collected and analyzed, it's time for someone, typically the investigator, to explain everything that has happened, thereby exposing the murderer and the motive. Normally a somber affair, this well-worn breed of dénouement unfolds as all of the suspects are gathered in one room and the detective methodically walks everyone through the events that have transpired, including, of course, the murder. Red herrings are explained away as just that, clues that may have appeared to implicate a suspect but in fact don't. Embarrassing secrets are exposed: innocent characters seem guilty because they are hiding a tryst, a theft, or some

8 Landis and Stoppard, "Transcript of Conversation."

other shameful event from their past. The murderer is often the one the audience least suspects.

Lynn's screenplay and Curry's performance turn this trope on its head, forcing dinner guests to run through a mansion in formal evening wear. This is a huge part of what draws kids to *Clue* when they discover it on television or home video. The Red Scare, sexual innuendos, and jokes about J. Edgar Hoover might be meaningless to a ten-year-old, but a man in a butler's uniform throwing another man into a bathroom? That they got. The action was intended to move so fast that Lynn included a note in the screenplay: "The speed of these scenes cannot be judged by the usual criteria." He wanted the words spoken "so fast that they may be completely unintelligible," resulting in "something like an under-cranked, speeded up section" of an old film.

With Wadsworth's reenactment came a major shift in the production schedule, especially as filming fell behind and Lynn looked for ways to catch up. It was no longer feasible to shoot in continuity, since the actors were running from room to room, stopping for just a few seconds in each spot. Mrs. Peacock might've been speaking for the whole gang when she asks, in sheer exasperation after learning that they were going back to the study for the umpteenth time, "Again?" Instead, the production began filming room by room, getting all the shots needed in each one before moving on to the next. The actors spent a few days in the study, then one in the dining room, all while Curry replayed the whole movie or the other actors filmed brief flashbacks—someone taking weapons out of the cupboard or sneaking out of a secret passage, for instance. Cast and crew spent the next week in the billiard room, study, kitchen, lounge, and dining room, then took the rest of July to film everything in the hall. One minute of screen time may have been shot across five separate days as Wadsworth bounced from the hall to the library, then to the kitchen, back out into the hall, and then on to the study.

Since this dizzying schedule included flashbacks to the murders, the actors—who had grown accustomed to proceeding largely in sequential order—were at times confused. On one day alone, late in July, they filmed scenes for three of the four different endings, including a flashback to much earlier in the film. It was easy to lose the plot for the day, and Lynn would step in and remind everyone of what they were shooting and what he needed from each actor. Brennan told a reporter that Lynn "instilled an enormous sense of trust" in all of the actors and that "when you ask him a question, he has an answer." As the film's writer, Lynn "understands it better than anyone else possibly could," she said.[9]

One creative idea for Wadsworth's reenactment that was ultimately abandoned was Lynn's vision of the camera racing into a scene ahead of the actors as they sprinted from room to room. Lynn explained the camera's action in the script's slugline: "INT. THE HALL (shooting towards FRONT DOOR)." The set was designed and built around this idea, but the lighting needs from one room to the next were too difficult to accommodate. The lighting in the hall might be perfect, but then, once the camera dollied into the study, the lighting requirements were different. If spending tens of thousands of dollars (or more) to design the set a certain way only to discover in the end that you cannot fulfill your vision sounds wasteful, Kemper reminded a reporter that "unfortunately, that's typical of our business."[10] He said that if producers would consult with cinematographers early in preproduction, they'd save a lot of money, but, he complained, they rarely do.

The guests' first stop in Wadsworth's retelling is the library. Throughout principal photography, the number of takes needed for each scene might range anywhere from one to a dozen (occasionally more), but usually required no more than three or four. Now that number would tick upward—still usually no more than six, but with all of the actors running through the set, filming became more complicated. A handful of brief scenes were dropped to save time. Originally, after Wadsworth leaves the library and gestures to the guests to follow him into the kitchen, there was to be a shot of everyone running into the hall after him. This was never filmed; instead, the film cuts to the kitchen as Wadsworth runs in and mimics the act of picking up the

---

9 Farber, "Off the Board."

10 Kahan and Turner, "Clue," 54.

knife the cook was sharpening. He's there for less than a few seconds before he sprints back into the hallway on his way to the front door to announce that Colonel Mustard has arrived.

Next, he runs back to the library, and the guests follow. He tells them that he gave them champagne (a reminder for the fourth ending) and then takes off again, back to the front door. By now, the guests have figured out what he's doing, and instead of running after him, they stand in the library doorway to watch him reenact Mrs. White's arrival. When he returns to the library, he gives the guests their first clue: Mrs. White and Yvette recognized each other, and not pleasantly. But as funny as Wadsworth's retelling of the night in Hill House is for longtime fans, it often feels confusing and disorienting for people watching for the first time. There's no way to pick up on all of the hints and explanations. This bedlam contributed to the feeling by some critics and audiences that *Clue* was akin more to *Murder by Death* than Agatha Christie: it might be funny, but it made no sense.

As he worked on the third draft of the screenplay, Lynn realized that reenacting everything from the movie would grow tiresome after a few minutes. As a result, he cut scenes from earlier drafts of the butler, after being followed into the dining room by the guests, disappearing into the kitchen and throwing open the hatch again to demonstrate what the cook and Yvette were doing. He also discarded a sequence in which Wadsworth runs back into the hall to admit Mr. Boddy through the front door. Instead, in the third draft, the guests grow impatient and tell the butler: "Get on with it!" Fortunately for the film's pacing, Wadsworth does, and the group quickly moves into the study. John Morris's music is so perfectly timed that these scenes almost function, as Lynn would say later, as a "choreographed musical sequence."[11] The shot of the guests' feet running across the hall to the study adds visual variety to the film and reinforces the urgency of the sequence.

The study remains the center of the action in *Clue*. Lynn cut more from the first draft, including Wadsworth's recreation of Mr. Boddy running into the conservatory to try and escape and Mr. Boddy going

11 Brandon and Lynn, "*Clue*: The Director's Commentary Track," 1:45:05.

into the hall to get the packages. Wadsworth switches off the lights to mimic Mr. Boddy's death, and Miss Scarlet, unperturbed by it all, lights a cigarette a split second before the lights come back on. This was originally planned as a longer moment to showcase her cavalier attitude, but close shots of Warren and of others looking at her were eventually cut. When the butler gets back up, much to everyone's relief, he at last explains what happened: Mr. Boddy was faking his own death. Professor Plum objects, insisting that Boddy was dead. In the first draft, Lynn included a joke about psychiatrists, telling Plum it wasn't his fault, since psychiatrists "know absolutely nothing about medicine." Lynn's wife, Rita, is a psychiatrist.

Wadsworth pulls on Boddy's ear to show Professor Plum where the bullet had grazed the blackmailer. Lee Ving slowly bobs his head back and forth after Curry lets go of his ear, still playing a corpse—a difficult shot to capture because shadows were thrown on the white lampshade behind the three actors. Wadsworth resumes his reenactment, including a scene in which Mrs. Peacock is slapped, which was filmed carefully so there was no danger Eileen Brennan would actually be hit, especially given the pain she was still experiencing from her car accident. In the cut ending that featured Wadsworth as the killer, earlier in the film when Boddy was faking his death, the butler had sneaked off through the secret passage and was nowhere to be found during Mrs. Peacock's screaming. How then did he manage to recreate this portion of the evening? It turns out that a scene that might work well for one ending may not fit as neatly with another.

Next, Wadsworth drags the guests to the billiard room to demonstrate how they responded when they heard Yvette screaming. He tells everyone that someone wasn't there with them when they went to check on the maid. Instead, that person was off murdering the cook. Except that in two of the four endings, Wadsworth is wrong (in one of them he's wrong; in another, he's lying). The butler does say that "maybe one of us was murdering the cook." That "maybe" has to do some heavy lifting.

Curry entered the billiard room on July 8; when he's running out into the hall, it's nine days later. Such was the impact on the shooting schedule once filming proceeded room by room. When Curry shot the scene of Wadsworth first walking across the hall of Hill House back on May 21, the floor looked new; now it was heavily worn, the result of two months of shooting, thanks to souvenirs left behind by shoe prints, heavy light stands, and dollies.

With everyone gathered in the kitchen for a demonstration of how the cook was killed, Wadsworth runs out, grabs a letter opener off the study desk, returns to the kitchen, and stabs the fake leg of lamb in the kitchen freezer. Then he stuns the guests by revealing the secret passage. The passages on Stage 17 were used sparingly. Building them on Stage 18 into the mansion set would have been impossible; in the board game, the passageways crisscross the house, implying that they are underground. While it would have been easier for the production team if the secret passages ran parallel along the set—the kitchen to the lounge and the conservatory to the study—they stuck to the original layout, as shown in the board game.

Wadsworth shows the guests that the passage ends in the study, behind the painting of William McKinley. Wadsworth then laughs at Mr. Green's suggestion that he could have been the one who committed the murders, since he knew about the secret passages. Left unclear, however, is how anyone other than the butler did know about the passages. Even Yvette, who was posing as a maid at Wadsworth's invitation, presumably wasn't familiar with Hill House. These scenes were shot on July 9, but getting them right required several retakes later in the day. One shot was labeled unusable because one cast member pulled a prank on the others—what that prank was is unknown. But it points to what the actors have said over the years: they had a lot of fun working with each other on *Clue*. McKean would later tell Adam Vary that while most of the actors were joking around in between takes, Curry was stuck trying to pull off an incredibly difficult performance. Curry remembered that he was working so hard that toward the end of shooting his reenactment, he needed to go "to the doctor and . . . take pills for a week, my blood pressure was so high."[12]

Wadsworth finally slows down long enough to explain to the guests

12 Vary, "Something Terrible Has Happened Here."

what happened. The murder victims were Mr. Boddy's informers, and that's why they were killed. A very pleased-with-himself Colonel Mustard finally gets it. The butler walks them through who knew Yvette, implicating Mrs. White, Miss Scarlet, and Mustard; each had a motive to kill the phony maid. In an early draft, Lynn includes a digression from Professor Plum explaining the "Vermont Headless Corpse Murder!" Plum tells the other guests that a headless corpse was found stabbed, and he clumsily indicts Mrs. White, since one of her husbands also was found with his head cut off and also because she knew Yvette. The other guests buy his weak accusation and join in accusing Mrs. White. After a few moments, however, attention turns to Colonel Mustard, who also knew Yvette . . . very closely. He was a regular at Miss Scarlet's home for the oldest profession, and Mrs. Peacock in particular will seem keen throughout the rest of the movie to implicate Mustard. She of course has her own reasons for deflecting suspicion from herself.

With this pause to explain things over, the reenactment ramps back up, and the guests dash off back to the kitchen, assuming Wadsworth will go there too. Instead, he has retaken the secret passage back to the icebox, and he falls out into Mr. Green's hands. McKean dropped Curry onto padding, turning him a little so that he would land on his side. Wadsworth explains that after they discovered the dead cook, the murderer slipped back through the secret passage to kill Mr. Boddy. Wadsworth is filling in the role of the amateur detective, but some of his knowledge about how the murders were committed goes beyond what has been shown to the audience. *Clue*, despite Hill and Landis's vision of allowing the audience to solve the mystery, doesn't always play fair.

The next scene, in which everyone is back in the study so that Wadsworth can show them how Mr. Boddy was killed, was one of the toughest shots in the film. On July 9, Lynn and company shot Curry fifteen times running from the painting hiding the secret passage, tripping McKean, picking him back up, then pushing him down again. On July 10, they did seven more retakes, for a total of twenty-two, the most in the film. The retakes went unused, and Lynn settled on a take from the previous day. The more challenging issue was the audio; the production team couldn't seem to get the sound right. Conversely, the shots in the hallway of Wadsworth stalking Green with the candlestick went quickly. It took three tries for Curry to hit McKean, and only one to throw him into the bathroom and have him re-emerge. It was McKean's idea to walk out of the bathroom drying his hands on a towel with the sound of the toilet flushing in the background.

Everyone moves to the front door, and Wadsworth reenacts the throwing away of the key. Mr. Green realizes that Colonel Mustard and Mrs. White's dead husband are connected via Yvette. The fake maid had affairs with both men and wormed government secrets out of them. McKean shot two takes, then slipped and nearly fell coming down the slick marble steps during takes three and four. Wadsworth tells the guests that like Yvette and the cook, the Motorist, Cop, and Singing Telegram Girl were Mr. Boddy's informers. The Motorist worked for Mustard and knew that he stole radio parts to sell on the black market; the Cop was bribed by Scarlet so she could run her brothel; and the Singing Telegram Girl was a former patient of Professor Plum's with whom he'd had an affair. Everyone still alive at Hill House had a motive to kill at least one of the victims.

Mrs. Peacock is disgusted by the news that Miss Scarlet had bribed the Cop, and Scarlet is in turn thoroughly fed up with Peacock's convenient prudishness. Her line "Oh, please!" in response to Peacock's outrage is absent from every draft of the script and was added by Lynn and Warren on the day of shooting. The three male guests bring the body of the Singing Telegram Girl (called the Western Union Girl in the screenplay) inside. The original plan was to have the camera shooting up from the floor as the men throw her body into the study so that it would sail into frame before crumpling on the sofa or crashing into the opposite wall. However, this proved too difficult to accomplish, and shooting was already behind schedule, so a dummy was nonchalantly dropped on the floor alongside the other corpses.

When Professor Plum asks how the murderer knew who the informers were, Wadsworth explains that they must have seen the evidence in the envelope that had been sitting on the desk in the study. This last scene in the study, another challenging one, required several takes as Curry walked around the room telling everyone what had happened.

The butler tells everyone a crucial detail: how the murderer got the weapons. After he locked the cupboard, he put the key in his pocket. When the group was in a huddle, the killer must've taken it out of his pocket and swapped in a duplicate so that Wadsworth wouldn't notice its absence. While a flashback was filmed showing Colonel Mustard taking the key to commit a murder in one ending, no flashbacks were filmed showing how the killers in two other endings—Miss Scarlet and Mrs. Peacock—were able to get the key.

The first draft of the script goes into more detail about how the murderer was able to make their way into the locked library to kill the Cop. Wadsworth had apparently left a master key in the lounge door and the murderer took it to access the other rooms. Scarlet suggests that "whoever has the key is the murderer," but in this first draft Wadsworth insists that they would have hidden the key. He searches a nearby potted plant and finds it. All of this was cut in the third draft. Instead, Wadsworth leaves the key in the library door, but without any explanation of this offered, audiences are left to spot it on their own.

Next comes the shot of Warren running toward the lounge to explain how she and Mustard had found the Motorist dead. As the camera pans, Curry runs to the lounge and then back again to tell them that the doorbell then rang . . . and then the doorbell rings. The shot continues—it's all one continuous take as Peacock marches up the steps to open the door, where she finds someone designated in the script as the Elderly Evangelist. When Howard Hesseman filmed his scenes in *Clue* over seven days, he was forty-five years old. His beard had already turned mostly gray, and no extra steps were taken to age Hesseman into the old man the script had called for. His costume—a trenchcoat with a suit underneath it and a matching fedora—would, in retrospect, suggest his role as a police chief or FBI agent. He is wearing a lapel pin that reads "We Did Remember Pearl Harbor." The phrase "Remember Pearl Harbor" was a rallying cry during World War II, and a Republic Pictures propaganda movie titled *Remember Pearl Harbor* was released in 1942.

Upon seeing the Evangelist, Lynn marvels in his audio commentary with Josh Brandon at how little the US has "changed in the last thirty years."[13] *Clue* is funny, and the performances by the actors make otherwise unlikable characters amusing and even appealing. A lot of what audiences and longtime fans see is the slapstick and the farce and the witty banter, but the film is also a scathing commentary on the United States of America. Lynn, a well-read British man, exposes hypocrisy disguised as patriotism, the willingness to do anything to make a buck, and America's repressed sexuality, classism, sexism, homophobia, and religious zealotry. Lynn penned the first drafts of the screenplay in 1984, just as Ronald Reagan was cruising to reelection by one of the largest margins in US history. America was awash in patriotic rhetoric and conservatism. National symbols were held up as evidence of a great and powerful country. The Statue of Liberty was undergoing a massive restoration in anticipation of its one-hundredth anniversary in 1986. But behind the show of strength, nostalgia, and patriotism were rising poverty, racial tension, environmental threats, unease over the Cold War, a raging drug epidemic, and an AIDS crisis that all too many Americans were happy to ignore. *Saturday Night Live*, toward the end of Reagan's presidency, aired a sketch with guest host Matthew Modine as "The Liberal," a man modeled on the Richard Kimble character in *The Fugitive*, lampooning how unpopular progressive politics had become.

Lynn, in an early draft of the script, wrote that Mrs. Peacock, fed up with the Evangelist, bellows at him, "Why don't you fuck off!" However, the line is softened in all the later drafts to, "Get lost!" before it became, "Our lives our in danger, you beatnik!"

After the interruption by the Elderly Evangelical, Wadsworth is ready to proceed, and the audience is finally ready to hear whodunit.

13 Brandon and Lynn, "*Clue*: The Director's Commentary Track," 1:55:20.

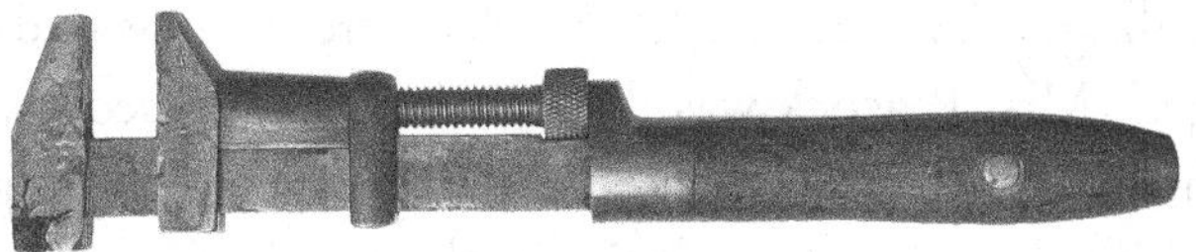

# 8. "OKAY CHIEF, TAKE 'EM AWAY"

"I looked at it, and I thought, *No, no, no, we've got to get rid of that.*"

-Jonathan Lynn[1]

*Clue*, in keeping with Debra Hill and John Landis's original vision, was written with four endings, shot with four endings, edited with four endings, and screened to test audiences with four endings. Each of these endings begins when Wadsworth turns the electricity back on as he runs through his manic retelling of what happened that evening. A power outage is a rather brilliant way to segue into each ending. Other writers who worked on *Clue*, each talented in their own way, couldn't solve the problem of four solutions. Lynn did.

Keeping track of the endings can be difficult, because the order in which they appeared changed at each stage—from script, to theatrical release, to home video. They were listed in one order in the screenplay and another in newspaper advertisements for theaters and then shown in an altogether different order for the VHS, Betamax, laser disc, and cable TV releases in 1986.

Here again are the endings of *Clue*, as they appear in the screenplay:

In ending A, Mrs. Peacock does it. In ending B, everyone does it. In ending C (deleted prior to the film's release because test audiences didn't care for it), Wadsworth is the killer. And in ending D, Yvette and

1 Farr, "Abnormal Interviews."

Miss Scarlet are the culprits. After ending C got dropped, the order switched. When newspapers in larger markets advertised which ending was playing in which theater, ending B—in which everyone did it—became ending A. Yvette and Miss Scarlet were the new ending B. And in ending C, Mrs. Peacock was the murderer. Confused? Wait, there's more: when the film was released on home video in August 1986, Yvette and Scarlet were the culprits in the first ending, Mrs. Peacock in the second, and everyone (except Mr. Green, of course) did it in the last, "here's what really happened," ending.

Let's, to paraphrase Wadsworth, consider the endings one by one, as they were originally conceived and listed in Lynn's screenplay.

### Ending A

Mrs. Peacock is, in the script, the least likable character. But Eileen Brennan played her as both hysterical and silly, and in doing so made her a funny addition to the guest list. Now, at least in this ending, the charade is dropped. Wadsworth reveals to everyone that she "murdered them all." Brennan is especially good here in her close-ups as Curry explains how she did it. She is cold and ruthless, displaying none of the vulnerability or empty-headedness that had defined the character up to that point. The scenes in the hall of Wadsworth exposing her and then her subsequent escape from the house were filmed July 22–24.

Wadsworth runs through the final three murders, then explains Peacock's "fatal mistake": she had said that monkey brains, the main entrée at dinner, was one of her favorite recipes, suggesting that she knew the cook. This line about a "fatal mistake" repeats in three of the four endings. In Lynn's third-draft script, there's a follow-up joke delivered by Miss Scarlet or Mrs. White, depending on the ending, in response to a comment that monkey brains cannot be found in Washington, DC: "Are there any brains to be found in Washington, DC?" The line was ultimately dropped and never filmed.

Wadsworth, despite his apparent omniscience when it comes to knowing how the murders were committed, is wrong about one thing: monkey brains are not, and never have been, popular in Cantonese cuisine. Claiming that Asians eat brains, eyeballs, hearts, and other organs has a long history in film and literature as a way of exoticizing these characters, to make them seem mysterious or dangerous. In *Clue* and such movies as *Indiana Jones and the Temple of Doom*, it's done for laughs, as white characters react with disgust to the alien food they are forced to consume either unknowingly or to be polite. Today, thankfully, it is recognized for what it is—racist, in addition to being inaccurate—and is done less frequently.

Wadsworth gets Mrs. Peacock to reveal herself as the killer; she pulls a gun, and Mr. Green reacts with shock as he strolls out of the bathroom, in a neat display of comic timing by McKean. Unlike in the other endings, no flashbacks show how the weapons were taken and the murders committed, though two were shot and went unused. On June 10, the production crew filmed a scene in which, as everyone else is huddled around the billiard room door after Yvette screams, Brennan sneaks behind them and raises a dagger on her way to the kitchen to kill the cook. A few days later, another flashback was shot, this one of Peacock's lower body in the secret passage just beyond the freezer after everyone else discovers the cook; she is on her way to the study to kill Mr. Boddy. But no footage was shot of Peacock sneaking up the cellar stairs or moving through the secret passage into the lounge to kill the Motorist.

Wadsworth reassures Mrs. Peacock that the police are not coming, and they can hide the bodies and go peacefully on their way. As she begins to leave, the remaining guests begin singing "For She's a Jolly Good Fellow." Madeline Kahn trills the high notes, standing out among the others and making the moment all the more hilarious. Mrs. White is giving Peacock a proper send-off. Lynn and the editors used the eighth and final take for the shot of the group serenading Mrs. Peacock as she flees from the mansion.

With the danger now outside, Professor Plum inquires about a cover-up. Wadsworth responds that the murders will all be hushed up by the FBI, evoking Sir Humphrey in *Yes Minister*, whose job more often than not was to convince Minister Hacker that it was in the public's best interest to know very little of what happens in government. The butler ends with a British joke about FBI director Hoover cleaning messes up because of his last name; in England, they don't vacuum, they "hoover."

Mrs. Peacock steps outside, anxious to get to her blue Packard. This scene was filmed in one day, on August 1, 1985. The first shot is a long take, nearly two minutes, to get Peacock as she leaves the house, heads toward her car, and is confronted by the Evangelist. Most of this was cut, however. In the final film, the Evangelist steps between Mr. Boddy's and Colonel Mustard's Cadillacs and tells Peacock that the kingdom of heaven is at hand. He draws his gun and holds her at bay as police lights flood the driveway. The officers move in, and Peacock is never seen again, though her voice is heard off-screen demanding that the cops stop manhandling her—"I'm a senator's wife!"

Before Lynn and the editors worked on it, the scene looked rather different: the Evangelist approaches Peacock before she gets to her car and asks why she has a gun. She offers an excuse about the house being so isolated. The dogs are visible to the right, and one take had to be discarded because the animal trainer's hand was visible holding the dog's collar. She continues to her car, but when the Evangelist calls her by her name, Mrs. Peacock asks how he knows it. After using the line that the kingdom of heaven is at hand, the Evangelist whips out his gun in a flash and fires a single shot at her. She collapses to the ground, dead.

During test screenings, Lynn decided this ending was a bit over the top. The gunshot and Peacock's death were removed, and some quick cuts and her voice-over bring her back from the grave to be arrested rather than killed. Eagle-eyed viewers might notice that as the cops run into the driveway from the bushes, the Evangelist has turned and is walking toward the house, but following a cut, he's back to standing where he was when he drew his gun. Two images from the deleted scenes were printed in the *Clue* children's storybook. The first shows Mrs. Peacock holding the revolver and speaking with the Evangelist; the second is of the Evangelist holding his literally smoking gun after he shoots her.

Lynn thought about how exactly to close this first ending, trying different things along the way. In the first drafts of the screenplay, the guests, still inside the mansion, hear the gunshot, and Wadsworth smiles as he tells them, "I thought it wouldn't take us long." By the third draft's revisions, the guests are outside when the Evangelist tells them that "she who lives by the gun shall die by the gun." Mr. Green's line "Mrs Peacock was a man?" was written during script revisions; however, the scenes of Wadsworth and Colonel Mustard slapping Mr. Green and Wadsworth asking if anyone would like dessert, were added later, during filming.

Having one murderer who killed everyone is a clean way to end the story, but how does Mrs. Peacock as culprit fit in with the rest of the film? Going through the murders in order, each death becomes more unlikely than the last if she is the killer. The first victim, and the reason she began the killing, was her old cook, Mrs. Ho. Peacock was the last person to leave the study while Yvette was screaming, so her slipping past the group in the billiard room to kill the cook in the kitchen seems the most plausible murder out of the six she committed. Given the jokes about Mrs. Ho's weight and how hard it was for three guests to lift her to put her on the couch, we might ask how the oldest person in the house was able to stuff the cook into the freezer.

Harder to swallow is the notion that Mrs. Peacock, who is standing in the kitchen doorway during the scene when Mr. Boddy was supposedly killed, snuck past everyone and back into the secret passage to kill the blackmailer in the study (and then carry him to the bathroom). Perhaps that's why the flashback shot of her moving through the freezer and into the secret passage was tossed. It might be easier for audiences to believe that she slipped out of the kitchen door and down the hallway to kill Mr. Boddy instead of using the secret passage.

But even if Mrs. Peacock didn't use the passage to kill Mr. Boddy, she certainly had to use it to murder the Motorist. While attempts to explain how some of the guests learned about the secret passages are made in other endings, none is offered here for how this woman, presumably a first-time visitor to Hill House, hundreds of miles from her home in Washington, DC, knows about them. First, she had to swap the key to the weapons cupboard while all the guests were huddled around Wadsworth. Then, when they split up to search the house (which she had adamantly opposed), she would have had to make her way past Professor Plum in the cellar, climb the stairs, enter the study, destroy the evidence in the fireplace, unlock the cupboard, grab the wrench, make her way back down the hall to the conservatory, take the secret passage to the lounge, murder the Motorist, return to the conservatory through the secret passage, and return to the cellar, all without being seen by her partner or by Colonel Mustard and Miss Scarlet as they searched the ground floor. If it's not impossible, it's also not likely.

After the gloved hand shuts off the power before the last three murders, there's a cut to Mrs. Peacock in the cellar. She backs into an air duct from the furnace and turns and begins hitting it with her purse, convinced it's Professor Plum or perhaps the murderer (or both). Other endings suffer from the same problem: after the power goes out, brief shots show characters in places they almost certainly wouldn't be if they had just shut off the electricity. In this case, it means Mrs. Peacock would've climbed the cellar stairs, shut off the power, returned back down the stairs, then gone back up again to retrieve the weapons and commit the murders. And there's one more problem with ending A: in real life, motive isn't always important to investigators. By definition, murder is an irrational act that often defies logic or reason. When one person has premeditatedly killed another, we are well outside the realm of normal or predictable behavior. But in detective stories, motive is central to the plot. It has to be, so that the detective can solve the mystery. The why is as important as the who, the how, and the when. What, then, was Mrs. Peacock's motive? In the case of the cook and Mr. Boddy, revenge for betrayal and blackmail. It's straightforward enough and makes sense, at least in the realm of murder mysteries. But why kill the other four? Wadsworth answers Peacock when she asks that same question: because Mr. Boddy may have told them about her. It's a terribly weak motive, especially considering that Mrs. Peacock watched the other guests learn her secrets when Wadsworth first explained why they were all being blackmailed. Why kill people who *might* have known when all around her are people who *did* know?

Still, toss out the cut to Mrs. Peacock back in the cellar when the power goes off and her character could have committed the murders, even as far-fetched as her motive was.

## Ending B

An "everyone did it" ending is a nice homage to the Golden Age of Detective Fiction, especially Christie and *Murder on the Orient Express*. But in this case, while some clues are hiding in plain sight, others are impossible to know or guess. We might deduce that the cook worked for Mrs. Peacock and that Peacock was missing in the billiard room when the others found Yvette screaming, but there are no hints that Miss Scarlet bribed the cop or that the Singing Telegram Girl had an affair with Professor Plum. Instead, viewers learn about the connections through exposition and are shown only later how the murders could have been committed. Hill's original vision of an expertly crafted whodunit that audiences could solve sitting in their seats was incompatible with a movie that needed to be around ninety minutes long and include multiple endings. A mystery writer has hundreds of pages to lay out all of their hints, traps, and red herrings. Lynn had an hour and a half.

Most of ending B was shot on July 15 and from July 23 to July 26, the bulk of it taking place in the hall. Scenes in other rooms were filmed earlier, when Wadsworth began reenacting the events of the evening. The butler starts by explaining that it was Professor Plum who killed Mr. Boddy. Wadsworth had previously explained that the person who killed Boddy had slipped through the secret passage in the kitchen while everyone else was distracted by the cook's body. A single shot shows Professor Plum (and Mrs. Peacock, for ending A to work) missing in the kitchen, but no flashback scenes were shot of Plum sneaking through the freezer and into the passage or killing Mr. Boddy.

Miss Scarlet exclaims that Professor Plum had to be the culprit because he was missing from the kitchen when Boddy was murdered, but Mr. Green quickly points out that Plum couldn't have killed Mrs. Ho because he was with them in the billiard room. He couldn't, in other words, have killed them both. But when Mrs. Peacock disagrees, trying to cast the blame on Plum, Wadsworth pivots, now accusing her of killing the cook. In a scene filmed on July 12, he takes them into the kitchen to explain how Peacock knew Mrs. Ho. In the first-draft screenplay, all the guests announce that they feel sick upon learning that they ate monkey brains. When asked if that's what they really ate,

Wadsworth replies, "I'm afraid so." This was deleted by the second draft.

Several more flashback scenes were shot for ending B, with Colonel Mustard figuring in them the most. As Wadsworth's voice-over explains how Mustard killed the Motorist, we see the colonel take the key from Wadsworth's pocket, enter the study to destroy evidence, unlock the cupboard, and then commit the murder. The shot of Mustard crossing the hall to the study was the earliest flashback filmed, on June 17; the rest were shot on separate days throughout the production. To help identify the flashbacks, John Morris came up with a cue that hovers between dreamlike and sinister, tipping off viewers that they've jumped back in time to earlier in the evening.

Next, it was Mrs. White's turn. On July 15, the production got a crane shot of Curry dragging Madeline Kahn partway up the stairs before he climbed the rest of the way up and stopped at the top. Wadsworth accuses Mrs. White of killing Yvette, and a flashback shows her carrying her shoes down the stairs, shutting off the power, getting the rope, and strangling the maid. Ten days later, on July 25, Kahn ad-libbed the most famous part of the movie, stammering about flames on the side of her face as the rest of the cast stares in amazement. She improvised the line in rehearsals, and, after her first take, Lynn thought about getting another with her saying the line originally as written. But Kahn was so good they didn't bother; instead, they got another take of her redoing the flames line. They shot just these two, and they used the second in the final film. It was so funny that Lynn took reaction shots of Mull and Christopher Lloyd looking from one to the other, positively baffled at her ranting. They also got a reaction shot of McKean turning to Wadsworth, then looking agape at Mustard and Plum as White ranted on, but it went unused. The cast and crew knew it was funny, but it's doubtful any of them realized at the time that it would become the most popular line—what Adam Vary calls "The Moment" among fans—in the entire movie.[2]

When Wadsworth moved on to accusing Miss Scarlet, Lynn

---

2 Vary, "Something Terrible Has Happened Here."

filmed two different versions of her in the dark, one a wider shot of her coming from the billiard room and the other a medium shot of Scarlet walking from the study. One would be used in this ending; another would be used in ending D. By and large, the production avoided reusing the same footage for each ending; one exception was the shot of Scarlet raising the lead pipe to hit the Cop over the head. Miss Scarlet, stunned at Wadsworth's inerrant deductions, asks him if he's Perry Mason. While the TV series starring Raymond Burr as the fictitious defense attorney was still three years away from the events of the movie, Erle Stanley Gardner had written over forty Mason novels by 1954 (sometimes as many as three a year), and those had been adapted for radio and several Warner Bros. movies.

The other guests turn on Mr. Green, convinced he must've killed the Singing Telegram Girl, since, as Colonel Mustard points out, "there's nobody else left." In this ending, Green, rather than Wadsworth, uses the ploy of finding the gun to finger the girl's killer. It was, the guests are stunned to learn, Wadsworth. Except he's not Wadsworth—he's Mr. Boddy. The man who pretended to be Mr. Boddy (Lee Ving) was the real butler all along. The shot of Curry moving from the library doorway to confront the guests was an eighty-second take, with reaction shots and close-ups of the other actors cut in. When Wadsworth/Boddy comes clean, Morris's music, spare throughout each of the endings apart from the flashbacks, returns, highlighting the danger to the guests. The man before them with the gun is the mastermind who had not only blackmailed them and tricked them into coming, but was now manipulating them into killing the only people who could turn on him.

The shot of Wadsworth crossing in front of the guests as the camera passes behind them needed only two takes. The crew took seven shots of Mr. Green shooting Wadsworth/Boddy and nine of Wadsworth firing back. Three of the nine were unusable because Curry's prop gun misfired.

Until Wadsworth reveals himself as Mr. Boddy, this ending was largely the same across all of the script drafts. After Boddy reveals his true identity, there are several changes from the first to the last draft. In the first draft, when the guests ask Wadsworth/Boddy what his motive for killing the Singing Telegram Girl was, he tells them he had to because "nobody else did." Professor Plum asks who was pretending to be Mr. Boddy (the man Plum killed earlier with the candlestick), and upon learning it was Boddy's butler, yells, "Shit!" Mr. Boddy shuts off the tape recorder that has been running the entire evening and gathers up the reels to ensure there is no evidence against him. But in this first-draft screenplay, he isn't done yet; he has one more bombshell. He's poisoned them all with the champagne he served at the beginning of the evening. That, he explains, is why they feel sick, not because they ate monkey brains. The blackmailer leaves through the front door but is confronted by the Evangelist, who addresses him by his real name—Mr. Boddy. Just as Mrs. Peacock did in ending A, Boddy asks the Evangelist how he knows his name; the Evangelist responds that "The kingdom of God is at hand," and he guns him down. As the real Mr. Boddy dies, the Evangelist tells him that he was sent by J. Edgar Hoover, who is an expert on Armageddon.

All of this was changed over the next two script drafts. The profanity is eliminated and the dialogue tightened and simplified. The poisoned champagne is dropped altogether, and the tape recorder is shut off when they all go to check on Yvette. In the second draft, Mr. Green is promoted to FBI agent, and he shoots and kills Wadsworth in the hall. It wasn't until a late revision just before filming began that another bit of dialogue was added, one that would become the last line in the movie when the three endings were put together for the home video version. Mr. Green smiles at the Evangelist, now revealed to be a police chief, and says, "I'm going to go home and sleep with my wife."

Audiences might be able to work out the first two murders in ending B, at least in theory. The sharpest-eyed viewers might spot that Professor Plum was missing in one shot in the kitchen when the cook was found dead. They might even have spotted the blood on Mr. Boddy's ear after he feigns death and worked out that Plum, who was gifted the revolver, had fired the bullet that just missed. A stretch, to be sure, since he told them that someone tried to grab the gun from him. It's a plausible lie, given that no one would want to use their own weapon to kill Mr. Boddy when the lights go out, since they would be immediately fingered as the murderer. But however easy it may or may not be to deduce, at least the clues are there.

The same is true for the murder of the cook. Mrs. Peacock did say, as Wadsworth explains in this ending as well as ending A, that she was eating one of her favorite recipes. To most viewers, it's a throwaway comment, or perhaps a baffling one. Only the keenest detective fiction fans, accustomed to major revelations disguised as harmless asides, might recognize it as a clue. Wadsworth went to great pains during dinner to hide the cook from Mrs. Peacock. And like the murder of Mr. Boddy, this death takes place while everyone is still on the ground floor. Peacock is the one missing when they all crowd into the billiard room to check on Yvette.

The murder of the Motorist by Colonel Mustard is difficult, but not impossible. He tells Scarlet he'll check the kitchen while she searches the ballroom. But this killing involves much more than sneaking through the secret passage in the conservatory to get to the lounge. Mustard has to steal the key from Wadsworth's pocket, convince everyone to split up, go to the study, destroy the evidence, get the wrench, go through the secret passage, kill the Motorist, and then make his way back down the passage to reunite with Miss Scarlet. It's tough to pull off, but doable.

The same cannot be said for two of the three remaining murders. Mrs. White's killing of Yvette, at least as depicted in the final film, is the unlikeliest—in this ending or any other. According to Wadsworth, she "hurried downstairs" and shut off the electricity. But seventeen seconds later, she is back upstairs in the dark nursery, yelling after a window blown open frightens her. Her yells echo through the house even as Yvette makes her way down the main staircase to the ground floor. From there, Yvette crosses to the billiard room and is told by her killer to close the door. The rope lands around Yvette's neck, and the noose tightens. Just a few moments later, after the Singing Telegram Girl is shot, Mrs. White is standing exactly where we last saw her, in front of the window by the large jack-in-the-box. In order for Mrs. White to have murdered Yvette, she would have had to make her way downstairs, turn off the power, grab the rope, gone back upstairs, scream when the window burst open, make her way back downstairs (while her screams were still emanating from upstairs) and into the billiard room before Yvette arrives. Then she would've had to go back to the nursery to stand in the exact same spot she was standing in before.

Miss Scarlet would have had a much easier time killing the Cop. She and Colonel Mustard get separated in the ballroom, and she could have made it to the study to get the lead pipe, then let herself quietly into the library (Wadsworth left the key in the lock) to bash the Cop over the head. But the final murder, Wadsworth's killing of the Singing Telegram Girl, is almost as unlikely as Mrs. White's killing of Yvette. Just as there are shots of Mrs. Peacock in the cellar and Mrs. White in the nursery after the power goes out, there are brief shots of Wadsworth upstairs in the dressing room that make it almost impossible for him to have been in the hall to shoot the girl. An entire scene was filmed in which Curry falls onto a table and is unable to get back up, but it was cut, and a note was added to the shot log telling editors not to use the footage after Lynn realized that too much screen time of Wadsworth upstairs would make it impossible for him to have killed the Singing Telegram Girl (or everyone, in ending C). Even so, it's difficult to believe Wadsworth has no problem finding his way out of the dressing room and the bedroom to get downstairs in time (apparently not passing Mrs. White on the stairs or Miss Scarlet in the hall) to kill the girl, then go back upstairs and promptly get lost once more until he ends up soaking wet in the shower.

Another issue with ending B: Why, if Wadsworth is in fact Mr. Boddy, would his butler agree to pretend to be him for the evening? Fans might dream up any number of reasons—money topping the list. But in the film, and across all the screenplay drafts, the question goes unanswered.

Finally, how did the guests know about the secret passages? When asked that question by Josh Brandon, Lynn's answer was simple: "I don't know."[3]

---

3 Brandon and Lynn, "*Clue*: The Director's Commentary Track," 2:06:15.

## Ending C

*Clue* fans I've spoken to have known for years of a fourth ending, but details were sparse. Over time, the internet provided some answers. Wikipedia, IMDB, and fan sites all include summaries of *Clue*'s fourth, deleted solution, taken from Lynn's screenplay, the *Clue* storybook that was issued in support of the movie, and Michael McDowell's novelization of the film. The now-out-of-print storybook and novelization both command significant sums of money from fans and collectors eager to see the ending with their own eyes. But the fact that it exists on paper doesn't solve the mystery of whether it was ever filmed. The answer is it was, and using the script, the shot list, unreleased publicity stills, and a few other sources, one can recreate ending C.[4]

After Wadsworth throws the power back on, he begins the same way he does in the other endings, walking everyone through the first murders. He runs to the front door to mimic the death of the Singing Telegram Girl, then announces that the killer ran back to the cellar. The guests take a second to realize the implication of what he's saying—the murderer was in the cellar? Once again, as in ending A, Mrs. Peacock tells him that Colonel Mustard wasn't searching the cellar. "No, but you were," comes the butler's reply. "So?" she asks. In ending A, when Wadsworth accuses Peacock, Brennan turns her on a dime into a cold, dangerous killer. This time, however, she is agitated and unnerved. It's then that Wadsworth makes a stunning accusation: she and Professor Plum "were in league with each other." Still standing in the hall, Wadsworth tells everyone that Mrs. Peacock was missing when the cook and Mr. Boddy were killed and that the cook used to work for her.

We cut to a wide shot of the dining room, facing toward the kitchen. Wadsworth runs in, moves around the table, and takes a seat on the left, his back to the windows. The others, having followed close behind, stand on the other side of the table. He goes through the monkey brains speech, and the camera cuts to a close-up of Wadsworth as he

4 All quotes from this recreation come from Lynn, "Clue," shooting script, 119C–127C.

rises. We cut to a medium shot of Mr. Green and Miss Scarlet standing in front of the dining room entrance. "Is that what we ate?" Green asks, referencing the money brains. Scarlet quips, "Are there any brains to be found in Washington, DC?" Another cut takes us to Mrs. Peacock and Professor Plum, who are standing across the table from Wadsworth in front of the small table to the left of the dining room doorway. They look front left to an off-screen Wadsworth, then right to Mr. Green and Miss Scarlet, also off-screen

Mrs. Peacock seems as if she's about to cry. She admits that Mrs. Ho was her cook but is adamant she didn't kill her. Plum chimes in, asking what any of this has to do with him. A dolly shot starts on Wadsworth and follows him as he crosses around the table and stops in front of Mr. Green, Miss Scarlet, Mrs. White, and Colonel Mustard. There is a reaction shot of Peacock and Plum watching Wadsworth suspiciously. The camera cuts back to the butler, who turns to face Professor Plum on his left, and tells him that he knew Mr. Boddy was still alive. He repeats the explanation from ending B: that Plum missed him with the gun and but killed him later when they were in the kitchen. Mr. Green, who is buying Wadsworth's solution, asks if it really had nothing to do with Mrs. White's dead nuclear physicist husband or Mustard's work on the bomb. Of course not, Wadsworth tells them, communism was a red herring.

But Mrs. White is still confused, wondering why Plum and Peacock would murder six people. The two answer in unison: "We didn't!" Unmoved, Wadsworth tells the assembled guests there is no other way it could have happened. Professor Plum is lost in thought. He's concentrating hard as the camera pans with him and he slowly walks out of the dining room and into the hall. The others follow; after a cut, we watch from the dining room through the kitchen hatch as Plum walks into the kitchen toward the freezer. We cut to a wide shot in the kitchen of everyone else entering and stopping on the landing. Then we go back to the long shot through the kitchen hatch as Plum looks to the others, standing off-screen on the landing. The professor addresses Wadsworth, telling him that as the butler, he was the only one who knew about the secret passages. Plum crosses to the kitchen table and explains that Wadsworth was also the one who held the matches when they drew lots; the butler could have arranged for Peacock and Plum to have been paired together. We cut back to inside the kitchen and the group on the landing. Mr. Green, very excited now, says "It's a frame-up!"

Wadsworth angrily denies that he's framing anyone. The camera cuts between wide shots of the group and close-ups of Professor Plum as he announces that it will be easy to find out if Wadsworth is telling the truth. Whoever has the gun is the killer. Wadsworth draws the gun from his pocket and congratulates Plum on his ingenuity. The others move off the landing away from Wadsworth in fear. Miss Scarlet asks him if he really killed the Singing Telegram Girl, but Professor Plum tells them that Wadsworth killed everyone. Shocked, Mr. Green asks if the butler really did it. Lynn intercuts between a close-up of Professor Plum and a group shot of everyone else, with Wadsworth standing off to the side. He is to the left, between Plum and the others. The professor explains to everyone that it was Wadsworth who knew about them all, Wadsworth who brought them to Hill House, and Wadsworth who had the key to the weapons cupboard and the locked rooms. In a close-up, Mrs. Peacock looks left to Wadsworth, who is off-screen, then right, to the others, all also off-screen. The camera cuts back to the group shot and creeps in on Colonel Mustard, who asks how Wadsworth could have killed the cook, since she was killed when they were checking on Yvette in the billiard room, and he was there with them.

The butler tells them that he was lying, and we cut to a flashback showing Wadsworth slipping into the secret passage from the study while the others gather around Mr. Boddy on the floor. His voice-over explains that he killed the cook earlier and that it was easy. Another shot shows him stepping into the kitchen to stab the cook, and then we see him running back down the secret passage. The brief flashback ends, and Mrs. White tells him that the police will arrive soon and he can't possibly get away with it. Wadsworth smiles and tells them the same thing he tells them in two other endings: no one has called the police; they aren't on their way.

Professor Plum has crossed to stand with Mr. Green and Mrs. White. We now cut among shots of those three, a medium shot of Wadsworth, and close and group shots of the others. Miss Scarlet realizes what Wadsworth means about the police not coming and yells out, "Of course not!" Mrs. White asks him why he did it, and he responds with a question of his own: Would they buy it if he told them his motives were noble, that he wanted to get rid of a blackmailer? Mr. Green says no, they wouldn't. Wadsworth merrily tells him he's right. Instead, his motives are rather disturbing.

"All my life has been spent in a struggle for perfection," the butler explains. "I tried to be the perfect husband, but my wife killed herself. I strove to be the perfect butler, but I was driven to killing my employer. So I resolved that, in doing so, I would commit the perfect murder. But there is no pleasure in my triumph without an audience to admire it. So, as none of you has the brains to expose me, I decided to expose myself." Colonel Mustard delivers the same line he gives in ending B—that he shouldn't expose himself with ladies present.

Professor Plum tells Wadsworth that the game is up, that the murders weren't perfect because there are six witnesses to his crimes. But Wadsworth isn't about to go quietly. He has one last trick up his sleeve: he tells the others that soon there will be a dozen bodies lying in the mansion. Mrs. Peacock states the obvious: there are six murders, not twelve. The butler begins laughing like a lunatic and tells them that the champagne they were served in the library when they first arrived was poisoned, and without an antidote, they'll die within three hours.

Wadsworth runs out of the kitchen. We cut to the lounge and a medium shot of the crazed butler as he races in and yanks the phone cord out of the wall. An insert shot shows the cord being ripped from the socket. Back in the hall, the guests have congregated in-between the lounge and the dining room and are watching Wadsworth in shock. He rolls past them, as if on roller skates, from left to right on his way to the library.

In an oral history of *Clue* for *Entertainment Weekly*, Michael McKean remembered of Curry that "at one point he was on a skateboard." Lynn retorted that McKean "has a wonderful imagination. Tim was not on a skateboard. I would remember that."[5] But McKean was partially right: Curry was filmed on roller skates for five of the seven takes of him racing from the lounge to the library to give the effect of Wadsworth appearing to glide through the house. Some of the shots were taken at a slower frame rate to make it appear as if he was moving at a high speed. The butler was crying out, "Ha-ha!" and laughing like a maniac.

Back in the library, the camera points toward the dead Cop on the table. Wadsworth runs in from left to right and grabs the phone, ripping the cord from the wall. The rest of the guests are gathered in the library doorway watching him. In a full shot, he tries to run out of the room, but the others block him. Just then, the doorbell rings. Wadsworth points his gun at the guests and tells them not to move. When he himself tries to leave, they tell him in unison that he just said "Don't move." He pushes through the group, and we cut to a high-angle shot looking down on the hall from the second floor. The guests are gathered at the library door as Wadsworth moves into the hall and toward the front door. Cut to a close-angle dolly shot on Wadsworth moving left to right to answer the door. He opens it; guess who's standing there? Yep, the Evangelist.

Wadsworth says, "I thought we told you to get lost." The Evangelist starts to argue; the butler shows him the gun. This time it's Wadsworth who's in for a surprise. The Evangelist grabs his wrist; the gun goes off, but nobody is hit. Eight cops burst through the front door, guns drawn. We cut to another high-angle shot and see the cops running into the hall. Another cut and we are back in a wide shot with the guests, who run up to the cops, all talking at once, begging for help and telling them they've been poisoned. We cut between this and the high-angle point of view down from the second floor as the cops tell them to put their hands up, pushing them up against the wall. Cops who have been searching the house burst out of the lounge, the billiard room, and the library, all at the same time, and the three say in unison, "There's a body in there!" Another policeman runs out of the study in shock and tells the others that there are three bodies in that room.

5 Lenker, "Red Herrings."

"Three more?" the other cops say.

Wadsworth is on his knees on the front landing, in-between the standing Evangelist and another policeman. The butler asks the Evangelist who he is, and the Evangelist flashes an FBI badge. He's there to clean up the mess, he says. Close-up on Wadsworth, who asks if that's why the FBI is run by a man called Hoover. The guests are frisked by the police, starting with Mr. Green and Mrs. White, with Mrs. Peacock and Colonel Mustard in the background. Mrs. Peacock asks the cop, "Do you know who I am, toots?" They are all looking to the right, where the Evangelist is off-screen holding Wadsworth at gunpoint. The FBI agent asks who's responsible for the murders, and the guests point and announce in unison that Wadsworth is. We continue to cut between the medium shot of the Evangelist and Wadsworth and a close-up of Wadsworth. The Evangelist asks if this is true, and Wadsworth, rising, announces that it was the perfect murder.

Another high-angle shot shows us Wadsworth moving everyone back to clear a space. He explains that he is going to retell the events of the evening all over again. We cut back to a medium shot of Wadsworth, once more at high speed. He's speed talking, telling the guests that Yvette was in the library and the cook was in the kitchen and the doorbell rang. He throws open the front door—but instead of mimicking what happened earlier, he runs outside and slams the doors in an effort to escape. We cut to the front portico as Wadsworth quickly locks the door. From on high, the camera shows us the cops and guests running to the front door and beginning to beat on it.

Wadsworth runs down the front steps, the camera dollying alongside him. He checks two cars before finding one that's unlocked. He starts to drive off, and we cut back inside the mansion to the conservatory. The cops and guests have realized there is no other way out. Using a two-camera setup, one inside the conservatory and one out, Lynn films the cops and guests breaking through the glass and running off-screen left to right in pursuit of Wadsworth. The camera outside the conservatory is filming at forty-eight frames per second to show the glass breaking in slow motion. Between the shattering window panes and the guests and the cops yelling, the noise is deafening.

Inside the car, the camera is close up on Wadsworth, who's laughing maniacally once again. His nose wrinkles. He begins to sniff, then turns and looks in the back of the car. A handheld camera picks up the action before a cut to the final shot, from Wadsworth's point of view: two Doberman are rising from the back seat, snapping and snarling.

Ending C was filmed over several days in July, with the final shots finished in August. While most of the other endings take place in the hall, with occasional flashbacks or brief visits to other rooms, ending C bounces through five different rooms, the front driveway, and the interior of a car. In many ways it was the toughest ending to shoot. Curry had to don roller skates, and the shot approaches varied more than in the other endings. But it didn't test well with preview audiences, who didn't find it as funny and who were confused by Wadsworth's motives. Lynn agreed with their assessment.

It started out much differently from what was filmed. In the first draft, Wadsworth's motivation is not perfection, but greed. He has decided to take over Mr. Boddy's blackmail scheme, convinced he could convert it into a million-dollar venture. He calls Boddy "small time" and tells the guests he no longer wants their money, which he considers chump change. No, he wants the secrets from the state department, from defense contracts, and from the government's nuclear program. In this early version, he hasn't poisoned them, and he is quite sane. Rather than run through the mansion pulling out the phones, Wadsworth calmly explains why he'll never be caught. The doorbell rings, and Wadsworth lets in the FBI and the police. But he denies everything when the guests tell the cops what happened. The final shot is the camera closing in on the clicking noise of the still-running tape recorder in the billiard room; Wadsworth's entire confession has been recorded.

An ending in which the butler did it is a nod to what is believed to be an age-old detective story trope. However, in reality, the butler rarely did it in traditional detective fiction. This ending suffers from many of the same problems as endings A and B. Once again, reasonable explanations exist for the early murders, while the details of how he pulled off the later killings are largely ignored. The flashback shows how Wadsworth killed the cook first, and it is possible to believe he killed Mr. Boddy. He had the key to the weapons cupboard, but how did he make it downstairs to kill the Motorist? And later, to shut off the power and kill three more people? None of it is really explained.

Although Paramount has never released ending C as a bonus feature on DVD or Blu-ray, it is possible to see a blink-and-you-miss-it clip. In a thirty-second TV spot advertising *Clue*, there's a cut to Professor Plum gesturing to himself and asking, "What has it got to do with me?" The TV ad is, as of this writing, available online at sites like YouTube and Internet Archive. Stills and promotional images from the fourth ending have made their way to the internet, including a photo from the children's storybook of the Evangelist punching Wadsworth in the stomach.

### Ending D

Ending D begins just as the other three do, with Wadsworth throwing the power back on and launching into his explanation of who did it, where it was done, and with what weapon. He stuns the guests by telling them that none of them killed Mrs. Ho or Mr. Boddy; it was Yvette. The events in the hall for this ending were filmed over three days, July 29–31. All of the flashbacks of Yvette committing the murders were filmed on different days, two in June and four in July. Considerable footage was taken of Curry reenacting the murders; ten takes were shot of Wadsworth mimicking how Yvette had sneaked into the study to swipe the knife. But nearly all of the footage of Curry recreating the murders was cut in favor of a voice-over explanation by Wadsworth as flashbacks were shown of Yvette stealing the dagger, stabbing the cook, returning to the billiard room, and later killing Mr. Boddy. Some of the deleted footage was heavy on physical comedy. Wadsworth explains that after Yvette took the dagger, she went into the dining room and through the swinging door into the kitchen to kill the cook. As Wadsworth reenacts this, the door smashes into Mr. Green and Colonel Mustard, throwing them back into the other guests before they can finally push their way through to the kitchen.

These shots were discarded in editing to maintain the film's brisk pace. Watching Curry ricochet from room to room could have been funny, but there was no need to show both the flashbacks (which had been planned all along) and Wadsworth's reenactment.

After Yvette kills the cook and screams—a phony scream in this ending—she returns with everyone to the study. When the others realize that the only other person in the house is the cook, they jump up, Yvette with them. But she isn't seen running down the hall, and she never appears in the kitchen. Unlike in ending A and B, where someone has to break away from the group to kill Mr. Boddy, Yvette stays behind in the study to follow him. She hides behind the sofa, and when Boddy rises, she follows and kills him with the candlestick. From there, she drags his corpse to the bathroom.

When Wadsworth is asked why she did it, he gives an odd answer: "To create confusion!" She was, it turns out, acting under orders—Miss Scarlet's. Scarlet is the mastermind in this ending, convincing Yvette to kill two people before Scarlet herself kills the rest of the victims—including the maid. More footage was taken of Curry showing how it was done. Once again he donned roller skates; Lynn called for thirteen of Wadsworth whizzing by the rest of the guests as he reenacted how Scarlet went from the study to the billiard room to kill Yvette. Two additional takes were filmed of Wadsworth without the skates, running by the guests instead. But this too was cut, along with eleven takes of Wadsworth demonstrating how Scarlet killed the cop in the library. Other reenactment footage of Curry also went unused. Instead, the butler's voice-over returns, and flashbacks show Miss Scarlet taking the weapons out of the cupboard, strangling Yvette, bludgeoning the Cop, and shooting the Singing Telegram Girl.

Confronted, Scarlet takes out the gun and confesses. She reveals that her real business is "secrets," an idea Lynn later said was inspired by Hitchcock's *North by Northwest*, when Cary Grant learns that the villainous Phillip Vandamm is "a sort of importer-exporter . . . of government secrets."[6] Trading in valuable US intelligence was part of the *Clue* plot from the beginning, and ending D remained largely unchanged throughout all versions of the script, with just a few minor revisions and one addition. In the first draft, Scarlet tells the others she is planning to blackmail them just as Mr. Boddy did, but now

---

6 Hitchcock, *North by Northwest*, 1:37:55.

she can hold murder over their heads as well. By the second draft, this line becomes the one spoken in the final film about Professor Plum's reputation not being helped when it's discovered that he was involved in six murders, including that of his former patient. The "one plus two plus two plus one" dialogue between Wadsworth and Miss Scarlet, now a fan favorite, was not added until a later revision, in April 1985. But it was an inspired idea, and a reaction shot of the other guests doing the math on their fingers was filmed, though it went unused. In the final movie, they can still be glimpsed in the background trying to add everything up.

Curry and Warren's showdown was filmed on July 30 and needed several takes, though only the last three were usable. After Wadsworth grabs the gun, the police rush in, detain everyone, and quickly search the house. As in ending C, some of the cops originally had lines announcing that they had discovered bodies in the various rooms. In the first draft, Lynn wrapped up this solution with a line from the Evangelist that appeared in other endings: "Mr. Hoover is an expert on Armageddon." In the third draft he switched it to Wadsworth's nod to *Gone with the Wind*, "Frankly Scarlet, I don't give a damn." In his later revisions, he added the chandelier falling behind Martin Mull.

The insert shots from earlier in the film of the chandelier hanging from the false ceiling and spinning after it was hit by the bullet were reused. Two cameras were set up to film the crash. The scene was shot in one take on July 31; one camera shot at thirty-four frames per second and the other at thirty-eight. Lynn felt more comfortable with this drop, since none of the actors were moving, so therefore no stunt doubles were used. The glass was a breakaway prop. All of the endings, including this one, stop with a freeze frame. In theaters, where only one ending was included at each showing, "Shake, Rattle, and Roll" played as the credits rolled. On the home video release, which includes all three solutions, Morris's score and title cards transition from one ending to the next.

Ending D, among die-hard *Clue* aficionados, is usually considered the fairest—that is, the most plausible. When Lynn submitted his third-draft screenplay to Paramount in January 1985, script reader Julie Lantz liked this ending the best and recommended that it be used if the studio decided to drop the multiple-ending plan. She especially thought the twist of Miss Scarlet using her brothel as a cover for spying was marvelous. While many fans I've spoken to prefer ending B, in which everyone "did it," ending D, while not without problems, makes the most sense. Of all the guests, Miss Scarlet as the killer—with the help of one of her sex workers—holds up best when compared with the rest of the movie. Warren played Scarlet as cunning and ruthless. She seems to be enjoying herself when others are squirming. For her to recognize the opportunity the evening presents—to kill off Mr. Boddy and his informers and essentially take over his business—is certainly in character. She explains that she is already in the business of secrets, and now is her chance to uncover even more. Her motive makes more sense than Mrs. Peacock's or Wadsworth's and blends well with the theme of corruption in capitalism.

The logistics of carrying out the murders also work best in this ending. Wadsworth goes to pains to show how everything was pulled off in ways that he doesn't for the other endings. He explains why they didn't hear the cook scream when she was stabbed; he points out that Miss Scarlet was on the ground floor, which made it easy for her to shut off the power; and he tells everyone that Yvette informed her of the secret passages. Yvette meeting Miss Scarlet in the billiard room with the power out also works well. Why would Mrs. Peacock or Mrs. White or Wadsworth think to go in there and wait for her? How would they know to ask her how things were going? But a prearranged meeting with her boss makes sense, though Yvette's surprise line "It's you!" is a little at odds with this idea.

Not everything works well. It's still a little unclear how Yvette was supposed to hide the cook's body in the freezer or drag Mr. Boddy to the bathroom, especially without being noticed while everyone was in the kitchen. Remember too that she was not a real maid and didn't work at Hill House; she was there only for that evening. So how, exactly, did she know about the secret passage?

Just as in the other endings, the person who killed the Motorist had to not only sneak away and know about the passage, they also had to steal the key to the cupboard from Wadsworth's pocket and destroy the evidence. In this case, Miss Scarlet makes the most sense, since she was on the ground floor. The shot of her slowly making her way across the ballroom floor to check behind the curtain while Colonel Mustard is in the kitchen doesn't give her a lot of time. We might also ask why she'd bother checking behind the curtain at all, given that she knows who the murderer is. But it's more likely that she, rather than someone who was upstairs or downstairs, could have killed the Motorist. The same is true for shutting off the power and killing the final three victims.

On August 8, the brief clip of Lesley Ann Warren firing the gun at the Singing Telegram Girl was filmed. It was the last day anyone from the main cast would be on set. Production moved August 9 to Franklin Canyon to film the Cop (Bill Henderson) finding the Motorist's car on the side of the road. Monday, August 12, was the final day of photography, to capture footage of those pesky dogs—jumping over the camera, snarling, and grabbing Wadsworth's coat. The last shot filmed was of two dogs rising up into the camera frame in the back of the car, ready to attack Wadsworth in ending C.

Principal photography finally wrapped, nine days over schedule. Postproduction came next; Lynn would have to commute between London and Los Angeles to finish his movie.

# PART III
## *THE LAST LAUGH*

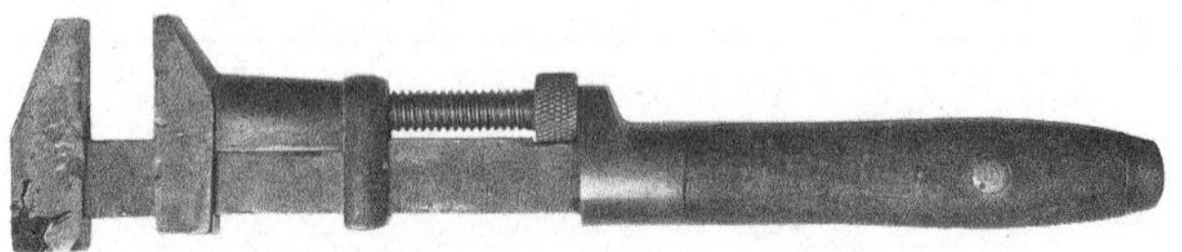

# 9. DÉNOUEMENT

"I saw the look of horror on the film publicist's face as I was talking."
-Jonathan Lynn[1]

After production ended, the producers threw a wrap party. It was a fun, if mostly low-key, event. One memorable attendee was Jonathan Lynn's son, Teddy, who had worked as a gofer on the set. He showed up with his hair outlandishly dyed, in hues of purple, red, and green. Everyone gawked for a moment, then Madeline Kahn approached him and "complimented him on it and danced with him for much of the evening."[2] The time with Kahn meant a lot to Teddy.

Although principal photography was complete and the actors would go on to other projects, much work remained to be done. Lynn would spend the next few months enmeshed in editing. A Writer's Guild of America arbitration hearing was set to determine writing credits for the movie. The sound needed to be completed—effects, Foley work, and ADR (automated dialogue replacement). Although *Clue* was not a visual-effects laden film, Bill Taylor and Syd Dutton needed time to prepare the matte painting of Hill House with the lightning strikes. John Morris would soon get to work recording the film's score. Paramount had hired Michael McDowell in June to write the novelization, and he was busy toiling away. Odd as it might seem for a movie filled with

1 Bygrave, "Man Whodunnit."

2 Madison, *Madeline Kahn*, 222.

murder, sexual innuendo, and jokes about the Red Scare, a children's storybook would be released. Test screenings would be scheduled to gauge audience interest and to help determine a marketing strategy. Advertising needed to be arranged—there would be a trailer, three TV spots, and ad buys in magazines and newspapers and on billboards and radio. Plans were being made for the stars of the movie to appear on late-night talk shows. Prints had to be duplicated and shipped to theaters across the country—normally a routine process but complicated here by the multiple endings. The world premiere in New York needed to be planned. *Clue*, in other words, was far from finished.

Plus, it wasn't the only thing Lynn had on his plate. Some six thousand miles away from Hollywood, filming was underway on the new season of *Yes Minister*, now retitled *Yes, Prime Minister* to reflect Jim Hacker's promotion to the head of the UK government. Juggling both projects, Lynn commuted from Los Angeles to London every week for ten agonizing weeks. If this sounds exciting, Lynn insists it was not. He had "never been quite so disorientated or exhausted" before.[3] In 1985, even on a direct flight, this meant Lynn was spending a full day in the air each week, plus making the long drives to and from Los Angeles International Airport and Heathrow Airport. He remembered once spending four days editing *Clue* in LA, then three in London working with Anthony Jay on their popular series, but it was probably closer to three and a half days in LA and two and a half days in London just to accommodate all of his travel. The eight-hour time zone difference meant the forty-two-year-old director would arrive in London nearly a full day after he left Los Angeles, then a few days later he'd fly out and get some of that time back. It was a dizzying schedule.

*Clue* producers and Paramount Pictures were required to submit a notice to the Writer's Guild of America of the proposed writing credits on the film, and they did so just two days after filming completed. Who gets ultimate credit as the writer can be contentious when more than one person has worked on the screenplay or contributed story ideas—which is almost always the case. Being a credited screenwriter

---

3 Lynn, interview with *Movies and Stuff*.

on a hit movie guarantees future work and potential earnings from sequels. In the case of *Clue*, the proposed story credit for John Landis, who was also an executive producer, triggered the guild's automatic arbitration process, set up to ensure that a producer isn't trying to score an unearned writing credit.

Although the WGA's review was not contentious on *Clue*, it still required Paramount Pictures to send notices of the arbitration to Parker Brothers and to agents, managers, and attorneys for Debra Hill, Landis, Warren Manzi, and Lynn. The first proposed credits were filed on August 14, 1985, for "Screenplay by Jonathan Lynn" and "Adaptation by John Landis and Jonathan Lynn," with the possible addition of "Based upon the Parker Brothers' Board Game 'Clue'®." Submitted for the arbitration were a copy of the board game and rule book, Hill's 1980 three-page treatment, both of Manzi's screenplays, three of Lynn's drafts and subsequent revisions, a transcript of Landis's pitch to Tom Stoppard given on February 7, 1983, and the final shooting script. All of this documentation established that none of Hill's original ideas were used, nor was anything from Manzi's screenplays that hadn't already come from Landis. But the transcript between Landis and Stoppard did show that the basic plot and the characters not in the board game were Landis's ideas. A month later, on September 16, the WGA legal department responded with the final writing credits: "Screenplay by Jonathan Lynn, Story by John Landis and Jonathan Lynn, Based Upon the Parker Brothers' Board Game Clue®."

While writing credits were being finalized, mixers, Foley artists, and sound editors were creating the film's soundtrack. Foley recreates the noises heard throughout movies that might not be picked up by microphones on set, especially sounds that sync up with the action visualized on-screen—footsteps across the hall, for example. The ringing telephone, the cook sharpening a knife, the front door slamming, the candlestick clattering to the ground—all of these would be either recreated by Foley artists or taken from stock sound-effects libraries.

Dubbing was another essential part of the sound process. ADR is a common practice; film footage might be perfect, but the dialogue could be off. Keeping the take is possible by rerecording the actors reading their lines in a sound booth under more controlled conditions than those on a noisy film set. All the actors would loop at least some of their lines. According to Michael McKean, all of Lee Ving's lines were dubbed with another actor. Ving's character is alive for only about twelve minutes of screen time, and he is quietly brooding for most of that, so dubbing his voice didn't represent an insurmountable challenge. Many of Mr. Boddy's lines are heard only after the camera has cut away from his face or his back is to the camera. Fans have speculated that the voice belongs to actor Joe Mantegna. Director Jeff Smith reached out to Mantegna, however, and confirmed that it is not his.

As editing continued, Lynn and editors David Bretherton and Richard Haines selected the takes they felt worked best as part of a cohesive whole. The film began to come together, with some shots and scenes snipped to keep the movie about ninety minutes long. A rough cut was assembled for producers and studio execs to watch and provide feedback to, and then another cut, this one incorporating that feedback, was made for test audiences. That version included a temporary score and did not have the matte painting effects, still unfinished.

Test screenings are easy to mock; in the never-ending pursuit of the broadest possible audience, movies can be dumbed down, sapped of creativity, and quickly forgotten as the drive to please everyone ends up pleasing no one. But Lynn welcomed the test screenings. He had been living and breathing *Clue* since the fall of 1983. He wrote the jokes, then rewrote them, tinkered with them, and finessed them to get the best possible script. He had heard those same jokes in rehearsals. He'd heard them spoken in take after take during filming. In the editing room, trying to find the best line, the best reading, the best moment, the jokes played over and over again. After such endless repetition, it's easy enough for someone to lose any accurate sense of what's funny and what's not, what's working and what isn't. Lynn therefore found the test-screening process valuable. "Nobody," he writes, "knows what is funny until we have seen and heard the audience's reaction."[4]

Lynn remembers only a few test screenings. Afterward, moves were

4 Lynn, *Comedy Rules*, 10.

made to tighten the movie even further, including additional cuts to the footage taken on Stage 17 in the upstairs rooms. But the biggest casualty was ending C—the one where the butler did it. Audiences scored it the lowest of the four. Lynn would say it was because it wasn't as funny. Over the years, he and the cast have been asked about it often, and no one seems to remember it well. Lynn would frequently say he couldn't recall it, and if he went beyond that answer, he'd only offer that it wasn't funny and didn't work. Some cast members remembered that it seemed to involve Curry, but never said much more than that. Rather than go to theaters with four different endings for audiences to choose from, *Clue* would go with three.

After the test screenings were held in September 1985, marketing was ramped up to promote the movie. Throughout the summer, newspapers and magazines had reported on *Clue*, the first movie based on a board game. Bigger media outlets and local Los Angeles papers had attended press day on the set before shooting began and incorporated the visit into their coverage. Others had arranged phone calls and interviews with Lynn and Hill. Smaller newspapers relied on the press kits Paramount had mailed out en masse. The kit was packaged in a black folder with a spinning wheel on the front and each of the actors' faces; spin the wheel to land on who might have done it. Inside were nineteen promotional photos of the actors, stills from the movie, and shots of Lynn directing on set. The stills included not just the seven main stars, but also Colleen Camp, Lee Ving, Bill Henderson, Kellye Nakahara, and Jane Wiedlin (Jeffrey Kramer was strangely absent). A thirty-two-page *Handbook of Production Information* was also included.

The handbook has been prized by *Clue* devotees eager to learn more details about the making of the movie. It features biographies of the actors, producers, and crew members. While short on plot points to avoid spoilers in the press, it offers details on the set design, boasting of the antiques collected for use in the film and the expense of the massive mansion on Stage 18. Reporters who opted to do a story on *Clue* for their local paper could, and often did, write an entire piece relying only on the studio-produced handbook and its preselected quotes and friendly information. Throughout 1985, well over one hundred papers either ran their own story on the movie or reprinted Associated Press reporter Bob Thomas's article on the production. Before Adam Vary's 2013 *Buzzfeed* oral history, much of what fans could find online about the making of *Clue* came from the *Handbook of Production Information*.

The stories churned out in 1985 were almost universally positive for Paramount and the producers. Journalists dutifully quoted Lynn and Hill. They wrote about the antiques and the elaborate set on Stage 18. Some of them got interviews with the cast and passed on funny quotes to their readers. It was all part of a familiar dance between studios and the press. Reporters knew that subscribers enjoyed light fare about Hollywood tucked away in the entertainment section, and studios knew that they could get free publicity. Best of all, these articles lent an air of mystery to the movie by reporting on the secrecy surrounding the endings. Depending on the story, *Clue* was either filmed with multiple endings so that even the cast wouldn't know whodunit or was filmed with one ending only but the stars signed NDAs expressly prohibiting them from revealing what happens. Or perhaps it was filmed with more than one ending but Paramount wasn't sure which it was going to do—should it use all of them, one of them, or some of them? The uncertainty around the ending was a ploy by Hill. Hollywood wasn't nearly as spoiler averse as it has become, but she wanted to keep audiences guessing, especially with three endings to see.

As these stories appeared, work continued on finalizing the film audiences would see in just a couple of months. Taylor and Dutton spent weeks finessing the effects and the matte painting. They juggled multiple projects at a time; they'd work on *Clue* for a few days, move on to something else, then return to the matte painting after a week or two. They performed dozens of camera tests, adjusting the intensity of the light and the flash of the lightning. The duo sent film to Lynn at the end of September, then provided several more shots throughout November. The last shot was turned in on November 22, just three weeks before the picture was scheduled to open.

Morris finished the score in mid-October and recorded it on the Paramount lot from October 21 to October 24 in the now-demolished Studio M. There were a total of seventy-two cues, including "Shake, Rattle, and Roll" and "Sh-Boom." Most of Morris's cues were less than a minute long, cutting in and out to add gravity or levity to scenes as necessary. The cues were named after dialogue or moments in the film. Cue 33, for example, played during Colonel Mustard and Miss Scarlet's discovery of the secret passage from the conservatory to the lounge. It is titled "I've Had a Good Life," lasts twenty-two seconds, and fades out after the fireplace slams shut. Musical scores released on CD or vinyl are prepared so as to sound more like a complete performance. This can be especially challenging for comedies, which tend to have shorter and more abrupt cues. They are combined into longer musical tracks, trimmed, and edited, and fade-ins and -outs are added. The *Clue* soundtrack was not released in 1985 and was unavailable until La-La Land Records released a limited edition CD in 2011.

Morris was born in Elizabeth, New Jersey, in 1926. He became enamored with the piano at a very young age, and his parents bought one for him. He went on to attend Juilliard, but his daughter would say that he was too shy to be a concert pianist. He worked instead as an accompanist and composer on Broadway. He first worked with Mel Brooks on *The Producers*, and he would go on to write the scores for all but two of Brooks's films. Morris was twice nominated for an Oscar, first for *Blazing Saddles* and then for David Lynch's *The Elephant Man* (1980). When Morris died in 2018 at age ninety-one, Brooks called him "my emotional right arm."[5]

Morris's score for *Clue* was meant to be playful and ironic. His scores for other parodies, including *Young Frankenstein* and *Haunted Honeymoon*, feature dramatic, sweeping music that simultaneously celebrates and pokes fun at old studio pictures. Musician Merrill Garbus notes how difficult this balance is, since the music has to be "a little too obvious. . . . Conducting an orchestra to play ironically isn't easy, but Morris does it in such a formidable way."[6] Lynn was pleased with the score and thought Morris was "a terribly nice man."[7] The director attended the recording sessions on the Paramount lot and got a call from producer Peter Guber asking him how it was. Lynn said

5 Sandomir, "John Morris."

6 Hobbs, "Know the Score." Emphasis in original.

7 Schweiger, "Mystery Music."

that it was "fine"—the wrong answer in Hollywood. Thirty minutes later, Guber's Ferrari sped into the studio lot, convinced the score was a mess. Lynn caught on that "great" in Hollywood doesn't apply to just Mozart or Beethoven, and he assured Guber the music was "great."[8] It *is* great, recognized by fans and critics (Kirk Ellis of the *Hollywood Reporter* called it "delightfully tongue-in-cheek") as one of the strongest parts of the movie.[9]

To supplement the press kits, Paramount created an advertising campaign for TV, newspapers, radio, and billboards. The marketing leaned heavily on the public's awareness of the board game and its iconic solution of who did it, with what weapon, and in which room. Paramount also emphasized the novelty of the three different endings.

Only one trailer was produced, using the soundtrack from *Airplane!* because Morris's score wasn't ready when the preview debuted in theaters. *Clue*'s trailer premiered a couple of months before the movie. Inspired by test-audience scores, the trailer and advertising campaign both focused on comedy over mystery. Test audiences liked the movie but were more invested in the laughs than in whodunit. Therefore, the trailer featured much of the film's physical comedy, including deleted scenes in which Mull slaps McKean and four of the characters crash into one another outside the cellar door. But unlike the rest of the ad campaign, the trailer didn't reference the multiple endings, nor did it nod at the board game. The weapons and the rooms were not mentioned at all.

The TV spots, however, crammed it all in. Paramount produced three television commercials—all a variation on whodunit, where, and with what. In each, Morris's music plays frantically as a narrator races to list all the characters, weapons, and rooms. At the end of each thirty-second spot, the narrator asks, "Or did the butler do it?" and then a cut shows Wadsworth answering, "No!" All three ads end when the narrator tells viewers that the movie is "a comedy with three different endings. Whodunit depends on where you see it." The TV spots played

8 Brandon and Lynn, "*Clue*: The Director's Commentary Track," 55:35.

9 Ellis, "Clue."

a few weeks before the movie debuted, letting viewers know it would open on December 13, and continued to air after the movie premiered.

Large newspaper ads greeting the movie's opening weekend asked "Was it . . ." followed by the names of the six suspects, "in the . . ." followed by all the rooms, and "with the . . . " followed by the weapons. Ads in big-city papers boasted that it was "a comedy with three different endings . . . whodunit depends on where you see it." A handful of medium-sized markets got two endings, and the newspaper ad mats were updated to "A comedy with two different endings . . . " Ads were created for weekday editions as well; "*CLUE*: The mystery comedy we dare you to solve" ate up a few inches in newspapers across the country. Other ads asked "Was it . . . " over a picture of a single character and weapon—often the noose at the end of the rope.

Both the ads and theater listings in cities where theaters received more than one ending made a point of printing which theater was showing which solution, designated by the letters A, B, and C. Remember, these endings were listed differently from the way they appeared in the screenplay or on the home video edition. In ending A, everyone did it; ending B, Miss Scarlet and Yvette; and ending C, Mrs. Peacock. Ads in the largest newspapers listed several theaters showing each ending. In the *Los Angeles Times*, for example, a full-page ad announced that ending A was playing in twenty-one theaters from Bakersfield to Oceanside, ending B was in twenty, and ending C could be found in seventeen. In most markets, however, each ending played in only a handful of theaters.

Movie-tie-in books had existed since the 1920s, though they were mostly reserved for the biggest films. By the 1960s and '70s, the promulgation of cheap paperbacks meant that nearly every movie released by a major studio had a tie-in novel. Most, including *Clue*, were stocked in bookstores and at supermarkets on metal racks by the checkout line. These books were based on the shooting script and were often released a few weeks before the film's premiere to generate interest. The thinking went that if someone saw the book in the store, they'd be reminded to see the movie, and people who were excited enough to buy the book were going to see the movie anyway. Spoilers were a concern for the press, since they had large audiences at their disposal. But they were not a major concern for readers; after all, no one in 1985 could take to Twitter or YouTube and tell millions of people the ending of a movie.

Most film novelizations come on the market and are quickly forgotten. But since they are based on the screenplay and not the final cut of the movie, they can include details or entire scenes that were dropped during shooting or editing. *E.T.*'s novelization includes a storyline about Elliott's mom and her romantic interest in Peter Coyote's character. For *Clue*, Paramount sought out a well-known horror writer: Michael McDowell.

McDowell was born in Alabama in 1950. He earned a bachelor's and master's degree from Harvard and a PhD from Brandeis. He wrote over thirty novels, usually horror, but he frequently genre-hopped and published under several pseudonyms. By the mid-1980s, he was writing for such television shows as *Alfred Hitchcock Presents* and *Amazing Stories*. His big Hollywood break came when he wrote the screenplay for *Beetlejuice* (1988). He reunited with director Tim Burton a few years later and was credited with adapting *The Nightmare before Christmas* (1993), though creative differences with Burton saw him replaced by writer Caroline Thompson. In the mid-1990s, McDowell was diagnosed with AIDS, and he lived out his final years with his longtime partner, theater scholar Laurence Senelick. McDowell died in Boston shortly after Christmas in 1999; he had been working on the screenplay for *Beetlejuice 2*. He was forty-nine years old.

Paramount contacted McDowell's agent in July 1985 to gauge the author's interest in novelizing *Clue* as a Fawcett Gold Medal Book—a paperback edition priced inexpensively to get into as many stores as possible. McDowell was offered $10,000 and 2 percent royalties. It wasn't bad, but he wanted a bigger cut of the royalties, so Fawcett countered with a larger advance if he'd stick with the 2 percent of net earnings. He accepted, received Lynn's screenplay in the mail on July 19, and got to work a week later. He was initially thrilled at the four different endings because he was told Fawcett "will publish it in four different editions" and he would "get more money for these three extra sets of endings," since die-hard collectors and mystery fanatics "will want all four books."[10] However, that plan was scrapped, and only one edition was published with all four endings.

Movie novelizations weren't exactly seen as Pulitzer Prize material; they had long been regarded as a quick way to earn a buck. McDowell worried that a *Clue* novel wouldn't be any good, but he stayed with the project. He was a prolific writer, and with Lynn's screenplay as his guide, he cranked out the first draft in a month. McDowell got minor edits back from his agent and publisher, and as he worked on his second draft, he was offered a chance to get to know the film better. He was living in Los Angeles at the time, and on September 9, he drove to Paramount to meet with Lynn and watch an early cut of *Clue*. When he got there, he realized that the showing would happen on the small screen of a Moviola editing machine. Lynn was in the middle of adding the temporary soundtrack for the cut to be shown to test audiences. McDowell took notes on costumes and production design for his second draft, but he was unimpressed with the movie. He had "doubts about the film," though he found Lynn to be "very smart." He thought that while Warren was "really wonderful," Kahn was "dreadful" and Curry was "not quite up to what he should have been."[11] Despite his reservations, he was being well paid for a job that took him less than nine weeks from start to finish. He turned in his final draft to his agent on September 23.

The book was released on November 12, a full month before the movie. The cover was wordy, anxious to catch buyers' eyes: "Paramount Pictures presents *Clue*, a novel by Michael McDowell, based on the screenplay by Jonathan Lynn—A delightful whodunit based upon the famous board game!" The bright red CLUE still sported the ® to let everyone know this was Parker Brothers' property. Six-and-a-half years after the book debuted, McDowell got his final royalty statement. The book had retailed for $2.95 and sold 35,784 copies. Because the *Clue* novelization has the most detailed description of the deleted fourth ending, fans have sought it out, but the days of snapping it up for

---

10 McDowell, Journal, July 19, 1985, in McDowell Collection.

11 McDowell, Journal, September 9, 1985.

$2.95 are long gone. Instead, it commands upward of $300 from used book dealers and at online auction sites.

*Clue* was rated PG and meant to appeal to families, and so the studio took the additional step of releasing a children's storybook. Other 1985 family movies—*The Journey of Natty Gann*, *The Goonies*, *Back to the Future*—also had editions for kids. Although the word "storybook" conjures up images of young children, these books were often marketed to fans of all ages who wanted to see stills from the movie, and the books' covers would advertise that dozens of images were available inside. For *Clue*'s children's tie-in, Paramount hired Ann Matthews to adapt Lynn's screenplay. While she toned down some of the more overt innuendo—Miss Scarlet runs an escort service—much of what appears in the movie is in the book. Professor Plum still has affairs with his patients, and people are still murdered left and right. While today the storybook doesn't sell for quite as much as the novelization, it still routinely fetches $200 or more from online sellers. Fans stay on the lookout for it because it contains images from deleted scenes and alternate takes, such as Mr. Boddy arriving at the front door, Yvette grabbing the champagne bottle in the library, and, most sought after, the Evangelist punching Wadsworth in the fourth ending.

One final ingredient in this marketing stew was booking the stars of the film on late-night talk shows. In the end though, only two appeared: Mull, on *Late Night with David Letterman*, and Kahn, on *The Tonight Show* when it was still under the famed care of Johnny Carson. Booking the stars proved challenged by the timing of the film's release: it was wedged between Thanksgiving and Christmas, a busy time for theaters but a quiet time in Hollywood, when stars, executives, agents, and publicists take time off and business slows until January. Reruns for most shows, including talk shows, were the norm around the holidays. While Mull was able to appear on Letterman's show on December 11, 1985, two days before the movie opened, Kahn didn't sit down with Carson until January 8, 1986, nearly four weeks after *Clue* premiered.

Kahn and Carson had a friendly rapport, and despite her introverted personality, she was a fun talk show guest. She leaned into what McKean described as her "reputation for being a little absent-minded" and as someone who was trying to keep up with life as it moved too fast around her.[12] On Carson, she bounced from topic to topic, always a bit disconnected from the questions the host was posing. She also revealed her penchant for privacy, as when he asked her if she lived alone and she bristled and told him "not to do this" because she doesn't like her life displayed to the public. When Carson asked her if she was having a good time on his show, she said, "It ain't bad," but then called the anticipation of appearing "scary" and likened it to surgery—the wait is worse than the event. Kahn ended her segment singing a song she had written titled "The Moment Has Passed."

Her appearance was by turns funny, engaging, and baffling. But what made for great late-night talk was not great for promoting *Clue*. Kahn seemed uninterested in discussing the movie. When Carson introduced her and said that Mrs. White was a "severely demented blackhearted widow," Kahn replied only that she wouldn't have described her like that. Toward the end of her appearance, before she sang, the time came to show a clip, and Carson asked her if it needed any introduction, to which Kahn said, "Oh, it probably does but . . ." and she trailed off. Carson, appearing genuinely thrown, said, "But you don't want to," and she told him, "Well, a woman has her own logic." At least the clip Paramount provided was perhaps the best to showcase the movie's humor. It was the scene in the kitchen when they find the cook dead and Mull interrogates Kahn, asking her how many husbands she's had.

Mull was a frequent guest on Letterman, sometimes filling in at the last minute when another guest canceled. The pair got along well and shared an absurdist sense of humor. Letterman began the segment by pulling out a toy gun and shooting a dart at the camera before he introduced Mull. The two talked about Mull's new book based on his cable TV special, *The History of White People in America*. Mull took his own shot at the camera with the dart gun (and missed), then spoke with obvious pride about his five-week-old daughter, Maggie. Only at the end of Mull's visit did the two get to *Clue*. Letterman said that filming three endings sounded expensive, and Mull retorted that it

---

12 Smith, *Who Done It?, 28:45.

must've "cost hundreds of dollars." Letterman asked Mull if he was the killer, and Mull demurred, but Letterman pressed until Mull confessed that in one ending he was "not a very nice guy." No clip was shown.

Mull's appearance had come the day after the world premiere of *Clue* in Times Square, a few blocks away from the Letterman taping at Rockefeller Center. Invitations were mailed with the cast on the front and the heading "It's not just a game anymore."[13] Paramount booked the Embassy Theatre on Seventh Avenue and Forty-Sixth Street. The Embassy opened as an ornate movie palace in 1925, but it had since become an unremarkable multiplex. Times Square was still a good decade away from its makeover as a family-friendly tourist destination; in 1985 there was no M&M's store to be found. Instead, magazine stands hocked Playboy and Penthouse, sex work was rampant, and robberies were not uncommon. Paramount picked the Embassy to accommodate showings of all three endings. After the movie screened, there was a party in a swankier part of town, at the Park Avenue Armory. *Entertainment Tonight* sent a reporter to interview the cast and later aired a segment on the film. It is the only video footage of the premiere known to survive. Lynn wasn't told there would be a red carpet and "had no idea what to expect. I didn't know there would be a barrage of reporters asking me questions, and I was not prepared."[14] At least the Armory was convenient for Kahn; she lived less than a mile to the north at 975 Park Ave.

The premiere was Tuesday night, followed a night later by Mull's appearance on Letterman. Two days later, *Clue* opened on 1,006 screens, a respectable number. Paramount had issued a press release back on July 15 setting opening day as December 13. The movie was shipped to theaters on five two-thousand-foot 35mm reels. Each theater would get the same first four reels, plus a fifth labeled ending A, B, or C. After all the proverbial blood, sweat, and tears, *Clue* was finally in theaters, playing before audiences and competing in a crowded holiday season.

It flopped.

---

13 Paramount Pictures, invitation to *Clue* premiere.

14 Lynn, correspondence with the author.

There had been few signs of trouble for *Clue* thus far. Almost all of the summer reports on the movie made it sound fun and intriguing. The ad campaign had gone smoothly, and nothing major had happened to alarm producers or Paramount since the Carrie Fisher fiasco. Only a handful of the briefest of articles held any skepticism. One notice in the Minneapolis *Star Tribune* raised an eyebrow: "Just when you thought you'd heard of everything, along comes a movie based on a board game." The single-paragraph report, hidden in the back of the entertainment section, went on to mention the multiple endings, presciently opining: "Sounds confusing." Another notice, again barely a paragraph long, called the three-ending plan "a distributor's nightmare," but otherwise reported the details of the movie without editorial comment. It wasn't until the reviews started coming in that producers might have realized they were in trouble.

Part of *Clue*'s mythology is that the initial reviews were terrible. Some certainly were—plenty of critics didn't care for it. Tom Matthews of *Box Office* magazine hated it so much that he spoiled all of the endings in his review (screenings for critics showed all three back-to-back) and told his readers he would "rescue you from having to see this thing three times."[15] But other critics liked it just fine. There weren't many raves, and no one predicted *Clue* would be a popular film in four decades, but it was by no means universally hated. Hollywood trade paper *Variety* gave it a glowing review, calling it "pure fun" with "terrific performances."[16] The other industry trade, the *Hollywood Reporter*, was more muted, but still found room to compliment much of the comedy, the fast pace, the set design, and the impeccable performances. Those critics who liked *Clue* praised its cast and comedy. Some mentioned that the three endings were clever, but nothing about the plot stood out to them nearly as much as the laughs. They liked the actors, they liked Lynn's wordplay, and some liked the slapstick.

But while a majority of critics didn't loathe *Clue*, they largely seemed indifferent to it, which in some ways was worse than the negative

15 Matthews, "Clue."

16 "Clue," *Daily Variety*, Dec. 12, 1985, 3.

reviews. They just shrugged and went on their way, uninterested in thinking about the movie beyond getting their review written. A slew of critics gave it two or two and a half stars. More than one critic quipped that the board game had turned into a "bored" game. Critics at the country's biggest papers neither hated it nor loved it. Janet Maslin of the *New York Times* thought it started out as fun but then began "to drag." She mentioned the many double entendres and warned parents that "'Clue' is substantially smuttier than its PG rating would indicate," then accused Lynn of "directorial misogyny" for his treatment of women.[17] Roger Ebert, probably the country's best known critic thanks to his TV show, *At the Movies*, with Gene Siskel, wrote that Paramount's handling of "it's multiple endings is ingenious." But, he continued, that ingenuity was wasted on a film that wasn't very good, and no one would "drive all over town and buy three tickets to see all the endings."[18] Siskel and Ebert gave *Clue* two thumbs down and advised audiences to see ending A (everyone did it), though Ebert added, "It'd probably be best if you didn't go to this movie at all." Siskel called the multiple endings a mistake, not because the concept was confusing but because "Think about it: literally anybody could've done it and anybody did do it. . . . That cuts the heart out of the tension of the mystery." It was Kevin Thomas of the *Los Angeles Times* who zeroed in on the problem, the same problem that had worried Jonathan Lynn for months: *Clue* needed to be seen with all three endings. "The best version of *Clue*," wrote Thomas, "is the one you're not going to see." He called it "a shame" that audiences couldn't see all three endings at once, "because the notion that a whodunit can just as easily have one ending as another is the perfect finish for what is intended as a spoof of the genre."[19]

Was it the critics who sunk *Clue* or was it the confusion of having to pick an ending? It was both. It also didn't help that the film had no big-name, bankable star. The bottom line is that for one reason or another,

17 Maslin, "Screen: 'Clue' from Game to Film."

18 Ebert, "Clue."

19 Thomas, "'Clue' as Whodunit."

audiences didn't want to see it. The movie pulled in a little over $2 million on its opening weekend, ranking sixth. The number one movie was *Rocky IV*, followed by *Jewel of the Nile* (the sequel to *Romancing the Stone*), *Spies Like Us, White Nights*, and *Santa Claus: The Movie. Clue* did manage to edge out another Paramount Christmas flop: *Young Sherlock Holmes*. By December 26, after its second full week in theaters, *Clue* had fallen to number twelve, sandwiched between *Young Sherlock Holmes* and *Back to the Future*, which had been playing in theaters for six months. It clawed its way back up to number ten in its third week, though still behind *The Color Purple* and Disney's rerelease of *101 Dalmatians*. By the end of its fourth week, on January 9, 1986, the day after Madeline Kahn appeared on *Tonight*, the writing was more than on the wall; it was etched into *Clue*'s tomb. It fell back to number twelve and stayed there through the next week. Then, it was gone. It had lasted barely a month in theaters.

*Clue* still got an international release, playing in a handful of European cities. But no one was under any illusions that it would somehow catch fire and evolve from flop to hit. Paramount had already announced in January that it would take a tax write-down on both *Clue* and *Young Sherlock Holmes*. Just how much did it lose? Thanks to Hollywood's byzantine accounting practices, it's impossible to know for sure. In newspapers and the trades, the budget was put at anywhere from $8 million to $11 million, but that number was being floated while the film was still in production. Fans today might hop on Wikipedia or IMDB and see reports that *Clue* cost $15 million to make (a reasonable guess, but still a guess, since Paramount has never released the true budget) and made nearly that much—$14.6 million—at the box office. Sure, it wasn't a blockbuster by any stretch, but, the thinking might go, it's hardly a flop if it came close to making all of its money back and certainly has made it back in the years since with home video rentals, cable TV licensing deals, and streaming rights. If only it were that simple.

While the precise calculus on each film is different, a general rule of thumb in 1985 was that a movie must make three to four times as much as its production budget in order to break even. If *Clue* cost $10 million by the time the film was in the can and postproduction was wrapping up, then roughly another $5 to $10 million would have been budgeted for P&A—prints and advertising. That money is used primarily for marketing, but also to produce duplicate prints of the film that would be sent around the country—over one thousand in this case—and later throughout the world for screening. Now the cost is running anywhere from $15 million to $20 million. Next, they have to split 50 percent of whatever the movie makes with exhibitors—the movie theaters showing the film. (These numbers have evolved over time to reflect inflation, technical changes like digitization, and shifts in power so that, for example, behemoth studios can often demand more than 50 percent of the cut, but they were the norm in 1985.) Even the most conservative estimates—if *Clue*'s total budget was $15 million including P&A—meant that it needed to make about $30 million at the box office just to break even. It didn't come close. Instead, it earned about $7.4 million after the cut with theaters.

Fortunately for Paramount and the producers, home video and cable TV rights helped. *Clue* came out on VHS, Betamax, and laserdisc on August 20, 1986, and included all three endings. Lynn shuffled things a bit to show that the everyone-did-it ending was how it "really happened." The VHS and Beta cassettes were "priced to rent," at $79.95, or well over $200 by 2023 numbers. By contrast, "priced to own" releases typically cost $29.95.

Paramount had one last advertising trick up its sleeve. On September 17, 1986, a month after *Clue* debuted on home video, a special starring Mull aired on CBS. *Clue*: *Movies, Murder, & Mystery* was essentially a one-hour clip show that took "a lighthearted look at America's fascination with mystery"—or so the producers said in a press release.[20] The special intersperses Mull's humorous asides with clips and interviews with stars such as Angela Lansbury and Peter Falk. The program got plenty of attention in newspapers, including a promotional image of Mull holding a magnifying glass up to his face, but like the movie it promoted, it flopped. *Variety* wondered what on earth was the point, especially since the clips shown were unlabeled—

20 "Tonight's Programs," *Ithaca Journal*, Sep. 17, 1986, 11B.

audiences couldn't identify which movies or TV shows they were from. It called the show "filler, presumably concocted as a promotion gimmick."[21] Out of 563 primetime specials from September 1, 1986, to August 31, 1987, it ranked near the bottom at 503.

Despite this setback, *Clue* performed reasonably well in the rental market. It landed on *Billboard*'s VHS rentals chart at number sixteen. It peaked in its third week on the chart at number eight, but stayed in the top forty for several weeks—well into November. It wasn't as popular as *Back to the Future* or *Spies Like Us*, but people were renting it. It didn't do as well on the sales chart, though this was no surprise given the purchase price. By its third and final week on the sales list, it had dropped to number thirty-seven, behind *Automatic Golf* and *Playboy Video Centerfold 2*.

A month after the home video release, *Variety* mentioned *Clue* in a story about a lavish party held on the old mansion set. Dom Pérignon champagne flowed into flutes and coupe glasses sipped by eighties Hollywood royalty. John Forsythe toasted Aaron Spelling as Linda Evans and Joan Collins looked on. But the party had nothing to do with Lynn's movie. Instead, *Clue*'s mansion had been repurposed; for the next three years, it would double as the Carlton hotel on *Dynasty*. Despite the very different decor, the set was instantly recognizable as Hill House. The layout was flipped for *Dynasty*, and the fictitious hotel guests entered through the ballroom doors, while the front doors of the *Clue* house became the hotel's exit to a dining patio. It was an unremarkable end for a grand set, another sign of how quickly *Clue* was tossed aside.

Nearly a year after its world premiere on December 10, 1985, *Clue* seemed destined to go the way of so many other movies: middling reviews, a few weeks in theaters, and then . . . gone, only to occasionally resurface in the bargain DVD bin. Lynn had developed a good reputation in Hollywood while working on his first feature. He'd managed to keep the cast happy and meet all of the producers' expectations. He was levelheaded and had navigated Hollywood

21 "*Clue: Movies, Murder, & Mystery*," *Variety*.

with aplomb. Just before *Clue* hit theaters, he told a reporter that he had several offers to direct more movies, including from Paramount, regardless of *Clue*'s box office receipts. But, he quickly clarified, "If *Clue* was a kind of cataclysmic disaster, that might present a problem."[22]

In a town where promises are a dime a dozen and you're only as good as your last picture, it was a problem. Lynn was set to direct *Roxanne*, starring Steve Martin. Less than two weeks after *Clue* premiered, he was "off the picture."[23] Although Curry would remember that Lynn "was miserable about it," the director had already mentally prepared for the possibility that things might not work out. "I told a well-known American journalist the other day that if I messed up *Clue* I could simply go back to doing what I was doing in England. I saw the look of horror on the film publicist's face as I was talking. You're simply not allowed to express such doubts in America—it brands you as a wimp and a loser—whereas in England, if you didn't express them, people would think you were insanely arrogant."[24]

Lynn did exactly what he had said he would. He went back to England and had success with the new *Yes, Prime Minister* series. He returned to directing theater, including *Three Men on a Horse*. But if he was done with *Clue*, it wasn't done with him, at least not entirely. A few months after his first film debuted on home video, a little-noticed event would change the trajectory of its reputation. On December 6, 1986, *Clue* premiered on Showtime.

---

22 Abramson, "Clue."

23 Vary, "Something Terrible Has Happened Here."

24 Bygrave, "The Man Whodunnit."

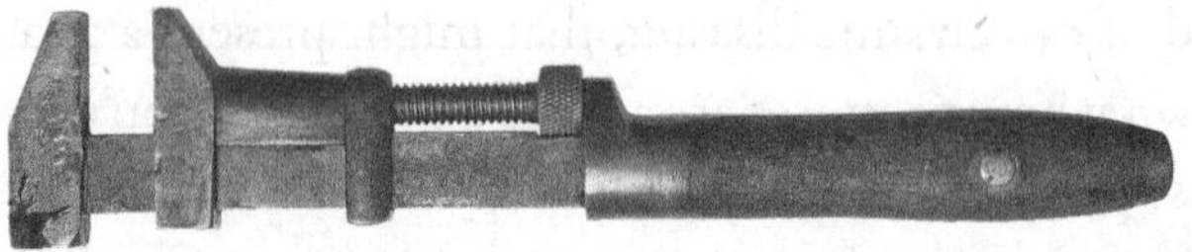

# 10. AN ENDING WITH A TWIST

"Some things have to be about actually caring for human beings."

-Jonathan Lynn[1]

Jonathan Lynn has spent most of his life thinking about comedy and what's funny and what isn't. He even wrote a book about it, *Comedy Rules*. But he gets at least one thing about comedy wrong—and it's his own movie that contradicts him. He writes that "nobody laughs at a comedy as much as when they see it for the first time. The second, third, fourth or umpteenth time contains no surprises."[2] But decades after it flamed out in theaters, people laugh at *Clue*. Often uproariously, and certainly much more than the first time they saw it and perhaps even more than the last time they saw it. They discover new jokes, and then they begin laughing at the anticipation of a line they know is coming up, which is the exact opposite of Lynn's comment that surprises are essential for laughs. Comedy, it turns out, can also be about familiarity, and for a lot of kids growing up in the 1980s and nineties, nostalgia is rooted in the pop culture they shared with friends and family.

It's difficult to overstate the importance of television in *Clue*'s transformation from flop to cult classic. Sure, some people saw it in the theater, but a lot more rented it on VHS or saw it on cable. In a (completely unscientific) survey of 135 *Clue* fans I conducted, 42

---

1 Lynn, interview with Gottfried and Santopadre, 1:28:10.

2 Lynn, *Comedy Rules*, 19.

percent said they first saw the movie when they rented it, and another 30 percent saw it first on cable TV. Those first viewings, fun as they may have been, might be dizzying; a lot is going on. The jokes fly fast and furious, and it can be hard to keep track of everything. Young people knew they liked the movie, especially the physical comedy, and plenty wanted to see it again. It was television that cemented *Clue*'s status as a cult hit. Television empowered the film's young fans, allowing them to see it again without pestering a parent to take them to the local video store.

*Clue* fandom didn't happen overnight; the film wasn't suddenly discovered by huge masses of people in 1986, 1987, or even 1988. Fandom's embrace of Lynn's movie unfolded over two decades, thanks to *Clue* becoming a TV staple.

Showtime and its sister network, The Movie Channel, obtained the rights to *Clue* for three years. It premiered at noon on December 6, 1986, and replayed at 8:00 p.m. Showtime aired it regularly until its rights expired. On November 29, 1989, *Clue* played on HBO for the first time. It also screened on HBO's sister channel Cinemax. In early 1991, it moved from cable to network television when it began playing on Fox-affiliated local stations. It also played overseas. It first aired on public television in Australia in 1989 on Network 10. On March 7, 1991, it aired on BBC1 in Lynn's home country.

*Clue* was, in many ways, ready-made for TV, especially basic cable. Its 97-minute runtime was perfect for a two-hour space with commercials. While many movies, even other PG-rated films, had to be edited for language, sex, or violence, *Clue* didn't. Thanks to Debra Hill's original contract with Parker Brothers, it had almost no profanity and, despite several murders, no shocking violence to speak of. While one shot of Mrs. White punching Mr. Boddy in the stomach instead of kneeing him in the groin was filmed, the footage was never swapped in for television. Boddy getting kneed was exactly the kind of thing that kids loved about the movie—and it was kids who were watching it.

A full 50 percent of the fans I surveyed saw *Clue* between ages nine and seventeen. Another 39 percent saw it before they were eight years old. In other words, nearly 90 percent of the fans I surveyed watched it before they were adults. In the 1980s and 1990s, kids were able to discover movies through cable that they otherwise would never have seen. Another Christmas 1985 Paramount flop, *Young Sherlock Holmes*, gained its own fans through repeated cable showings. Of course, not all movies found an audience through cable. There are no sellout midnight screenings of *Brewster's Millions* or *Private Resort.* Cable did boost fan appreciation of other movies, including *Weird Science* and *Better Off Dead*, but no other movies from 1985 save for *Back to the Future* and *The Goonies* have had the staying power of *Clue*. Kids tuned in again and again.

It wasn't just that they watched it; it was also *how* they watched it. Many *Clue* fans have memories of staying home from school sick, lying on a couch converted into a bed by a loving mom or dad rushing out the door to make it to work on time—pillows, blankets, maybe some crackers and Sprite to help settle an upset stomach. Also, a TV viewer's best friend: the remote control, and with everyone else out of the house, it was all theirs.

Most cable subscribers had access to fewer than fifty channels back then, and kids had no problem memorizing what network was on which channel. This was long before the days of networks with multiple channels—there was no MTV2 or HBO Signature. Kids knew which channels they were interested in—Lifetime was their mom's channel and CNN had nothing of use for them, especially during the boring Iran-Contra hearings in the summer of 1987. But they could flip through the stations with ease, jumping to the ones with the good stuff. They also knew that most programs began at the top of the hour. They could fetch the *TV Guide* or the local paper with the day's listings. Smaller papers would list cable channels only in the Sunday edition, while larger papers might have them every day.

*Clue* on a sick day was a chance for a kid to laugh without being interrupted and told to take out the garbage or clean their room. If they were pulling a Ferris Bueller and faking it, the chance to spend time away from school with a favorite comedy was just the break they needed. Sometimes kids found *Clue* after school at that reliable friend's house—the one with the premium cable channels. Still others trudged to that local grocery store with a video rental department or to a Blockbuster to check out that film their friends had raved about.

This kind of nostalgia has played a massive role in the popularity of not only *Clue*, but a great deal of contemporary pop culture. One might argue that nostalgia used to spring up organically; now it is largely manufactured by corporations seeking to cash in the audience's love of the content they grew up with. Movie studios, especially Disney, lean into this connection. Films and TV series call back to beloved shows from the 1970s, eighties, and nineties, even the 2000s, winking at and nudging audiences along the way: remember this thing you saw as a kid? It is all designed to exploit Gen Xers' and millennials' chase for a nostalgia high.

It's easy to recall childhood memories that have been buffed by the patina of time, but recapturing the past is elusive. No one can quite feel like they did as a kid. Movies, when seen through a kid's fresh eyes, are dazzling. But then we grow up, and life's years flow over us, eroding our innocence. Over time our memories deepen and become romanticized. But trying to recapture a particular moment in time over and over again is a bit like trying to relive a vacation by staring at pictures. It might initially spur some nice feelings, but eventually they slip away, along with the potency of those first emotions.

This profound emotional attachment to films from our youth leads some of us down a path of intense devotion. A few devotees, eager to learn more about the movies they love, have taken it upon themselves to make fan documentaries. The list is impressive: *Pennywise: The Story of IT*; *The Shark Is Still Working: The Impact and Legacy of Jaws*; *Cleanin' Up the Town: Remembering Ghostbusters*; *Never Surrender: A Galaxy Quest Documentary*; *The Death of Superman Lives*; and *Back in Time*, about the impact and legacy of *Back to the Future*. Some of these filmmakers covered production costs through the crowdfunding website Kickstarter.

Jeff Smith's *Who Done It? The Clue Documentary* is one such fan film. When he began, he reasoned that he had a film degree that he wasn't using, so he might as well make a movie about *Clue*. After all, how hard could it be? How long could it take? Nearly six years, as it turned out. Smith reached out to the cast and crew and gained insights into the film that no one else had ever reported. He spoke to Lynn twice and interviewed Michael McKean, Lesley Ann Warren, Jeffrey

Kramer, Colleen Camp, costume designer Michael Kaplan, casting director Jane Jenkins, and fans of the film. He's the only person who has managed to get Lee Ving to talk about *Clue*. Smith embraced the metafilm approach, appearing throughout the documentary himself, lending it personality and an air of authenticity.

This continuing need to feel a deeper connection to the pop culture we love can make criticism feel strangely personal. We are talking about a movie—one fans had no part in writing or making. But they come to identify with it so strongly that criticism of the movie feels like criticism of the fan. Nostalgia and fandom, allowed to simmer too long, can congeal into a toxic stew of entitlement and rage. The internet has created an immediacy to all of this. On social media anyone can (and most people do) have an opinion. Hot takes of movies are as common as photos of someone's fancy dessert.

The issue of toxic fandom might seem out of place in discussions about an eighties movie like *Clue*; after all, it existed long before the internet. But fans of the movie do debate its treatment of women, its portrayal of a gay man, and its use of an overweight Asian woman as a cook who made monkey brains for dinner. Nostalgia exists within an evolving world, and while *Clue* fans love the movie, they recognize that time marches on, and so do societal attitudes.

Take Mr. Green's final line: "I'm going to go home and sleep with my wife!" It's a favorite moment in the film for many people, often quoted and often laughed at. But other fans dislike it because it appears to erase Green's identity as the sole LGBTQ+ character in the movie, rendering his queerness a mere act in an undercover sting and identifying him as a hero only once he is "outed" as straight. Still, other fans are just grateful Mr. Green exists at all, a rare gay portrayal in a mainstream eighties Hollywood movie, and a likable one at that. To their credit, the producers and Paramount never challenged Lynn over Mr. Green. When asked about the jokes at Green's expense in a 2020 interview, Lynn said that while he might not "make those same jokes today," he thinks "they're pretty harmless." He then mentions cancel culture, saying he's "not terribly in favor" of it and thinks the "criteria should simply be: are [the jokes] funny?"[3]

No one seems poised to cancel *Clue*. Fans recognize it for what it is: a movie from the mid-1980s that was portraying the mid-1950s. Some *Clue* fans shrug at the antiquated gender dynamics and accept it as part of watching a movie that is nearly forty years old, portraying an era that is nearly seventy years old. Others are a bit more uncomfortable with it, though it doesn't diminish their love of the film. Still others are defensive at the suggestion that one of their favorite movies has any issues at all.

Most comedy has a shelf life; it is of a particular moment. *Saturday Night Live* sketches from the 1980s often land with a thud today. For every *Caddyshack* or *Dumb and Dumber*, there are a dozen comedies that come and go, quickly forgotten. This makes *Clue*'s ongoing relevance all the more remarkable. Its themes of secrecy, judgment, and political paranoia continue to resonate. And it isn't the only content Lynn wrote that remained relevant long after its creation. In October 2022, as England struggled with political turmoil, Prime Minister Liz Truss resigned after only forty-five days in office, the shortest tenure of any prime minister in British history. Jokes and commentary abounded, and clips from *Yes Minister* popped up across social media, garnering hundreds of thousands of views, likes, favorites, and retweets. Forty-two years later, a TV show about the British government seemed as relevant as ever.

Lynn's political commentary is dense and multifaceted. The irony of *Clue* is that one of the reasons it bombed in theaters has helped guarantee its status as a cult classic. It does too much to really succeed in a single viewing. It's a loop of comedy, a mystery, a parody, and a farce, one layered on top of the others.

Comedy and mystery might seem at first glance like an unholy marriage. The best comedy feels natural, inevitable, organic. It's hard sometimes to imagine that the characters in *Clue* are really talented actors delivering well-rehearsed lines rather than a bunch of funny people standing around riffing off of one another.

---

3 Alter, "*Clue* at 35."

Mystery is another beast altogether. The best whodunits are like well-oiled machines, with multiple moving parts interlocking at just the right moment to pull off the seemingly impossible. If comedy feels organic, mystery feels surgically precise. But in fact, most comedy is carefully, painstakingly crafted. Writers can agonize for days over the right punchline, the best word, the perfect way to tell a joke.

Comedy and mystery work together because audiences understand them both. The popularity of *Knives Out* (2019) and its follow-up, *Glass Onion* (2022), is further proof of how these two genres can fit together so perfectly. (In one of the funniest parts of *Glass Onion*, private detective Benoit Blanc lambasts Clue as a stupid game.) Thanks partly to these movies, there appears to be a resurging interest in golden age-style murder mysteries. What's old is new again. There are adaptations of Agatha Christie's most famous Poirot novels from Kenneth Branagh that despite middling reviews continue to find audiences. But there are also original movies, such as *See How They Run* (2022) and TV series from *Only Murders in the Building* (2021) to *The Afterparty* (2022). Mysteries, just as they did for readers a century ago, recovering from the trauma of World War I, give audiences comfort today. In these stories, chaos is turned into order. At the end, as the detective stands in front of the suspects and recounts exactly what happened; the opaque becomes transparent as the fog is lifted. Everything is revealed, and it all makes sense. Despite murder and mayhem, by the end, normalcy is restored. If only life were that way. Being able to laugh along the way, to laugh in the face of death, only offers even more reassurance. It's another form of nostalgia, comfort repurposed for a difficult era.

*********

The cast and crew of *Clue* went on to other work, in some cases eager to put the theatrical flop behind them. Michael McKean has perhaps had the most diverse career since *Clue*. He's had turns both hilarious and dramatic, including a critically acclaimed stint as Chuck McGill in *Better Call Saul*. He's appeared in over fifty movies, often in comedic supporting roles. For a period in the 1990s, it was not uncommon for McKean to be in three or four movies a year. He married actor Annette O'Toole in 1999 and continues to appear on stage, on television, and in movies.

Martin Mull and Lesley Ann Warren, who became friends on the *Clue* set, have worked together a half-dozen times since 1985. They appeared in episodes of *Community* and *The Cool Kids* as well as the *Psych* homage to *Clue* alongside Christopher Lloyd. Warren has been in more than eighty films and TV series since 1985, working almost nonstop for the past thirty-eight years. Interviews with her reveal a peaceful acceptance of what Hollywood is and what it isn't. She notes that "naturally as you get older" the offers for leading roles dwindle, but that there is plenty of room "to find joy and the excitement" in creating your own role when offered a supporting part.[4]

Likewise, Mull has stayed busy, appearing more often in television but also taking roles in comedic movies such as *Jingle All the Way* and *Mrs. Doubtfire*. He had a recurring role on *Roseanne*, but otherwise has demonstrated a knack for popping up in long-running sitcoms with rabid fan bases that nevertheless struggle in the ratings, including *Community*, *Brooklyn Nine-Nine*, and *Reno 911!*. His most popular recurring role may be Gene Parmesan, the "far from the best" private detective on *Arrested Development*. He worked with his daughter, Maggie, "just swollen with pride," on the series *Dads*, but he thinks of himself as "pretty much 99 percent a painter."[5]

Lloyd, like many of his costars, has continued to work nearly nonstop, including repeat performances in *Back to the Future II* and *III*. He also appeared in *Who Framed Roger Rabbit* as a creepy villain and in *The Addams Family* as Uncle Fester. In 2021, at age eighty-three, he appeared in four movies. In recent years, Lloyd has spent a lot of time on the fan convention circuit, occasionally reuniting with his *Back to the Future* costars, speaking, posing for pictures, and signing autographs.

Tim Curry appeared in *The Hunt for Red October*, *Home Alone 2*, *McHale's Navy*, and *Charlie's Angels*, among others. But nothing captured audiences quite like his portrayal of Pennywise the Clown

---

4 "Lesley Ann Warren," *Film Talk*.

5 Wojciechowski, "Fox's *Dads* Star Martin Mull."

in the two-part made-for-TV movie *IT*, adapted from Stephen King's novel. While Curry's performance was appreciated at the time, it has since grown in stature; it's even cited in academic journals examining why some people are terrified of clowns. Curry is a private man who rarely comments on his personal life. In July 2012, he suffered a major stroke, but so close-knit are his family and friends that the news did not leak until the following May. By then he had been in physical therapy for several months. In June 2015, at age sixty-nine, he received a Lifetime Achievement Tony Award. Today he does occasional voice work and appears at fan conventions and signs autographs.

Colleen Camp continues to appear in movies and TV series. She reunited with Lynn in *Greedy*, a comedy starring Kirk Douglas, Michael J. Fox, and a scene-stealing Phil Hartman. Camp has also produced several films.

Following *Clue*, Jeffrey Kramer largely stopped acting and turned to producing. He had two massive hits with *Ally McBeal* and *The Practice*.

Lee Ving went on to appear in a handful of TV series and movies for the next fifteen years. He was often cast as the villain or the attractive bad boy, as in *Who's the Boss?* He's since moved away from acting, but he continues to perform as the lead singer of Fear.

Jane Wiedlin's first movie was *Clue*, and she's since continued acting. She was Joan of Arc in *Bill and Ted's Excellent Adventure*, and she's done voice-over work in animated features and series. She's spoken openly about her mental-health struggles and is active in PETA. In 2020, she was part of a documentary that premiered at the Sundance Film Festival on the Go-Go's, and a year later the band was inducted into the Rock & Roll Hall of Fame.

Bill Henderson spent the next twenty-two years working in over two dozen movies and TV shows, but *Clue* turned out to be one of his more prominent roles. He continued to sing and appeared on several jazz albums. He retired from acting at age eighty and passed away in 2016, two weeks after his ninetieth birthday.

Howard Hesseman appeared in dozens of movies and TV shows after *Clue*, many well-known, some less well-known. He rarely gave interviews, and when he did, he sounded misanthropic and disappointed at the state of the world, but never despairing or miserable to be around. He would follow up his observations about the banality of life with a self-deprecating joke. Even the simplest questions sent him off on tangential ruminations about everything from fandom to human nature. When he died in January 2022, he had been with his partner, Caroline Ducrocq, for forty years.

Over the fifteen years after *Clue*, Kellye Nakahara appeared in a handful of small speaking roles in about a dozen movies and TV shows. She also worked as an artist with her own studio. She loved her adopted *M*A*S*H* family, and she would host gatherings of the cast and crew. She'd laugh as she recalled Alan Alda strolling up her driveway in Pasadena balancing a pasta salad in his arms for their latest potluck get-together. She passed away February 16, 2020, of cancer.

John Landis shot *The Three Amigos* in 1986, then went on trial for the *Twilight Zone* accident. In May 1987, he was found not guilty of involuntary manslaughter. He would go on to make *Coming to America* in 1988, but a decade later, his output had slowed considerably. In 2010 he directed *Burke & Hare*, a British comedy starring Andy Serkis and Simon Pegg. Landis has worked in television and made a handful of acting appearances, but in the mid-1990s he acknowledged that the helicopter accident had damaged his career.

Eileen Brennan continued to work after *Clue*, appearing in a movie or TV series every year for the next twenty years. She had a handful of recurring roles, including in *Will & Grace*, for which she was nominated for an Emmy. She continued to recover from her car accident, though in 1989 she fell off the stage during a performance of *Annie* and broke her leg. In 1990, she successfully underwent treatment for breast cancer. She spoke openly about her addiction to painkillers.

After *Clue*, Debra Hill partnered with Lynda Obst and gave Chris Columbus his first directing job, *Adventures in Babysitting*, starring Elisabeth Shue. It was a modest hit, and Columbus would go on to direct *Home Alone*, *Mrs. Doubtfire*, and the first two Harry Potter films. Hill and Obst signed a production deal with Disney that gave Hill freedom to work on other projects. She hired Terry Gilliam and Robin Williams for *The Fisher King*. It was, perhaps, her most celebrated film, at least within the industry. While the reviews weren't universally enthusiastic, *The Fisher King* was nominated for several awards and appeared on dozens of best-of lists at the end of 1991. Mercedes Ruehl in particular was singled out for her performance, and she won the Academy Award and Golden Globe for Best Supporting Actress. Hill produced specials for Disney and worked on her own movies. The last was Oliver Stone's 2006 film, *World Trade Center*.

Hill never had the child she told reporters that she wanted. In the early 2000s, she began to feel ill. Like a lot of people who work hard and push themselves, she initially attributed it to fatigue and put off seeing a doctor. When she finally went to a doctor, the news wasn't good: colon cancer. She began treatment, but circulation to her legs was cut off, and both were eventually amputated, though it didn't stop her from throwing a disco party and hitting the dance floor in her wheelchair. On Christmas Day 2004, she was rushed to the hospital in an ambulance. She never came home, passing away on March 7, 2005. A decade and a half later, Lynda Obst remembered Hill on different sets, her eyes darting around the room, taking in everything, "with her arms on her hips, like Peter Pan arriving in Neverland," ready to tackle anything.[6]

Madeline Kahn remained choosy about roles. Her film work included a few voice-over parts and a turn as Martha Mitchell in Oliver Stone's *Nixon*. She appeared in a handful of made-for-TV movies and series before landing the part of Pauline on *Cosby*, the sitcom that aired on CBS from 1996 to 2000 (not to be confused with the NBC sitcom *The Cosby Show*). This was two decades before Cosby's reputation would be shattered by sexual assault charges, and Kahn called it "the best job I ever had."[7] She also worked on the stage and won multiple awards, including a Tony, for playing Gorgeous Teitelbaum in *The Sisters Rosensweig*. In August 1998, she fainted, and subsequent tests revealed that she had ovarian cancer.

Kahn's cancer had spread throughout her abdomen. True to her personality, she told almost no one apart from her brother and a few close friends, including her longtime boyfriend, John Hansbury. She

---

6 Ryzik, "Overlooked No More."

7 Madison, *Madeline Kahn*, 299.

continued to work on *Cosby*, where it was obvious she was sick with something but everyone tiptoed around it, since she had told no one what her illness was. She underwent three surgeries and three rounds of chemotherapy treatment. In October 1999, Hansbury proposed to Kahn, a gesture of both romance and practicality; her lawyers said her estate would be easier to manage if she were survived by a spouse. They were married at Mount Sinai Hospital in New York, a mile north of her apartment on Park Avenue. There was nothing more to be done, and on December 3, 1999, she died. Obituaries and remembrances filled newspapers, and at least a few said that her "flames" speech was a highlight of her career. Fourteen years later, when Mel Brooks was asked about her, he began to cry. "The funniest and most intelligent comedienne . . . nobody could approach the magnificence and wonder of Madeline Kahn."[8]

Lynn did what he said he would do if *Clue* was a flop: he returned to England and had success in television and theater. But he wasn't done with film. Four years after *Clue*, he directed *Nuns on the Run* for HandMade Films, a British production company co-owned by George Harrison. Two years later, he directed what many regard as his best film, *My Cousin Vinny*. Even now the movie is thought of as one of the most accurate representations of the American legal system on celluloid. Lynn pushed hard for a relatively unknown Marisa Tomei to be in the movie. The studio balked, but Lynn prevailed, and Tomei won the Oscar for Best Supporting Actress.

Lynn went on to direct several other movies, all comedies, and all with varying degrees of farce and slapstick. His biggest box office success was *The Whole Nine Yards*, starring Bruce Willis, Matthew Perry, and Amanda Peet. He also did well with *The Distinguished Gentleman*, a political comedy with Eddie Murphy, whom Lynn liked working with. While some of his movies have more fans than others, they typically appeal to audiences more than critics. Even *My Cousin Vinny* initially opened to middling reviews, though now it is better regarded. Lynn's movies seem to follow a pattern: they're released to critics, who rarely

8 Brooks, interview with Gross, 18:00.

love them or rarely hate them but often give them two stars or a C+. The films struggle at the box office, but the audiences who see them like them. After some time and distance, they all seem to find at least some fans who, upon repeat viewings, like them more and more. Even the much maligned *Sgt. Bilko*, starring Steve Martin, Dan Aykroyd, Phil Hartman, Chris Rock, Glenne Headly, and Debra Jo Rupp—has its fan base, though nothing rivaling that of *Clue*.

Lynn eventually moved from London to New York, and his career has remained as diverse as ever. He's written novels, plays, and his memoir and adapted *Yes Minister* for books and the stage. He's been married to his wife, Rita, for over fifty-five years.

*********

In 2010, NPR's pop culture correspondent, Linda Holmes, wrote that when people learned she hadn't seen *Clue*, they looked at her as if "I was announcing I hadn't heard music or never walked barefoot through a field of grass."[9] Three years later, two events cemented *Clue*'s status as a cult classic. The first was when the TV series *Psych* celebrated its hundredth episode with an homage to *Clue*, reuniting Lloyd, Warren, and Mull. The episode, titled "100 Clues," was done well—original in its own right but with plenty of references to the film for fans. Lloyd's character is named Martin Kahn. There's a cabinet in which items are locked away, a falling chandelier, a corpse in a freezer, gargoyles in the rain, a singing telegram girl, and more. The episode allowed fans to vote live for one of three different endings. Two were aired, and a third was included on the DVD release as a bonus.

But it wasn't just the episode itself that made an impact. Mainstream publications like the *A. V. Club* and the *Hollywood Reporter* covered the episode in ways that would have seemed impossible twenty-five years earlier: They were writing about people celebrating *Clue*. Gone was the snark over making a movie out of a board game. Gone was any mention of *Clue*'s dismal performance in theaters. Rather, *Clue* was treated as a movie that deserves celebration.

---

9 Holmes, "Charm of Remembrance."

The second 2013 event occurred on September 2. That morning, word began to spread on Twitter: Adam Vary had written an oral history of *Clue* for *Buzzfeed.* Fans of the film were ecstatic. His own story of discovering *Clue* as a kid mirrored that of many other fans. He was hanging out with friends in the early 1990s when, surfing through channels, they stumbled across a movie with a bunch of grown-ups running around a mansion in suits and dresses. Vary's oral history was the first time a lot of fans learned . . . well . . . anything about how *Clue* was made. He interviewed Landis, Lynn, and nearly all of the surviving actors (Ving declined to speak to him). Curry was still recovering from his stroke, but he went on record with Vary later, and the article was updated. Vary's *Buzzfeed* piece cemented *Clue*'s status; it had graduated from guilty pleasure to acknowledged classic.

Over the years, fans have been eager to snatch up artifacts from the film, including scripts, call sheets, and storyboards. Costumes worn by Kahn and Brennan were sold at auction. But items directly from the film are hard to come by. Because *Clue* flailed at the box office, not many items were preserved. After it had served its purpose as the Hotel Carlton on Dynasty, the set was unceremoniously scrapped. Props were returned to the Paramount prop department; Camp regretted not snagging one of Yvette's costumes for herself.

In the years since, fans have found artwork by other fans or relied on websites that detail exactly what weapons were used in the movie so that they can find their own copies. Promotional photos taken from the press kit or, on occasion, even complete press kits with the *Handbook of Production Information* are offered for sale online, and collectors snatch them up. Original posters or harder-to-find foreign-language lobby cards also surface from time to time. The storybook and novelization, while not offered for sale regularly, do turn up often enough that a fan eager to own them can find one or both books. In 2011, La-La Land Records released John Morris's soundtrack on CD. It too sold out, and is now commanding decent sums on the reseller market. In 2016, Mondo released a limited edition vinyl of the score with new artwork and seven different colors for the records to match the character tokens from the game, along with black for Wadsworth. More recently, Enjoy the Ride Records has reissued the soundtrack on vinyl and cassette. Memorabilia isn't rampant, but it's not so scarce that fans can't find something to enjoy.

The Clue game continues to spawn new properties, and keeping track of them all can be challenging. There are game shows, a musical that debuted in 1995, several books, and two comic book series—all of which are based on the board game, not the film. The exception is *Clue on Stage*, a direct adaptation of Lynn's movie. While it did not perform well enough in early performances to earn a Broadway run, it is popular among community theater groups and high schools. It is adapted by Sandy Rustin and follows the movie closely, with references to the board game added and nods to audiences' familiarity with Lynn's film. Quite the opposite of Lynn's original plan, the actors are usually dressed in their game-token color. It also includes a handful of jokes from the screenplay that were cut from the final film.

Much to some fans' dismay, a new movie is in development. It was first announced in 2011, and every few years a new story emerges that swears it's still happening. Details are scarce; it's not even clear if it will be a remake of the 1985 film. A few reports seem to point in the direction of a reboot over a remake. Studios are always on the lookout for a new franchise, and a few reports suggest that 20th Century (owned by Disney) might see *Clue* as a chance to make the current renaissance of whodunits into a hit property.

Despite all of this—the other adaptations, the proposed reboot, and the passionate fan base that the 1985 movie has generated over nearly forty years—Paramount Pictures has shown little interest in capitalizing on *Clue*'s popularity. Digital home video releases, including the DVD and Blu-ray, have no bonus features. When Lynn asked Paramount about recording an audio commentary, the studio wasn't interested. When I reached out to Paramount to license photographs for this book—pictures they had already designated for promotional use—I was (very politely, it must be said) turned down. While it is understandable that *Clue* isn't the highest priority for the studio that produced *The Godfather* and *Chinatown*, it seems a shame not to do more with the property. A digital release with the fourth ending and additional deleted scenes would delight fans.

What spurs devotion to a nearly forty-year-old movie? There are many explanations, but the reassurance of laughter tops the list. *Clue*—farce, parody, screwball comedy—might seem silly, but there is nothing silly about being able to laugh. Sitting with friends and family, the people we love, laughing and bonding over a movie is a gift too often taken for granted in a world drowning in "content." Alongside directors, writers, and actors are YouTubers, TikTokers, Instagrammers, and influencers of every stripe, all competing for a piece of our attention. It's little wonder that many people embrace the familiar—choice fatigue is real. Really, who can be blamed for saying, "The hell with it; let's watch *Clue* again," knowing they will have a good time?

# SELECTED BIBLIOGRAPHY

Articles on *Clue*

Abramson, Dan. "Clue—A Whodunnit with Three Differences: the Conclusions." *Screen International*, January 18, 1986, 22.

Alter, Ethan. "*Clue* at 35: Jonathan Lynn Reveals How Carrie Fisher and Rowan Atkinson Were Almost Cast in the Classic Board Game Movie." *Yahoo! Entertainment*, December 14, 2020, yahoo.com.

Archerd, Army. "Just for Variety." *Daily Variety*, April 25, June 18, 20, August 6, December 4, 1985, and September 25, 1986.

Attanasio, Paul. "'Clue': It's for the Boards." *Washington Post*, December 13, 1985, B1.

Bentley, Rick. "'Tis the Cinema Season." *Town Talk* (Alexandria, Louisiana), November 24, 1985, C-9.

Blyth, Jeffrey. "UK's Lynn Winds Up 'Clue' in Hollywood." *Screen International*, August 24, 1985, 74.

Brough, Rich. "Clue." *Park Record* (Park City, Utah), August 14, 1986, 20.

Bygrave, Mike. "The Man Whodunnit." *The Guardian* (London), July 11, 1985, 11.

"Clue." *Film Journal*, January 1, 1985, 6-A.

"Clue." *Screen International*, May 24, 1986, 20.

"Clue." *Sydney Morning Herald*, April 17, 1986, 12.

"Clue: Movies, Murder, & Mystery." *Variety*, September 24, 1986, 110.

"Col. Mustard & Co. Bite the Bullet in Motley 'Clue.'" *Pantagraph* (Bloomington, Indiana), December 28, 1985, 36.

Conway, Jeff. "Lesley Ann Warren Reflects on 35 Years of 'Clue' and a Lifelong Journey in Hollywood." *Forbes*, December 29, 2020, forbes.com.

Cosford, Bill. "Prof. Plum? Or Maybe Mr. Green?" *Miami Herald*, December 15, 1985, 16D.

Craft, Dan. "Happy Holidays, Moviegoers." *The Pantagraph* (Bloomington, Indiana), November 30, 1985, 5.

Crain, Mary Beth. "Clue." *LA Weekly*, December 20, 1985 (clipping).

Crockett, Lane. "Whodunit?" *The Times* (Shreveport, Louisiana), July 5, 1985, B1.

Darling, Cary. "'Clue': Director Jonathan Lynn Brings the Board Game to Life." *BAM*, December 20, 1985, 26–27.

DeBrosse, Jim. "The Real Mystery in Film 'Clue' Is Why You Should Pay to See It." *Cincinnati Enquirer*, December 17, 1985, D9.

Dobuler, Sharon Lee. "Carpenter, Hill Plan 'Clue' after N.Y. Escape." *Hollywood Reporter*, October 23, 1980.

Ebert, Roger. "Clue." *Chicago Sun-Times*, December 12, 1985, rogerebert.com.

Ellis, Kirk. "Clue." *Hollywood Reporter*, December 12, 1985, 3.

"Ex-Go Go's Member . . ." *Variety*, August 14, 1985, 29.

Farber, Stephen. "Off the Board, onto the Screen for *Clue*." *New York Times*, August 25,

1985, H15–16.

Feineman, Neil. "Cutting Edge: It's All in the Game." *San Francisco Examiner*, September 15, 1985.

"Film Assignments." *Daily Variety*, July 1, 1985, 6.

"Filming in the U.S." *Daily Variety*, May 24, 1985, 10.

"Films in the Future." *Daily Variety*, February 15, 1985, 20.

Gould, Kim. "'Clue' Lacks Mystery and Suspense of Game." *Anniston* (Alabama) *Star*, December 21, 1985, 6.

Greenberg, James. "Hollywood Hopes to Lure Holiday Crowds with Baker's Dozen Assortment of Comedy, Drama, Adventure, History, and Musical Drama." *Daily Variety* Fifty-Second Anniversary Issue, October 29, 1985, 14, 15, 24, 52.

Haithman, Diane. "Clue's Played on a Hollywood Set." *Detroit Free Press*, August 25, 1985, 3E.

Harmetz, Aljean. "There's No Mystery in Clue's Transition from Game to Film." *New York Times*, February 5 1985, C13.

Hobbs, Thomas. "Know the Score: Merrill Garbus on the Joys of Clue." *Little White Lies*, October 19, 2019, lwlies.com.

"Hollywood Soundtrack." *Variety*, August 21, 1985, 21.

Holmes, Linda. "The Charm of Remembrance: 'Clue' Did It in the '80s, with the Slapstick." NPR, July 6, 2010, npr.com.

Honeycutt, Kirk. "Audiences Have Plenty of 'Clues' to Go on—and Plenty of Endings." *LA Daily News*, December 13, 1985, 13.

Ivie, Devon. "Lesley Ann Warren Answers Every Question We Have about *Clue*." *Vulture*, July 28, 2021.

Jones, Brin Hamer. "Screen Scene." *Pontypridd* (Wales) *Observer*, June 19, 1986, 10.

Kahan, Saul, and George Turner. "Clue Is More Than a Game." *American Cinematographer* 67, no. 1 (January 1986): 48–57.

Kempley, Rita. "'Clue': Game for Almost Anything." *Washington Post*, December 13, 1985 (clipping).

Kilday, Gregg. "Board Games." *Los Angeles Herald Examiner*, May 14, 1985, A2.

Knode, Helen. "Clued In." *LA Weekly*, November 14, 1985, 6.

Lally, Kevin. "Clue." *Buying & Booking Guide*, January 1, 1986, 57.

Lenker, Maureen Lee. "Red Herrings, Skateboards, and Carrie Fisher: An Oral History of Mystery Classic *Clue*." *Entertainment Weekly*, March 13, 2023, ew.com.

Mann, Roderick. "'Night of the Iguana': The Play as a Pick-Me-Up." *Los Angeles Times*, October 12, 1985, part V, 1.

———. "Old Films Clue Curry in on New Role." *Los Angeles Times*, July 13, 1985, D6.

Maslin, Janet. "At the Movies." *New York Times*, November 22, 1985, C10.

———. "Screen: 'Clue' from Game to Film." *New York Times*, December 13, 1985, C16.

Matthews, Jack. "Coca-Cola—A New Formula at Columbia?" *Los Angeles Times*, June 19, 1985, 4 (section 4).

Matthews, Tom. "Clue." *Box Office*, February 1, 1986, R-20.

McReadie, Marsha. "Deadly Dull." *Arizona Republic*, December 14, 1985, C14.

Mills, Bart. "Brennan Takes Setbacks in Stride." *Calgary Herald*, December 12, 1985, E1.

Natalie, Richard. "The Countdown to 'Clue,' the Movie." *Los Angeles Herald Examiner*,

May 20, 1985, C3.
"New York Soundtrack." *Variety*, August 28, 1985, 28.
"Only Stars Have Clue to Whodunit." *Austin American-Statesman*, June 30, 1985.
"Par to Roll Pic Version of Parker Bros. 'Clue.'" *Variety*, February 13, 1985, 5.
Phillips, Michael. "Murder Buffet." *City Pages* (Minneapolis–St. Paul), December 23, 1985.
Rabkin, William. "A Peek Behind the Scenes of 'Clue.'" *UCLA Daily Bruin*, October 30, 1985, 22–25.
———. "Whodunnit?" *Starlog*, January 1986, 37–39.
Rainer, Peter. "This Murder Mystery Doesn't Have a 'Clue.'" *Los Angeles Herald Examiner*, December 13, 1985, 8.
Rambeau, Catharine. "Board Game turns to Bored Game in 'Clue.'" *Detroit Free Press*, December 13, 1985, 3C.
Rico, Diana. "Miss Scarlet Did It in the Library with a Wrench?" *Daily News* (New York), September 1, 1985.
"Rushes: *Clue*." *Time*, December 23, 1985.
Sabulis, Tom. "Summer Movie Doldrums May End with Fall Heavy Hitters." *Minneapolis Star Tribune*, September 29, 1985, 9G.
Seiler, Andy. "Why Make It a Movie? 'Nary a Clue." *Central* (New Brunswick) New Jersey Home News, December 20, 1985, 16.
Siskel, Gene. "Did the Butler Do It? 'Clue' Offers 3 Answers." *Chicago Tribune*, December 13, 1985, 7A.
Schweiger, Daniel. "Mystery Music: John Morris Gets a Clue." Liner notes, *Clue* Motion Picture Soundtrack, composed and conducted by John Morris. Burbank, CA: La-La Land Records, 2011, compact disc.
"Short Takes." *Daily Variety*, May 23, 1985, 19.
Scott, Vernon. "Actress Returns to Sex Symbol Role." *South Florida Sun-Sentinel*, December 13, 1985.
Stanley, John. "'Clue' the Movie—The Story of Whodunit," *San Francisco Examiner*, December 8, 1985, Datebook section, 29–30.
Taggart, Patrick. "Variety Marks Season's Films." *Austin American-Statesman*, December 8, 1985, Show World section, 1, 38.
Thomas, Bob. "A Whodunnit with All the Clues." *Honolulu Advertiser*, July 14, 1985, C-15.
Thomas, Kevin. "'Clue' as Whodunit Spoof Lacks Spiff." *Los Angeles Times*, December 13, 1985, Part VI, 14.
UPI. "Brennan to Star in Comedy Film." *Charlotte News*, June 13, 1985, 3D.
"U.S. to Europe." *Variety*, January 16, 1980.
Vary, Adam B. "Something Terrible Has Happened Here: The Crazy Story of How *Clue* Went from Forgotten Flop to Hollywood Triumph." *Buzzfeed*, December 10, 2015, buzzfeed.com.
Walsh, Michael. "Movie as Good as Game." *The Province* (Vancouver), December 15, 1985, 54.
Williams, George. McClatchy News Service. "Here's a Hint, 'Clue' Fans: Laughter Is the Movie's Best Weapon." *Record Searchlight* (Redding, California), December 16, 1985, C-11.

Wixson, Heather. "Communism Was a Red Herring: 30 Years Later, *Clue*: The Movie Is Still Comedic Perfection." *Daily Dead*, December 13, 2015, dailydead.com.

Periodicals, Newspapers, Journals, Book Chapters, and Websites

"1986–87 Primetime Specials Ratings." *Variety*, September 30, 1987, 72–74, 88.

Alterman, Loraine. "Martin Mull's Fabulous Furniture." *New York Times*, June 3, 1973, 27.

American Film Institute. *Clue* (1985). Catalog of Feature Films, catalog.afi.com, accessed March 12, 2021.

Appelbaum, Ralph. "Working with Numbers." *Film and Filming*, September 1979, 20–24.

Art of Murder, The. Fan website at theartofmurder.com. Includes memorabilia, articles, and transcripts.

Associated Press. "Debra Hill, 54, Film Producer Who Helped Create 'Halloween,' Dies." *New York Times*, March 8, 2005.

———. "Inventor of Clue Dies in Mystery Worthy of His Popular Board Game." *The Journal Times* (Racine), December 2, 1996.

Bailey, Jason. "Review: Bodies Bodies Bodies." *Crooked Marquee*, August 4, 2022, crookedmarquee.com.

———. "'Twilight Zone: The Movie' and the Deadly Accident That Plagued It." *New York Times*, June 25, 2023, nytimes.com.

Barnes, Mike. "Actress Eileen Brennan Dies at 80." *Hollywood Reporter*, July 30, 2013, hollywoodreporter.com.

———. "Bill Henderson, Jazz Vocalist and Actor, Dies at 90." *Hollywood Reporter*, April 6, 2016, hollywoodreporter.com.

———. "David L. Lander, Squiggy on 'Laverne and Shirley,' Dies at 73." *Hollywood Reporter*, December 5, 2020, hollywoodreporter.com.

Bart, Peter. "Exec Comes Full Circle after Descent into Despair." *Variety*, February 7, 1993, variety.com.

*Bath* (England) *Weekly Chronicle and Herald*. Various issues, 1937–50.

Billen, Andrew. "Dark Art of Novelization." *The Observer*, March 28, 1993, A14.

"Bio." Jane Wiedlin, janewiedlin.com.

"Biography." Tim Curry, timcurry.co.uk.

Borrelli, Christopher. "Movie Novels Are Still Around, and They Aren't All Trash—Just Ask the Chicagoans Who Wrote Them." *Chicago Tribune*, March 30, 2020.

Boseley, Sarah. "In the Ground, of Natural Causes, Cluedo's Inventor, Anthony Pratt." *The Guardian* (London), November 27, 1996.

Chandler, Raymond. "The Simple Art of Murder." Originally published in *The Atlantic*, December 1944. Reprinted in Raymond Chandler, *The Simple Art of Murder*. New York: Penguin Random House, 1988.

"Credibility Gap Returns." *Los Angeles Times*, January 21, 1971, Part IV, 12.

"Debra Hill." Obituary, *The Independent*, March 9, 2005.

"Debra Hill, 54." Obituary, *Los Angeles Times*, March 8, 2005.

"Debra Hill Leaves Paramount Post." *Variety*, April 27, 1992, 4.

"Donald O. Stewart, Screenwriter, Dies." *New York Times*, August 3, 1980, 32.

Eller, Claudia. "Producer of 9/11 Movie Had Her Own Tragic Story." *Los Angeles Times*, July 27, 2006.
Ely, Robert. "Martin Mull Has Interest in Fine Art, Penchant for Humor." *St. Petersburg Times*, December 7, 1979, 9D.
Erwin, Fran. "From 'Bird Girl' at Busch Gardens to Movie Star, Her Career Takes Flight." *Valley News* (Van Nuys), May 26, 1977, Section 3, 1.
"'Escapes' Producer Hill Emphasizes 'Preplanning' as Key to Success." *Film Journal*, July 6, 1981, 84.
Farr, Nick. "Abnormal Interviews: My Cousin Vinny Director Jonathan Lynn." Abnormal Use, March 13, 2012, archived at web.archive.org.
"Fear Riot Leaves Saturday Night Glad to Be Alive." *New York Post*, November 3, 1981, 7.
Fox, Margalit. "Warren Manzi, Author of New York's Longest-Running Play, Dies at 60." *New York Times*, February 14, 2016.
Freedman, Richard. "Double Bill: Tonight's 'Halloween' Horrorthon Based On Writer's Teen Memories." *Spokesman-Review* (Spokane), October 30, 1981, 6.
Freeman, Marc. "'M*A*S*H' Finale, 35 Years Later: Untold Stories of One of TV's Most Important Shows." *Hollywood Reporter*, February 22, 2018, hollywoodreporter.com.
Gates, Anita. "Eileen Brenna, Stalwart of Film and Stage, Dies at 80." *New York Times*, July 30, 2013, nytimes.com.
Harris, Will. "Christopher Lloyd on Playing a Vampire, a Taxi Driver, a Toon, and More." *A.V. Club*, October 12, 2012.
Henderson, Kathy. "Michael McKean Savors the Taste of Superior Donuts." *Broadway Buzz*, October 26, 2009, broadway.com.
Hertzfeld, Laura. "Jonathan Lynn on 'Yes, Prime Minister,' Working with Michael McKean again, and Why U.K. Political Shows Are so Darn Popular." *Entertainment Weekly*, June 12, 2013.
Hilburn, Robert. "Fear." *Los Angeles Times*, June 13, 1982, 68.
Hill, Michael E. "Lesley Ann Warren." *Washington Post*, February 24, 1985.
"Hill Was Pioneer Femme Producer." Obituary, *Variety*, March 14–20, 2005, 64.
Hirsch, Lisa. "Debra Hill: Don't Call This Busy Hyphenate 'Honey.'" *Variety*, June 2–8, 2003, A6.
"Historical Pasadena Mansion Destroyed by Fire." PRWeb, December 5, 2005, prweb.com/releases/2005/12/prweb317995.htm.
Hughes, Mike. "'Halloween' Empire Branches Out—To TV and New Movie." *Argus-Leader* (Sioux Falls), October 29, 1981, 12C.
Itzkoff, Dave. "Surprise of a Salesman: Christopher Lloyd." *New York Times*, August 25, 2010.
Johnson, Charles. "'Schlock' Really Is." *Sacramento Bee*, October 14, 1973.
Kilday, Gregg. "Producer Hill: Her Escape Is Her Work." *Sunday News* (Lancaster), August 2, 1981, F-4.
King, Susan. "In 'Knock Knock,' Actress Colleen Camp Has a Cameo—and a Producer Credit." *Los Angeles Times*, October 3, 2015.
Lavin, Cheryl. "Martin Mull." *Chicago Tribune*, September 3, 1994.
"Lesley Ann Warren." *Film Talk*, February 18, 2016.
Lucas, Tim. "David Cronenberg's *The Dead Zone*." *Cinefantastique*, December/January 1

983–84, 24–31, 60–61.

Marquard, Bryan. "Warren Manzi, at 60; Wrote NY's Longest-Running Play." *Boston Globe*, February 18, 2016, B8.

McCloskey, Tim. "The Life and Times of Philly Hardcore Pioneer Lee Ving." *Philadelphia Magazine*, October 30, 2015, phillymag.com.

McFarland, Kevin. "Psych: 100 Clues." *A.V. Club*, March 28, 2013.

McKean, Michael. "A Biographical Snippet." Flotation Device: The Homepage of Michael McKean, michaelmckean.com.

Mills, Nancy. "Miss Hill Successful Unknown." *Indianapolis News*, September 30, 1982, 24.

Oliver, Myrna. "Michael McEachern McDowell; Horror Novelist also Wrote Movie Chillers." *Los Angeles Times*, December 31, 1999, A24.

Olsen, Mark. "Actress Known for Tough, Soft Quality." *Los Angeles Times*, July 31, 2013.

O'Neil, Tom. "The Envelope." *Los Angeles Times*, December 15, 2008.

Pollock, Dale. "Spielberg Philosophical Over E.T. Oscar Defeat." *Los Angeles Times*, April 13, 1983, Part VI, 1.

———. "Writers: The Line Louder than Words." *Los Angeles Times*, May 29, 1981, G1.

Reinke, Malinda. "Being a Party to 'Murder' becomes a National Rage." *Fort Lauderdale News*, December 8, 1985, A1, A8.

Rosenfield, Paul. "5 Films, 5 Hits . . . but Money Isn't Everything." *Los Angeles Times*, September 15, 1982, Part VI, 1–2.

Rule, Vera. "Son of a Pitch." *The Guardian*, March 12, 1999, theguardian.com.

Ryzik, Melena. "Overlooked No More: Debra Hill, Producer Who Parlayed 'Halloween' into a Cult Classic." *New York Times*, May 22, 2019.

Sandomir, Richard. "John Morris, Composer for Mel Brooks's Films, Dies at 91." *New York Times*, January 28, 2018.

Shales, Tom. "Mull's Life after Death on 'Mary Hartman.'" *Washington Post*, February 25, 1977.

Smith, Jack. "A Pasadena Mansion Bears Testament to Dreams of Nobility in the House That Jack Built." *Los Angeles Times*, April 10, 1985.

Smith, Liz. "Treatment Is Prescription for Carrie." *Daily News* (New York), May 12, 1985, 10.

Specter, Michael. "Funny? Yes, but Someone's Got to Be." *New York Times*, April 8, 1993, C1, 6.

Stanley, John. "Avoiding the Horror Cliches in 'Dead Zone.'" *San Francisco Examiner*, October 16, 1983, 25.

"Struck by Lightning." *Variety*, September 26, 1979, 56.

Summerscale, Kate. "Jack Mustard, in the Spa, with a Baseball Bat." *The Guardian*, December 19, 2008.

Sutcliffe's ad, *Courier-Journal* (Louisville), January 22, 1950, sec. 3, pg. 5.

Taubman, Howard. "Theater: 'Cambridge Circus' Arrives." New York Times, October 7, 1964, 53.

Thompson, Anne. "Producer–Writer Debra Hill Dies." *Hollywood Reporter*, March 14, 2005.

Treneman, Ann. "Mr. Pratt, in the Old People's Home, with an Empty Pocket." *The I*

*ndependent*, November 12, 1998.
Variety. Box office reports for December 13, 1985–January 19, 1986.
Weintraub, Robert. "A New Dimension of Filmmaking." *Slate*, July 26, 2012, slate.com.
Wile, Rob. "It's the 30-Year Anniversary of the Greatest Wall Street Movie Ever Made: Here's the Story behind It." *Business Insider*, June 27, 2013.
Wilson, Earl. "True Blond." *Morning News* (Wilmington), October 31, 1974.
Windeler, Robert. "Lesley Ann Warren Washed Jon Peters out of Her Hair, but Barbra Is Her Soulmate." *People*, February 28, 1977.
Wojciechowski, Michele. "FOX's *Dads* Star Martin Mull: The Accidental Comedian." *Parade*, September 27, 2013.

Books

Aldridge, Mark. *Agatha Christie on Screen*. London: Palgrave Macmillan, 2016.
Carlson, Marvin. *Deathtraps: The Postmodern Comedy Thriller*. Bloomington: Indiana University Press, 1993.
Chandler, Raymond. *The Notebooks of Raymond Chandler*. New York: Ecco, 2015.
Donovan, Tristan. *It's All a Game: The History of Board Games from Monopoly to Settlers of Catan*. New York: St. Martin's Press, 2017.
Doyle, Sir Arthur Conan. *The New Annotated Sherlock Holmes*. Edited with annotations by Leslie Klinger. 3 vols. New York: W. W. Norton, 2005–06.
Edwards, Martin. *The Golden Age of Murder: The Mystery Writers Who Invented the Modern Detective Story*. London: HarperCollins Crime Club, 2015.
———. *The Life of Crime: Detecting the History of Mysteries and Their Creators*. London: Collins Crime Club, 2022.
———. *The Story of Classic Crime in 100 Books*. Scottsdale, AZ: Poisoned Pen Press, 2017.
Farber, Stephen, and Marc Green. *Outrageous Conduct: Art, Ego, and the Twilight Zone Case*. New York: Arbor House, 1988.
Fisher, Carrie. *Wishful Drinking*. New York: Simon & Schuster, 2008.
Fleming, Charles. *High Concept: Don Simpson and the Hollywood Culture of Excess*. New York: Doubleday, 1998.
Freeman, Hadley. *Life Moves Pretty Fast: The Lessons We Learned from Eighties Movies*. New York: Simon & Schuster, 2016.
Griffin, Nancy, and Kim Masters. *Hit and Run: How Jon Peters and Peter Guber Took Sony for a Ride in Hollywood*. New York: Simon & Schuster, 1996.
Haycraft, Howard. *Murder for Pleasure: The Life and Times of the Detective Story*. First published 1941, updated and enlarged 1951. Mineola, NY: Dover Publications, 2019.
Hearing before the Special Subcommittee on Investigations of the Committee on Government Operations. United States Senate, Eighty-Third Congress, Second Session, Pursuant to S. Res. 189. Washington, DC: Government Printing Office, 1954.
James, P. D. *Talking about Detective Fiction*. New York: Knopf, 2009.
Larson, Randall D. *Films into Books: An Analytical Bibliography of Film Novelizations, Movie, and TV Tie-Ins*. Lanham, MD: The Scarecrow Press, 1995.
Lee, Hermione. *Tom Stoppard: A Life*. New York: Alfred A. Knopf, 2021.
Lehman, David. *The Perfect Murder: A Study in Detection*. New York: The Free Press, 1989.

Lewisohn, Mark. *The Beatles—All These Years, Extended Special Edition: Volume One: Tune In*. London: Little, Brown, 2013.

Lynn, Jonathan. *Comedy Rules: From the Cambridge Footlights to Yes Prime Minister*. London: Faber and Faber, 2011.

Madison, William V. *Madeline Kahn: Being the Music, a Life*. Jackson: University Press of Mississippi, 2015.

Manzi, Warren. *Perfect Crime: A Thriller in Two Acts*. Revised ed. New York: Samuel French, 2020.

Matthews, Ann. *Clue: The Storybook*. New York: Simon & Schuster, 1985.

McBride, Joseph. *Stephen Spielberg: A Biography*. New York: Simon & Schuster, 1997.

McDowell, Michael. *Clue: A Novel*. New York: Fawcett Gold Medal, 1985.

McFadden, Brian. *The Real Woman behind Halloween, The Fog, Escape from New York, and More: Pioneering Filmmaker Debra Hill*. N.p.: Kohner, Madison, and Danforth, 2019.

"Motion Picture Production Code," March 31, 1930. Hollywood: MPAA.

Nashawaty, Chris. *Caddyshack: The Making of a Hollywood Cinderella Story*. New York: Flatiron Books, 2018.

Nesteroff, Kliph. *The Comedians: Drunks, Thieves, Scoundrels, and the History of American Comedy*. New York: Grove Press, 2015.

Obst, Lynda. *Hello, He Lied—and Other Truths from the Hollywood Trenches*. New York: Little, Brown and Company, 1996.

———. *Sleepless in Hollywood: Tales from the New Abnormal in the Movie Business*. New York: Simon & Schuster, 2013.

Orbanes, Philip E. *The Game Makers: The Story of Parker Brothers from Tiddledy Winks to Trivial Pursuit*. Boston: Harvard Business School Press, 2004.

Parlett, David. *The Oxford History of Board Games*. Oxford: Oxford University Press, 1999.

Poe, Edgar Allan. *Annotated and Illustrated Entire Stories and Poems*. Edited by Andrew Barger. N.p.: Bottletree Books, 2008.

Sabin, Roger, Ronald Wilson, Linda Speidel, Brian Faucette, and Ben Bethell. *Cop Shows: A Critical History of Police Dramas on Television*. Jefferson, NC: McFarlane & Co., 2015.

Shogan, Robert. *No Sense of Decency—The Army–McCarthy Hearings: A Demagogue Falls and Television Takes Charge of American Politics*. Chicago: Ivan R. Dee, 2009.

Simmons, Matty. *Fat, Drunk, and Stupid: The Inside Story behind the Making of Animal House*. New York: St. Martins, 2012.

Sims, Michael. *Arthur and Sherlock: Conan Doyle and the Creation of Holmes*. New York: Bloomsbury, 2017.

Symons, Julian. *Bloody Murder: From the Detective Story to the Crime Novel*. 3rd revised ed. New York: Mysterious Press, 1992.

Thompson, Leroy. *Fairbairn-Sykes Commando Dagger*. Oxford: Osprey, 2011.

Vallan, Guilia D'Agnolo. *John Landis*. Milwaukie, OR: M Press, 2008.

Watson, Victor. *The Waddingtons Story: From the Early Days of Monopoly, the Maxwell Bids, and into the Next Millennium*. England: Northern Heritage Publications, 2008.

Weller, Sheila. *Carrie Fisher: A Life on the Edge*. New York: Sarah Crichton Books, 2019.

Manuscripts and Archival Sources

Art Directors Guild. Collection, 1937–2000. Collection 1539, Margaret Herrick Library,

Academy of Motion Picture Arts and Sciences.
Casting Company. Casting Notebook. Casting Records, 1980–2007, Collection 1715, Margaret Herrick Library, Academy of Motion Picture Arts and Sciences.
Cinefantastique. Magazine Records, 1951–2004. Collection 1759, Margaret Herrick Library, Academy Motion Picture Arts and Sciences.
*Clue*. Core Collection, Production Files. Margaret Herrick Library, Academy Motion Picture Arts and Sciences.
*Clue* Production Elements. Visual Effects by Illusion Arts. 22 parts. Pickford Center for Motion Picture Study, Academy of Motion Picture Arts and Sciences.
*Clue* Revised Shooting Schedule, August 1, 1985. Copy in author's possession.
County of Los Angeles, Registrar–Recorder/County Clerk. "Debra Gaye Hill," Certificate of Death, 3200519010547.
Hill, Debra. "Clue." Treatment, August 21, 1980. Fd. C-579, Paramount Pictures, Scripts Collection, Margaret Herrick Library, Academy of Motion Picture Arts and Sciences.
Historic American Buildings Survey, Creator. Max Busch House, 160 South San Rafael Street, Pasadena, Los Angeles County, CA. Pasadena California Los Angeles County, 1933. Library of Congress, loc.gov.
Illusion Arts Collection. *Clue* Visual Effects Sample Reel. W107485, Pickford Center for Motion Picture Study, Academy of Motion Picture Arts and Sciences.
Landis, John. Papers, ca. 1973–1998. Collection 507, Margaret Herrick Library, Academy of Motion Picture Arts and Sciences.
———, and Tom Stoppard. Transcript of conversation, February 7, 1983, fd. C-592, Paramount Pictures, Scripts Collection.
Lynn, Jonathan. "Clue." Preliminary draft screenplay, undated (ca. spring 1984). Fd. C-580, Paramount Pictures, Scripts Collection, Margaret Herrick Library, Academy of Motion Picture Arts and Sciences.
———. "Clue." First-draft screenplay, May 4, 1984. Copy in author's possession.
———. "Clue." Second-draft screenplay, June 4, 1984. Box F-319, collection 073, Film Scripts, UCLA Arts Special Collections, UCLA.
———. "Clue." Third-draft screenplay, January 1985. Box F-319, collection 073, Film Scripts, UCLA Arts Special Collections, UCLA.
———. *Clue*. Shooting script. Based on a story by John Landis and Jonathan Lynn, February 8, 1985, with revisions March 26, 1985, April 10, 1985, and July 9, 1985. Fd. C-588, in Paramount Pictures, Scripts Collection, Margaret Herrick Library, Academy of Motion Picture Arts and Sciences.
Manzi, Warren. "Clue." Preliminary screenplay, 1981. Fd. C-581, Paramount Pictures, Scripts Collection, Margaret Herrick Library, Academy of Motion Picture Arts and Sciences.
———. "Clue." First-draft screenplay, March 29, 1982. Fd. C-582, Paramount Pictures, Scripts Collection, Margaret Herrick Library, Academy of Motion Picture Arts and Sciences.
———. "Clue." First-draft screenplay, August 1983. Box F-319, collection 073, Film Scripts, UCLA Arts Special Collections, UCLA.
McDowell, Michael. Collection. PCL MS 138, Manuscripts, Browne Popular Culture Library, Bowling Green State University.

"Notes on Nationwide Dialing." American Telephone and Telegraph Company, Department of Operation and Engineering, 1955.

Paramount Pictures. *Clue* Development File. Paramount Pictures, Scripts Collection, Margaret Herrick Library, Academy of Motion Picture Arts and Sciences.

———. *Clue* press kits, 1985. Fd. 61, Landis, Papers, Margaret Herrick Library, Academy of Motion Picture Arts and Sciences; *Clue*, Core Collection, Margaret Herrick Library.

———. Invitation to *Clue* premiere, December 10, 1985. Fd. 60, Landis, Papers, Margaret Herrick Library, Academy of Motion Picture Arts and Sciences.

———. Script Department, "Clue," shot list, ca. September 1985, copy in author's possession.

———. Scripts Collection. Margaret Herrick Library, Academy of Motion Picture Arts and Sciences.

———. Writing Credits. Correspondence between Rosanne Wright and the Writers' Guild of America, August 14 and 19, September 16, 1985, fd. C-591, Paramount Pictures, Scripts Collection, Margaret Herrick Library, Academy of Motion Picture Arts and Sciences.

Stoppard, Tom. Correspondence with John Landis. In Stoppard, Papers, 1937–2000. MS-4062, box 127, fd. 4, Harry Ransom Center, University of Texas at Austin.

Interviews, Podcasts, Movies, and Audio Commentaries

Brandon, Josh. Interview with the author, June 8, 2021.

Brandon, Josh, and Jonathan Lynn. "*Clue*: The Director's Commentary Track." Smodcast podcast, episode 377, June 12, 2017. Introduced by Kevin Smith, thatkevinsmithclub.com, mp3 copy in author's possession.

Brooks, Mel. Interview with Terry Gross. "Mel Brooks: 'I'm an EGOT, I Don't Need Anymore.'" *Fresh Air*, NPR, May 20, 2013.

Camp, Colleen. Interview with the author, June 24, 2021.

Carson, Johnny. *The Tonight Show Starring Johnny Carson*. Episode 5,466, January 8, 1986. Transcript in author's possession.

Coleman, Lani, and David Wallett. Interview with the author, September 19, 2021.

Conway, Tim, and Lang Elliott. Audio commentary. *The Private Eyes*, Blu-ray. Directed by Lang Elliott. Henstooth Video, 2010.

Hatch, John. Survey of *Clue* Fans. Conducted online, March 22–May 1, 2022. Results in author's possession.

Hesseman, Howard. Interview with Terry Gross. "TV Actor Howard Hesseman." *Fresh Air*, NPR, August 29, 1988, rebroadcast February 4, 2022.

Hickey, Andrew. "Sh-Boom by the Chords." *A History of Rock Music in 500 Songs* podcast, episode 18, February 4, 2019. 500songs.com, mp3 copy in author's possession.

Hitchcock, Alfred, dir. *North by Northwest*. Metro Goldwyn Mayer, 1959.

Jensen, Emily. Interview with the author, June 15, 2022.

Johnson, Rian. In-theater audio commentary. *Knives Out*, digital edition (iTunes), 2019.

Letterman, David. *Late Night with David Letterman*. Episode 607, season 5, episode 126, December 11, 1985. Digital recording in author's possession.

Lloyd, Christopher. Interview with Brad Gilmore. *Back to the Future: The Podcast*, March 11, 2021.

Lynn, Jonathan. Correspondence with the author, March 2021. Copies in author's possession.
———. Interview with Gilbert Gottfried and Frank Santopadre. *Amazing Colossal Podcast*, September 3, 2018, gilbertpodcast.com.
———. Interview with *Movies and Stuff*, December 2015. YouTube, uploaded December 11, 2015, youtube.com, accessed January 7, 2022. MP3 copy of interview in author's possession.
———. Interview with Nick Higham. *Meet the Author*, September 17, 2011, BBC News, available at bbc.com.
———. Interview with Roy Plomley. *Desert Island Discs*, BBC Radio, October 20, 1984, available at bbc.co.uk, MP3 copy in author's possession.
McKean, Michael. Interview with Andy Richter. *Three Questions with Andy Richter* podcast, January 27, 2020.
———. Interview with Gilbert Gottfried and Frank Santopadre. *Amazing Colossal Podcast*, April 4, 2016, gilbertpodcast.com.
Mull, Martin. Interview with Marc Maron. *WTF with Marc Maron* podcast, November 25, 2018.
Nakahara, Kellye. Interview with Jeff Maxwell and Ryan Patrick. *M*A*S*H Matters* podcast, episode 14, April 30, 2019.
———. Interview with Rachel Martin. "Nurse Kellye of 'M*A*S*H' Still Gets Fan Mail for Breakthrough Role." *Weekend Edition Sunday*, NPR, April 3, 2016.
Reid, Tim. Interview with Adrienne Faillace, May 20, 2021, Television Academy Foundation, at interviews.televisionacademy.com.
Siskel, Gene, and Roger Ebert. *At the Movies*, season 4, episode 15, December 21, 1985.
Smith, Jeff, dir. *Who Done It? The Clue Documentary*. It Looks So Fake Productions, 2022.
Warren, Lesley Ann. Interview. YouTube, uploaded March 20, 2019, youtube.com/watch?v=bkOlG9dsHhU, accessed June 25, 2021.
Wiedlin, Jane. "A Talk with Jane Wiedlin." Retro Junk, August 23, 2010, retrojunk.com.
———. Interview with Howard Gluss. *Engaging Minds*, undated, beond.tv.

# ABOUT THE AUTHOR

John Hatch is an editor and author who has written about the American West, memory in history, and pop culture. He has documented the roles of Paramount Pictures and Cecil B. DeMille in placing Ten Commandments monuments across the United States in the 1950s to promote DeMille's film *The Ten Commandments* (1956). He has also researched the early development of film in the Progressive Era and moral crusades against nickelodeons and cinemas. He lives in Salt Lake City with his wife, Joy.

## ALSO AVAILABLE

## AT TUCKERDSPRESS.COM

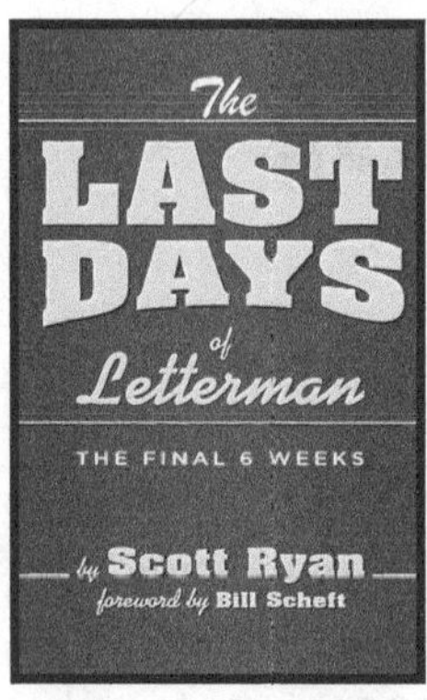